THE RETURN OF
ORDINARY CAPITALISM

THE RETURN OF
ORDINARY
CAPITALISM

NEOLIBERALISM, PRECARITY, OCCUPY

SANFORD F. SCHRAM

OXFORD
UNIVERSITY PRESS

OXFORD
UNIVERSITY PRESS

Oxford University Press is a department of the
University of Oxford. It furthers the University's objective
of excellence in research, scholarship, and education
by publishing worldwide.

Oxford   New York

Auckland   Cape Town   Dar es Salaam   Hong Kong   Karachi
Kuala Lumpur   Madrid   Melbourne   Mexico City   Nairobi
New Delhi   Shanghai   Taipei   Toronto

With offices in

Argentina   Austria   Brazil   Chile   Czech Republic   France   Greece
Guatemala   Hungary   Italy   Japan   Poland   Portugal   Singapore
South Korea   Switzerland   Thailand   Turkey   Ukraine   Vietnam

Oxford is a registered trade mark of Oxford University Press
in the UK and certain other countries.

Published in the United States of America by
Oxford University Press
198 Madison Avenue, New York, NY 10016

Library of Congress Cataloging-in-Publication Data
Schram, Sanford.
The return of ordinary capitalism : neoliberalism, precarity,
occupy / Sanford F. Schram.
pages   cm
ISBN 978-0-19-025301-1 (hardback)—ISBN 978-0-19-025302-8 (paperback)
1. Neoliberalism.   2. Economic policy.   3. Equality.   4. Public welfare.   I. Title.
HB95.S37   2015
330.12'2—dc23   2014046018

1 3 5 7 9 8 6 4 2

Printed in the United States of America
on acid-free paper

And the seasons they go round and round
And the painted ponies go up and down
We're captive on the carousel of time
We can't return we can only look
Behind from where we came
And go round and round and round
In the circle game
—Joni Mitchell, "The Circle Game"

A Klee painting named "Angelus Novus" shows an angel looking as though he is about to move away from something he is fixedly contemplating. His eyes are staring, his mouth is open, his wings are spread. This is how one pictures the angel of history. His face is turned toward the past. Where we perceive a chain of events, he sees one single catastrophe which keeps piling wreckage and hurls it in front of his feet. The angel would like to stay, awaken the dead, and make whole what has been smashed. But a storm is blowing in from Paradise; it has got caught in his wings with such a violence that the angel can no longer close them. The storm irresistibly propels him into the future to which his back is turned, while the pile of debris before him grows skyward. This storm is what we call progress.
—Walter Benjamin, "Theses on the Philosophy of History"

CONTENTS

★

LIST OF FIGURES AND TABLES

★

PREFACE

The essays in this volume reflect my recurring efforts to use political and social theory to understand how social welfare policy affects ordinary people, especially those on the bottom of the socioeconomic ladder. This time I focus on neoliberalization, including its marketization of the U.S. welfare state, the growing economic "precarity" that results for many of Americans, and role of protest movements especially Occupy Wall Street in framing an agenda for progressive responses. I want to thank Mimi Abramovitz, Jason Adams, Elisabeth Anker, Dana Becker, Dianne Butera, Sam Chambers, Rom Coles, Jodi Dean, Mitchell Dean, Andrew Dilts, Grant Duncan, Lennie Feldman, Rich Fording, Jack Gunnell, Allan Irving, Jeff Isaac, Michael Lee, Bettina Leibetseder, Nancy Love, Annie Menzel, Mark Mattern, Lawrence Moss, Christopher Parker, Andy Polsky, Joan Schram, Eric Sidoti, Micol Seigel, Basha Silverman, Amory Starr, Deborah Stone, Pam Stone, Rodney Taveria, Charles Tien, Rashid Taylor, Shyama Venkateswar, John Wallach, and Anna Yeatman for offering constructive criticisms. Once again Frances Fox Piven and Joe Soss provided ongoing encouragement and critical commentary that served to make my writing much better each time I shared it with them. I also want to acknowledge the support of the US Studies Centre at the University of Sydney and the Political Science Department, Roosevelt House, and the Faculty Development Fund at Hunter College, CUNY, for their support of this project. I am especially appreciative of all the great work on this book that was done by my Oxford University Press editor, Angela Chnapko, who believed in my vision and helped to make it become a reality. I also want to thank the anonymous reviewers whose extensive commentary provided the basis for significant improvements in the final manuscript.

Gwen Colvin managed the production of the book in style. Once again, Brianne Wolfe provided superb copyediting, for which I am deeply grateful. In addition, her insightful commentary on the substance of the book helped improve the narrative at critical junctures. Chapter 3 is based on "Occupy Precarity," *Theory & Event* 16, 1 (2013); chapter 4 is a revision of "The Deep Semiotic Structure of Deservingness: Discourse and Identity in Welfare Policy," in *The Argumentative Turn Revisited*, Frank Fischer and Herbert Gottweis, eds. (Durham, NC: Duke University Press, 2012), pp. 236–68; and chapter 5 is a revised version of Sanford F. Schram and Basha Silverman, "The End of Social Work: Neoliberal Paternalism in Social Policy Implementation," *Critical Policy Studies* 6, 2 (2012): 128–47.

THE RETURN OF
ORDINARY CAPITALISM

THE RETURN OF ORDINARY CAPITALISM

NEOLIBERALISM AS THE NEW NORMAL

In today's world of increasing inequality there is growing concern about whether and how we can respond.[1] Ideally, we will be moving to better times. With many people out of work and decreasing numbers of jobs paying a decent wage, pressure grows for small steps such as enacting increases in the minimum wage and for larger ones such as providing some kind of basic income guarantee.[2] Yet how we can build from the small steps to the larger ones, I would suggest, is the critical question. It may well be that the old approaches to pushing for political change need to be revised in light of our current predicament.[3] Using theoretical concepts across a number of areas of study provides a basis for that revision. From social movement theory, we need to take seriously the distinctive insight that movements for change inevitably arise within a particular place and time, unavoidably reflect those conditions even as they respond to them, and ultimately end up more often than not producing change within the existing structure of power more so than overcoming it.[4] From theories of social change, we might conclude that movement politics is best premised on a reflexivity that appreciates that the path to a more equitable society is never smooth, that the arc of political change is both cyclical and linear, and that with each swing back politics reflects where it came from. From public policy theory, we gain appreciation that each swing of the cycle can be seen as producing its own sort of "path dependency" in social welfare policy that stays in place until interrupted by a "critical juncture" where change can occur.[5] Whether we are at a critical juncture is very much an open question and how we respond if we are is subject to intense debate.

In a Time of Inequality

The Great Recession of 2008–9 was the worst economic downturn since the Great Depression of the 1930s. By the time its most devastating effects began receding in late 2012 and the economy's improvement became noticeable in 2013, many people were beginning to exhale a sigh of relief that things might return to normal after an extended period of massive hardship for individuals and families throughout the United States.[6] Yet it seemed that a new normal was emerging where economic opportunity for most people was not quite what it once was. In this transformed economy, the wealthy become ever more wealthy, while the middle class shrinks and people with lower incomes—the working class and poor—were being disciplined to be market-compliant actors in an economy that left them with dwindling opportunities for achieving a decent standard of living.[7] As if these negative trends were not enough, mainstream political discourse diverted attention away from growing economic inequality and precarity and has steadfastly instead focused on the alleged dangers of high levels of public debt. The resultant manufactured austerity did nothing but accelerate the trend whereby growing numbers of people who suffered diminished economic prospects were made all the more subject to disciplinary practices of the state that punished them for their failure to succeed in a transformed economy.[8]

These changes take place during a time of neoliberalism when there is increased emphasis on people practicing personal responsibility by applying economic logic to all forms of decision making across a variety of spheres of life.[9] Neoliberalism disseminates economic rationality to be the touchstone not just for the market but for civil society and the state as well. Most dramatically it has led to wholesale revision in public policy in a number of domains to be more consistent with market logic in the name of better promoting market-compliant behavior by as much of the citizenry as possible. People are expected to practice personal responsibility by investing in their own human capital to make themselves less of a burden on society as a whole or face the consequences of the heightened disciplinary regime.[10] As a result, post–Great Recession, the return of "ordinary capitalism" provided a new neoliberal normal of growing inequality and reduced economic opportunities for most Americans.[11] Under neoliberalism, the state buttresses markets rather than counters them and inequality grows virtually unabated, as not a bug but rather as a feature of this latest iteration of the return to ordinary capitalism.[12]

Joseph Stiglitz has written that these trends post–Great Recession are actually reflective of a long wave of state-induced economic transformation:

> For thirty years after World War II, America grew together—with growth in income in every segment, but with those at the bottom growing faster than those at the top. The country's fight for survival brought a new sense of unity, and that led to policies, like the GI Bill, that helped bring the country even closer together. But for the past thirty years, we've become increasingly a nation divided; not only has the top been growing the fastest, but the bottom has actually been declining.... The last time inequality approached the alarming level we see today was in the years before the Great Depression.... If we are to reverse these trends in inequality, we will have to reverse some of the policies that have helped make America the most economically divided developed country and, beyond that, to take further actions to lessen the inequalities that arise on their own from market forces.[13]

The new normal therefore was a long time in the making and public policy helped make it happen.[14] The effects of the Great Recession have been serious indeed but they are symptomatic of a larger economic restructuring where social welfare policies most significantly are revised to work consistently with the logic of the market rather than to counter it. This economic restructuring has not happened overnight, but instead, has come incrementally with economic downturns successively presenting opportunities to offload workers, outsource jobs, and rebuild firms so that they can more efficiently and profitably, if also more heartlessly, participate in the neoliberalization of the global economy. As a result, people on the bottom of the socioeconomic ladder have increasingly been forced to try to survive on the limited options the transformed economy offers them or come under the purview of an increasingly disciplinary state.

While the new normal represented a break with the past, it also reflected continuity especially for selected marginalized populations, low-income African Americans in particular.[15] In fact, the return of ordinary capitalism post the Great Recession has but intensified preexisting long-term inequities in income, housing, health care, social welfare, and criminal justice, as well as overall well-being, for many African Americans.[16] A case could be made that these persistent racial disparities were not simply the result of failed public policies but that race itself was a critical constitutive ingredient in the ongoing rollout of a neoliberal paternalistic regime of poverty governance.[17] Race facilitated the institution of policies designed to contain low-income populations and manage their poverty problems so that they did not become a burden for the rest of society.[18] Further, those policies (from welfare-to-work to mass incarceration) help reinscribe race as a marker of who is innocent and who is guilty, who is deserving and who is not.[19] In other words, persistent racial disparities in quality-of-life indicators were not a failure of the neoliberal paternalistic regime of poverty management but were instead its very raison d'etre, reflective of a systematic effort to exploit racial divisions as a way of justifying advanced marginality among low-income African Americans (and other people of color).[20]

Thomas Piketty has suggested that the 1945–73 period that Stiglitz references (i.e., what is often called the "Great Compression"), when wages rose with economic growth and there was a reduction in inequality, was actually an anomaly in the history of capitalism.[21] While African Americans and other racial and ethnic minorities did not benefit as much as whites during this period, for the bulk of Americans this was a distinctive time where, to turn a phrase, a rising tide was lifting most boats, if not all.

Yet on the basis of examining several hundred years of data across several countries, Piketty concludes that the normal course of affairs for ordinary capitalism is where the returns from capital exceed economic growth so as to concentrate wealth at the top and increase inequality. In other words, most often a rising tide lifts the boats of the well-off much more than anyone else. From this perspective, we have indeed post the Great Recession returned to the normal course of affairs for ordinary capitalism where the economy grows but so as to increase the concentration of wealth at the top. The aftermath

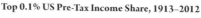

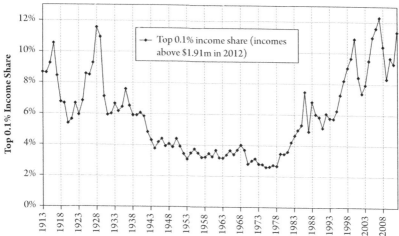

Source: Emmanuel Saez and Gabriel Zucman, "Wealth Inequality in the United States since 1913: Evidence from Capitalized Income Tax Data" (Cambridge: National Bureau of Economic Research, Working Paper, 20625, October, 2014).

Figure 1.1   Wealth at the Top, 1913–2012.

of the Great Recession has included an acceleration of that trend since the mid-1970s with the economy growing to create more inequality by concentrating wealth at the uppermost top of the income distribution, to the point of producing a new Gilded Age of "patrimonial capitalism" where the returns from capital help ensure that inherited wealth is the main driver of this extreme inequality (see figure 1.1).[22] Piketty calls for a global wealth tax as the only solution to the inevitability of increasing concentration of wealth at the top.[23] This is surely a utopian gesture, as Piketty himself recognizes, for there is not even a governmental body in existence to collect this tax.

Piketty's analysis therefore has an air of inevitability, that obdurate impersonal economic forces will be sustaining the new normal long into the future. Yet as ordinary people of all backgrounds persist in struggling to come to grips with this new normal, we must ask whether it is inevitable that economic forces will continue to generate greater levels of inequality and whether the ordinary people are in fact powerless to respond politically.

THE ARC OF HISTORY: LINEAR VERSUS CYCLICAL

Before we confront this dire situation of economic necessity and turn to timely issues of political possibility, perhaps we first need to consider more timeless, fundamental questions of political philosophy. Answers to these more foundational questions may well determine just what it is we have reason to think is politically possible and how we can act to achieve it.[24]

I say we need to ask more philosophical questions about political possibility for a basic reason. Failed attempt after failed attempt to mobilize concerted action to push back against the onslaught of reactionary policymaking must at some point force us to step back and try to understand how political change is possible in the current era. This step back creates the opportunity to reflect on the issue of change more systematically. In other words, today we may need to be asking questions like what is the course of history, what is its trajectory, is it always moving forward, in a progressive, developmental way toward something better? Is it reasonable to think we can build on what came before to reduce suffering, oppression, and subordination? Does it make sense to think of ourselves as progressives, not just meaning people who want things to change in a positive direction but also in the sense that it is reasonable to have an expectation that over time things improve in some sort of progressive, developmental fashion?

Martin Luther King famously said that the "arc of the moral universe is long, but it bends toward justice."[25] As inspiring as that thought is, we need consider its complexity. History's arc is long such that it only eventually bends toward justice. The arc of history is then not necessarily linear. In fact, we might take this argument a step further and challenge progressives (either as people on the left or just people who assume and believe in progress) to recognize that history is better understood as not linear at all, but as something that is more cyclical, where change in one direction is over time counteracted with a shift back in the other direction?

Capitalism's greatest critic, Karl Marx, himself famously rejected G. W. F. Hegel's suggestion that history repeats itself.[26] The myth of eternal return, as Mircea Eliade as well as Friedrich Nietzsche and others before him called it, was for Marx just that—a myth.[27] Eliade in particular worried that the people of the modern age thoughtlessly cast aside myth to adopt an unquestioning commitment to a linear notion of history that made them oblivious to its dangers, while ignoring the value of archaic notions of rebirth, resurrection, or even just cyclical repetition. If fact, the very idea of historical time, of time itself passing by, is not itself, as it were, timeless. Instead, its inception in all likelihood originally created a crisis—the crisis of time, or what do people do once they see themselves as existing in time, from birth to death, where stabilizing the basic conditions for existence is threatened by the ineliminable reality of life in flux.[28] Once time came to be an idea that could not be dismissed, in other words, once people saw themselves as existing in history, a crisis ensued about how to respond. Over time, many have proposed theories of history to help understand how to live in historical time. Marx's own theory of history, historical materialism, like many others in the second half of the nineteenth century, during a time of enchantment with the idea of progress, saw history as inevitably on an upward trajectory of progressive improvement.

It is not only the secular Left that has emphasized history as destined to lead to progress. Carl Schmitt also rejected cyclical theories of history as archaic. Schmitt said: "Following Karl Löwith, we are convinced that paganism is not at all capable of any form of historical thought because it is cyclical. The historical loses its specific meaning with the cycles of eternal recurrence. We know that the Enlightenment and the positivist belief in progress was only secularized Judaism and Christianity, and it obtained its 'eschata' from these sources."[29] Schmitt believed in progress but he also saw secularization as an adaptation that reworked religion rather than simply left it behind. Schmitt saw modernity's orientation toward progress as being legitimized by virtue of its being the secularization of religion's age-old messianic creed that predated modernity. Secularization was an adaptation of religion's belief in a moral universe.[30]

Yet not everyone has agreed with the progressive view of history. Cyclical theories have been commonly used to explain less global processes of political change.[31] For instance, concerning social welfare policies designed to compensate people for economic disadvantage in a capitalist economy, Frances Fox Piven and Richard Cloward argued that the welfare policies of the state served political and economic functions and alternated over time in emphasizing one over the other as circumstances dictated.[32] When there was political stability the state emphasized enforcement of the capitalist work ethic and sought to incentivize taking any jobs that were available (even those that left you in poverty). When things become politically unstable, the state liberalized welfare policies to placate those left behind by the capitalist system so as to re-create the conditions for political acquiesce (that still often left the poor without many economic prospects). Yet with each swing back in the pendulum, the return is never quite the same as what came before, especially if social welfare policies had become firmly established in the state and over time garnered public support from people who had become accustomed to receiving assistance when needed.[33] Writing in 1982 in response the beginning of the rightward shift in U.S. politics, Piven and Cloward noted:

> Contemporary developments in American public relief seem to confirm this cyclical pattern. Once the protests movement of the 1960s waned, real benefit levels began to fall, as state legislatures refused to raise grant levels despite rapid inflation.... On the other hand, the great expansion of other social welfare programs initiated in either the 1930s or the 1960s was not aborted with the ebbing of protests in the 1970s.... We do not underestimate the scale and force of the contemporary corporate mobilization against the entitlement programs. Nevertheless, we think many different groups will join in resisting, and that this time they will prevail.[34]

Then seems to still be now. The battle over the welfare state has continued, demonstrating persistent support for its basic idea even as it has been subject to retrenchment. In response to every attempt to assert the ascendency of the market, people find a way to mobilize in resistance as Karl Polanyi suggested when he noted the inevitability of what he called the "double movement," where marketization inevitably leads to a push back for social protections from the effects of too much marketization.[35]

In the end, it is arguably the case that political cycles and economic cycles are very much interrelated.[36] The issue of cyclical political change is most often in response to a change in economic conditions. And it is well established that economic trends are themselves cyclical, even if there is not agreement on how they work or the role of politics in responding to economic downturns.[37] At the least, capitalist economies are widely recognized to be cyclical, with booms and busts that Joseph Schumpeter famously suggested laid the basis for a process of "creative destruction."[38] Implicit in this idea is the understanding that a new period of growth is possible by destroying what came before (in this case an economy where there were stable, decent paying jobs for many, but by no means all, in the middle and working classes). Yet today the return to a growing economy surely does not imply anything like the economy of the boom years of prior periods. Instead, the Great Recession has created an opportunity to accelerate the structural shifts in the economy that have been developing for over thirty years. This structural shift involved the deindustrialization and outsourcing of increasing amounts of manufacturing jobs to other parts of the globe, so that there has been an evisceration of manual labor markets, an implosion of wage rates on the lower rungs of the occupational ladder, and a proliferation of more temporary jobs in the service economy that blossomed as the wealthy came to have more disposable income in an increasingly unequal society. Overall, the emerging economy is one that offers far fewer sources of security for most people laboring in the United States.

So the return to ordinary capitalism is always a return to disruptive change that poses real risks especially for those on the bottom of the socioeconomic ladder whose everyday experience has always been like a canary in a coal mine alerting us to negative effects that reverberate over time throughout society.[39] This time the experiences of those on the bottom are telling us that the return to ordinary capitalism is a return to economic shifts that are profoundly destabilizing for the society as a whole. What has emerged this time is a new, more financialized economy that makes money for those at the top while everyone else is weighed down by multiplying forms of debt, whether in home mortgages, student loans, credit cards, or medical bills.[40] We have shifted from "public Keynesianism" where the government takes on debt to stimulate the economy to a "privatized Keynesianism" where the government's job is to encourage everyone else to take on personal debt in order to sustain the economy.[41] We become less interested in people for their contributions to the productivity of labor and more interested in them as human capital that can enhance the profitability of financiers. The result just heightens the precarity of ordinary citizens.

After years of conservative social welfare policies, the increasingly unequal economy has worked to create its own vicious cycle. Growing economic inequality has helped fuel increasing political gridlock on issues of social welfare. A derailed policy process forestalls momentum to address problems wrought by the changing economy. The end result is many people without real prospects for securing a decent standard of living.[42] The arc of history has bent in a rightward direction for a long time now. A post–World War II economy that grew in ways that diminished the distance between classes has been replaced in the last thirty years by one that widens that distance. The process of creative destruction has once again produced a return to ordinary capitalism; after an economic downturn, the economy starts to

grow again but as transformed. This time the new normal is an intensifica-
tion of the inequity of a neoliberalized political economy.

While there may be no going back, how we go forward in response is
open to question. Marx may have denied that history repeats itself; however,
in the very same essay he also denied that people could act outside history
and ignore the conditions they confronted at any one time: "Men make their
own history, but they do not make it as they please; they do not make it
under self-selected circumstances, but under circumstances existing already,
given and transmitted from the past."[43] History might not repeat itself but
people (women as well as men, on the right as well as on the left) cannot
escape the force of history and inevitably are affected by it when seeking to
act collectively to change things.[44] Marx asserted: "The tradition of all dead
generations weighs like a nightmare on the brains of the living."[45] As Avery
Gordon has suggested:

> The way of the ghost is haunting, and haunting is a very particular way of
> knowing what has happened or is happening. Being haunted draws us
> affectively, sometimes against our will and always a bit magically, into
> the structure of feeling of a reality we come to experience, not as cold
> knowledge, but as a transformative recognition.... The ghost is not simply
> a dead or missing person, but a social figure, and investigating it can lead
> to the dense site where history and subjectivity make social life.[46]

The past informs the present; it is its condition of possibility, constraining
and enabling at the same time. It haunts us like a specter and gives shape to
the future we seek to bring into being, for worse as for better.[47]

The issue of history's trajectory and the conditions under which people
can exercise agency to move it one way or another has haunted the Left from
Marx's time on.[48] What Hegel called the "cunning of reason" suggested that
people could be unwitting agents of larger historical forces.[49] Attempts to
beat back the neoliberalization of society today need to consider the issue of
agency with caution for the philosophical quandaries posed here. In addition, there is need to consider how that agency, if it can be activated, is to be
used. For a long time, the expectation was that political action logically was
to be focused on how to further progress that would move us forward to
a higher stage of development. Yet it seems of late there is growing interest
in Walter Benjamin's perspective that political action on behalf of the

oppressed is best focused on resistance to disrupt the forces of acceleration into the future. Benjamin wrote: "Marx says that revolutions are the locomotive of world history. But perhaps it is quite otherwise. Perhaps revolutions are an attempt by the passengers on this train—namely, the human race—to activate the emergency brake."[50] There is evidence that today the progressive response to the political change is more often in resistance to its negative trajectory than pushing for accelerating change forward.[51]

These reflections provide a basis for understanding how to respond to the forces working to produce today's neoliberalized inequality. At a minimum, there is good reason to think about responses that grow out of a perspective that combines the linear and cyclical views of history as well as economic determinism and political agency, emphasizing how with each swing back we must of necessity account for and reflect the conditions to which we are reacting. Those conditions leave a trace, or, better, inscribe a signature, on our efforts to move back toward the other pole of the political continuum.[52] Today's efforts to redress the excesses of an age of inequality must of necessity take those conditions into account as they swing back toward a more progressive politics. If there is to be anything like what Polanyi called the "double movement," it must take into account and work through, but in no way ignore, the powerful presence of neoliberalism today.[53] Failure to do so will result in a politics out of time, disjointed from the conditions it must confront and haunted by the ghosts of failed efforts that preceded it.

THE LONG WAVE OF STRUCTURAL ADJUSTMENT

Politics helped create the current situation and it is crucial to the response. What kind of politics and what forms it takes are in need of examination. Piketty suggests that the Great Compression from 1945 to 1973 was actually an anomaly when economic growth was correlated with increased wages and reduced inequality.[54] If that is true, then a neoliberalized economy post–Great Recession represents a return to that ordinary capitalism that in the normal course of affairs increasingly concentrates wealth at the top. Yet as noted that did not occur overnight. Instead, it came about incrementally with the rolling out of a long wave of structural adjustment as part of a politically motivated cyclical swing away from social liberalism. Economic downturns provided the opportunity each time to build on prior changes to create the current highly inequitable system. For instance, over the last five U.S.

recessions since the oil crisis of the 1970s, the economy has always recovered more slowly than from the prior recession (as measured by job growth over the first forty-eight months postrecession).[55] The increased sluggishness in recovery has most likely been due to major corporations seizing the opportunity to not bring back laid-off workers so as to allow for a restructured firm in each case to move further into the global economy where first-world workers are an uncompetitive burden. This would not necessarily be fatal for sustaining an occupational structure that could enable most workers to earn a decent living for themselves and their families. Yet that structure would require systematic planning in the halls of government to move laid-off workers into alternative employment that offered comparable wages and benefits. Instead, in the United States, the state's role in responding to restructuring has been woefully insufficient to keep pace with globalization of the economy.

As a result, wages have been stagnant for workers in the bottom half of the occupational structure for more than thirty years now, with manual-skill workers seeing major diminutions in the real value of their pay. From 1947 until the 1973–79 period, wages grew with productivity and the slogan "a rising tide lifts all boats" was not an entirely inaccurate description of the U.S. economy (see figure 1.2).[56] But in the 1973–79 period, the Great Compression, where a growing economy and increased wages worked together to reduce inequality, came to an end. The decoupling of wages from economic growth began at this point in earnest. In the thirty-plus years since, while productivity increases accelerated, wages have stagnated. One major consequence of an economy that grows without creating economic opportunities for ordinary workers is widening inequality that has in recent years achieved unprecedented heights, perhaps going beyond even what the gap between the rich and everyone else was like just in the years prior to the Great Depression.[57] In the process, an "opportunity gap" (in access to education and other developmental services) has continued to widen over the last several decades between the children of well-off and those with lower-income parents, guaranteeing that growing inequality is not likely to be reversed any time soon.[58]

Since the 1980s, the economy has continued to grow, if not nearly as strongly as during the preceding thirty years, but as noted wages for the bottom half of the occupational ladder have been stagnant and even fell in real terms for the least skilled. The decoupling of growth and wages has helped

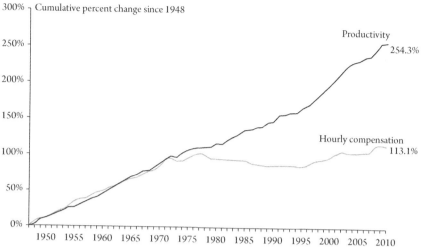

Figure 1.2 The Great Uncoupling: Economic Growth and Wages, 1950–2010. http://www.epi.org/publication/ib330-productivity-vs-compensation/. Reprinted with permission from Lawrence Mishel, *The Wedges between Productivity and Median Compensation Growth*, figure A, Economic Policy Institute Issue Brief #330, 2012.

contribute to growing inequality. For Piketty, this is normal: economic growth in capitalist economies normally leads to greater inequality, and the Great Compression was actually anomalous.[59] Sheldon Danziger has estimated that if the decoupling had not occurred, the reductions in poverty that came before would have continued, bringing the poverty rate down to basically zero. This, however, is not what has happened. Instead poverty has joined with inequality as a large problem of the current period. Danziger's estimates are striking: figure 1.3 indicates the persistence of poverty in spite of the rate of economic growth post-1973 and the projected declines in poverty that would have occurred if wages and economic growth had stayed connected.[60]

A neoliberal economy that involved growing reliance on automated production, increased outsourcing to foreign countries, declining negotiating power for labor with decreasing union membership, and other relevant factors weakening the position of ordinary workers conspired to decouple their wages from economic growth. The transformation was however not as Margaret Thatcher asserted when she invoked the acronym TINA (There Is No Alternative).[61] Instead, a concerted effort was made by economic and political leadership to weaken labor's power and free the economy to grow

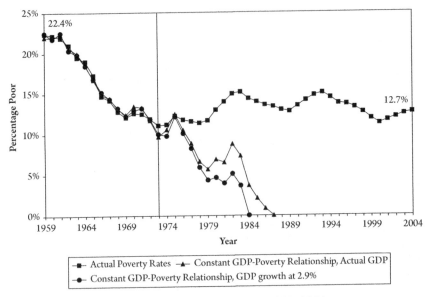

Figure 1.3 Official and Predicted Poverty Rates, 1959–2004.
Based on data in Sheldon H. Danziger, "Fighting Poverty Revisited: What Did Researchers Know 40 Years Ago? What Do We Know Today?" *Focus* 25, 1 (2007): 3–11.
Focus, Institute for Research on Poverty © 2007 by the Board of Regents of the University of Wisconsin.

in ways that inevitably increased inequality. The transformed economy was not one where a rising tide lifted all boats.[62]

Michael Katz succinctly summarized these developments:

> After the mid-1970s progress against poverty stalled. The 1973 oil crisis ushered in an era of growing inequality interrupted only briefly by the years of prosperity during the 1990s. Productivity increased, but, for the first time in American history, its gains were not shared by ordinary workers, whose real incomes declined even as the wealth of the rich soared. Poverty concentrated as never before in inner city districts scarred by chronic joblessness and racial segregation. America led western democracies in the proportion of its children living in poverty. It led the world in rates of incarceration. Trade union membership plummeted under an assault by big business abetted by the federal government. Policy responded by allowing the real value of the minimum wage, welfare benefits, and other social protections to erode. The dominant interpretation of America's

troubles blamed the War on Poverty and Great Society and constructed a rationale for responding to misery by retrenching on social spending. A bipartisan consensus emerged for solving the nation's social and economic problems through a war on dependence, the devolution of authority, and the redesign of public policy along market models.[63]

The long wave of structural adjustment not only eviscerated economic opportunities for working people, it also accelerated the concentration of wealth at the top, especially among corporate executives and their families, accelerating a shift toward a more patrimonial form of capitalism. By 2012, the average compensation for chief executive officers of major U.S. corporations was 354 times the average earnings of workers.[64] That was an approximately tenfold increase from thirty years before and many times the CEO-worker ratios of other advanced capitalist economies. As a result, the economy grew to concentrate wealth among the elite who now are increasingly transferring it to their descendants so as to produce a return to the patrimonial capitalism of the gilded age.[65] Levels of inequality not seen in a century are being unleashed by the transformed economy (see table 1.1).

Relying on Karl Polanyi, Fred Block and Margaret Somers have argued that the market always needs to be understood as embedded in the broader

Table 1.1   International Comparisons in CEO/ Worker Pay, 2012.

U.S.	354
Australia	93
Canada	206
France	104
Germany	147
Japan	67
Sweden	89

Source: http://www.aflcio.org/Press-Room/Press-Releases/ U.S.-CEOs-Paid-354-Times-the-Average-Rank-and-File-Worker- Largest-Pay-Gap-in-the-World. Note: 2012 U.S. CEO-to-worker pay ratio calculated based on AFL-CIO analysis of average CEO pay at 327 companies in the S&P 500 Index, which disclosed 2012 CEO pay data as of April 1, 2013, as provided by Salary.com. 2012 U.S. rank-and-file worker pay calculated from the U.S. Bureau of Labor Statistics' Current Employment Statistics Survey—Table B-2: Average hours and earnings of production and non-supervisory employees on private non-farm payrolls.

society and is deeply affected by state policy and social practices.[66] Wolfgang Streeck has argued that the increasingly unequal economy is the result of concerted effort to "disembed" the market from the state and civil society.[67] Yet regardless of whether we choose to see the market today as embedded, it is important to emphasize that the changes in the economy over the thirty years of the long wave of structural adjustment were not simply the result of inexorable economic forces. The rapidly growing concentration of wealth at the top among the corporate elite and their descendants was not the result of economic activity alone. There is compelling evidence that much of the gain by the wealthy came from economically unproductive tax cuts that contrary to arguments made at the time actually may have slowed economic growth while doing little more than lining the pockets of the rich. The findings from one highly cited analysis are: (1) tax cuts over the last fifty years in the United States have been a major source of growing inequality, (2) these tax cuts did absolutely nothing positive for economic growth, and (3) the optimal top marginal tax rate could increase to as high as 83 percent to encourage growth in an equitable fashion.[68]

At the same time the public policy was concentrating wealth at the top, it was also moving the economy to where people increasingly relied on debt to get by. It is not just that beginning in the mid-1970s, wages stopped growing with the economy, ending the Great Compression, thereby stalling progress against poverty, producing more economic hardship for growing numbers of ordinary workers, and increasing inequality. A growing dependence on credit led to heavier debt burdens for many in the form of increased credit card debt, home mortgages, student debt, and medical debt. Increases in bankruptcies and eventually defaulted mortgages became growing concerns of the most recent period. The burden on the young who came to find it increasingly difficult to advance economically without college degrees meant that growing student loans started to slow their taking on home mortgages (figure 1.4). As a result, a deleterious credit economy emerged where people's grim economic prospects became a prime profit opportunity for the financial industry and one of the remaining drivers available for spurring economic growth.[69]

Other evidence buttresses the claim that the Great Recession did not cause the lugubrious trends of recent years. These trends have been developing for thirty years as part of a long wave of structural adjustment. Further, those long-term changes were not the result of economic activity alone but were

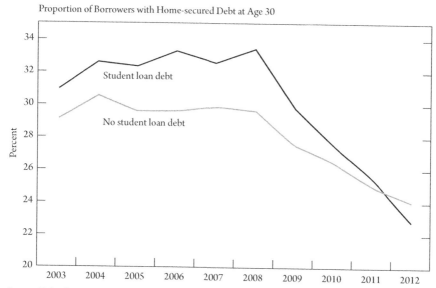

Proportion of Borrowers with Home-secured Debt at Age 30

Source: Federal Reserve Bank of New York Consumer Credit Panel/Equifax

Figure 1.4 Proportion of Borrowers with Home-Secured Debt at Age of Thirty. Federal Reserve Bank of New York Consumer Credit Panel/Equifax. Reprinted from Meta Brown and Sydnee Caldwell, "Proportion of Borrowers with Home-Secured Debt at Age of 30," Federal Reserve Bank of New York, *Liberty Street Economics* blog, April 17, 2013, http://libertystreeteconomics.newyorkfed .org/2013/04/young-student-loan-borrowers-retreat-from-housing-and-automarkets.html.

spurred on by explicit public policies that redistributed upward. The Great Recession has, however, created a pretext to accelerate the negative trends in ways that makes their effects that much harder to reverse. Corporations are seizing the opportunity to accelerate their participation in a globalizing economy that provides less stable, decently paying jobs for ordinary Americans here at home while production increasingly is done elsewhere and finance, insurance, and investment in other people's production become the fastest growing and most profitable parts of the U.S. economy.[70]

Corporate America's exploitation of the Great Recession to accelerate economic change is just part of the equation that makes the transformation that much more difficult to reverse. Another important part of this diabolical formula is that growing economic inequality has led to growing political inequality. As a result, this system of inequality becomes self-perpetuating because the wealthy can use their wealth to dominate the policy process while others are increasingly weighed down with debt that becomes a preoccupation, discouraging them from taking chances politically as well as economically.[71] Today, a transformed economy is producing an entirely different kind of politics, polarized between the haves and the have-nots and in which those with the wealth and power push for hollowing out the welfare state and promoting more disciplinary approaches for managing the economically disadvantaged. The result is unprecedented gridlock, whereby the wealthy use their gains from the transformed economy to block government action to address the inequities being created.[72]

Growing inequality produced an influx of money into politics that has led to gridlock born of political polarization that was the result almost entirely of the Republican Party moving increasingly to the right.[73] In fact increased inequality and political polarization are historically correlated. Figure 1.5 shows a pattern over time for political polarization in the U.S. House of Representatives that parallels the curvilinear trend for inequality over the course of the twentieth century. Today, the unprecedented levels of inequality are in no small part due to concentrating resources among the wealthy (most especially among the top 1 percent or even the top .1 percent), who have not been reluctant to use them to increase the partisan polarization

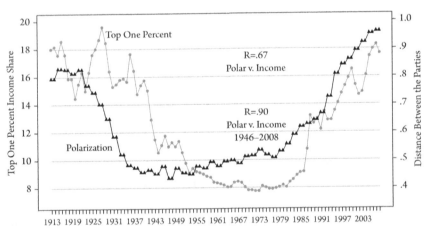

Figure 1.5 Top 1 Percent Income Share and U.S. House of Representatives Party Polarization, 1913–2008.
Nolan McCarty, Keith T. Poole, and Howard Rosenthal, *Polarized America: The Dance of Ideology and Unequal Riches* (Cambridge, MA: MIT Press, 2006), Figure 1.2, page 8, © 2006 Massachusetts Institute of Technology, by permission of The MIT Press.

that has contributed to the blocking of meaningful policy responses to the persistent economic hardship so many ordinary Americans confront on a daily basis. As a result, politics today intensifies the long-standing pattern of public policy representing the interests of the rich at the expense of the poor.[74] In an age of patrimonial capitalism, economic inequality translates into sustained political inequality. The result is rule by an economic oligarchy.[75]

Hollowing out the Welfare State

Within any political-economic cycle, public policy in general but social welfare policy in particular demonstrates a durable consistency that has been labeled by policy analysts as "path dependency."[76] Once policies have been enacted they are likely to gain acceptance, especially if they generate what Paul Pierson and others have called "policy feedback," where the policies' positive effects feedback and affect how the mass public as well as policy-making elites assess the policy.[77] Once a policy gains acceptance in this way, it becomes more embedded in the political-economic system and less likely to be quickly overturned even with partisan changes of those in elected positions. Yet over time when political conditions change, especially in response to economic difficulties, it becomes possible to break out of a path dependency where politics arrives at a "critical juncture."[78] At this point, the possibilities for serious policy revision arise.

Today, with mounting concerns over the increasingly inequitable character of the changing economy, we may be coming to the end of the path dependency that perpetuated the policies that redistributed wealth upward while imposing discipline on those left behind. For too long, attempts to move beyond these neoliberal policies that emphasize market-compliant behavior in spite of dwindling prospects for earning a decent living have stalled in the face of what Jacob Hacker has called "policy drift."[79] The inaction of policy drift becomes its own form of action, and social welfare policies by default become less responsive to changing needs for assistance. For instance, the minimum wage laws lag behind what is needed to support a family. The lack of state-subsidized child care makes it more difficult for the growing numbers of single mothers to sustain the double shift associated with simultaneously being the breadwinner and the homemaker. The growth of insecure jobs that provide no benefits including pensions make Social

Security retirement funds from the government the only basis of income in old age for a growing number of Americans.

One major reason for policy drift over the last three decades is that the battle over the welfare state has become more polarized and as a result public policies have not been updated to address the changing economic circumstances, leaving more people to suffer the consequences of their growing economic precarity. In an age of political polarization and the resulting gridlock, policy drift becomes its own way of retrenching the welfare state by inaction. As a result, the welfare state is hollowed out even as its policies remain in place.

To say that the welfare state is being hollowed out, however, can be a bit of an understatement. Policy paralysis has extended for so long that inequality has not only increased but for the first time in the history of recorded statistics life expectancy in the United States is now falling for people on the bottom of the socioeconomic order.[80] Kathleen Geier has noted that the economic deterioration is affecting whites as well as blacks: "Between 1990 and 2008, white women without a high school diploma lost a full five years of their lives, while their male counterparts lost three years. [D]ecreases on this scale have not been seen in the U.S. since the Spanish influenza epidemic of 1918. . . . In the U.S., the period between 1990 and 2008, which is a period that saw such steep declines in life expectancy for the least well-off white people, is also a period during which economic inequality soared."[81] Part of the explanation is today's distinctive form of policy drift—that is, the failure of public policy to address the consequences of a transformed economy.

The hollowing out of the welfare state highlights how neoliberalism has emphasized attacking what is politically vulnerable.[82] A big part of this political vulnerability is associated with long-standing efforts to resist aiding the less fortunate on grounds that they are not deserving of assistance. Class, race, and gender have been key buttons that politicians and others have been able to push to suggest that those in need of assistance have failed to conform to white, middle-class standards of work and family. The political rhetoric of demonization has played its role in delaying confronting the need to address the fallout from the transformation of the economy.[83]

Yet in the end, we must recognize that the hollowing out of the welfare state is not just the result of policy inaction born of path dependencies. Instead, draconian policy changes explicitly imposed on ordinary people are at work as well. To choose but one troubling example, massive cutbacks in mental health programming that have continued for several decades have made prisons and jails key places where we warehouse people with mental health problems, without providing real treatment for their conditions. As poignantly noted by one criminal justice official, "the situation now mirrors years past when large numbers of the mentally ill were put in prison rather than institutions where they could be treated."[84] The deterioration of mental health funding that has made our jails operate as nineteenth-century asylums (where we hide the mentally ill but do not treat them). This is bound to make people wonder about just exactly what type of political economy we are reverting to after the Great Recession.[85] The new normal has its own abnormalities; ordinary capitalism today is jarringly inequitable. Cyclical change away from the liberal, Keynesian countercyclical welfare state to a neoliberal, market-compliant disciplinary state has had its worst effects on those who could least afford it. In the process, the emerging "anti-state state," as Ruth Wilson Gilmore calls the neoliberalized regime of the current period, off-loads its welfare state functions via devolution by repurposing state prisons and local jails to take on new responsibilities for managing the poor and warehousing those disproportionately nonwhite populations who often get criminalized just for being poor.[86]

DRIFTING TOWARD NEOLIBERALISM

So it is within this not-so-predetermined political-economic context that the Great Recession has provided an opportunity for the acceleration of thirty-year-old trends that actually are indicative of the inequities endemic to capitalism itself. Capitalism has always meant economic insecurity for workers, but trade unions, the welfare state, and regulatory intervention previously combined to contain the risks associated with capitalist labor markets, even if to a lesser degree than in other advanced industrial economies. Yet now in an era of a globalized economy where financial products are the major source of profit in the United States, the declining influence of labor, the welfare state, and economic regulation joined to expose workers to great uncertainty about their ability to secure stable employment at decent wages.[87] In fact, the end of the economic meltdown stemming from the Great Recession heralded a return to an intensifying trend whereby a growing number of different types of people confronted a widening variety of forms of precarity: students with debt and no job prospects; the long-term unemployed, who were increasingly just plain unemployable; homeowners whose homes could only be sold at a massive loss; as well as growing numbers of people living in deep or extreme poverty. Even those well off but below the uppermost reaches of the labor market (the "99 percent" as they have come to be called) had reason to be less than sanguine about the return to the new normal because of concerns about their reliance on debt to continue to sustain their lifestyle.

The resulting economic insecurity for growing numbers of Americans is, however, not just an economic problem, it is also, and perhaps as noted a political problem.[88] Debates over increased inequality are on the surface largely economic.[89] On the surface, the issue is often couched as whether growing inequality not only produces more economic hardship and poverty but also slows economic growth.[90] It is likely that economic inequality has not only contributed to increased economic hardship for those on the bottom but has also undermined economic growth. Yet there is also the political dimension. Increased inequality creates disproportionate resources for the wealthy to dominate the political process in order to prevent increased taxation and spending that are needed to fund economic recovery programs and help address the economic misery being endured by people on the increasingly unequal economic ladder.[91]

As a result, growing economic inequality produces a paralyzed political process where policy drift becomes the norm.[92] Given the political paralysis that inequality has helped fund, government has been unable to address the economic misery the structural shift has inflicted. Lane Kenworthy has noted that across capitalist economies where governments have acted to compensate people for the growing inequality wrought by the structural shift, there has been less negative fallout than in countries like the United States where less government response has left people more vulnerable.[93] Edward McCelland has eloquently captured this point:

> The shrinking of the middle class is not a failure of capitalism. It's a failure of government. Capitalism has been doing exactly what it was designed to do: concentrating wealth in the ownership class, while providing the mass of workers with just enough wages to feed, house and clothe themselves. Young people who graduate from college to $9.80 an hour jobs as sales clerks or data processors are giving up on the concept of employment as a

vehicle for improving their financial fortunes: In a recent survey, 24 percent defined the American dream as "not being in debt." The lesson of the last forty years is that we can't depend on the free market to sustain the middle class without government intervention.[94]

In other words, the Great Recession has proven to be a pivotal moment not just economically but also politically. Just as the roots of the economic transformation stretch back before the Great Recession, the influence of wealth to forestall state action to address issues of social welfare has been growing for just as long.[95] The growing inequality has led to massive expenditures in lobbying by the wealthy to lower taxes, reduce regulation of business, and limit social welfare legislation. As a result, the United States is moving to a tiered society. At the top, there is a limited stratum of upper-class and upper-middle-class people, ensconced in positions of corporate oversight and needed professional occupations. At the bottom is everyone who is increasingly deemed as not deserving of the state's support, in part because they failed to position themselves as successful participants for the globalizing economy and are therefore seen as a burden that a globally competitive corporate sector cannot and will not carry. At the extreme, those in poverty are cast aside as disposable populations who are to be monitored, surveilled, disciplined, and punished more than they are to be helped.

The hollowed-out welfare state has less to offer those disadvantaged by economic transformation. Increasingly what it does have to offer is not so much assistance as discipline, discipline focused on getting people to internalize market logic and accept personal responsibility for the need to find whatever means, however limited, to get by in the changing economy.[96] This is the core of what is being called neoliberalism, a new liberalism that restructures the state to operate consistently with market logic in order to better promote market-compliant behavior by as many people as possible.[97]

Neoliberalism most fundamentally is about making economic rationality the basic ethic for everyday living in all areas of life.[98] It blurs the boundaries between the market and the state and civil society as well. It is a philosophy that prioritizes people learning to be economically minded about everything they do so they can more profitably develop their human capital and become less in need of relying on the government for assistance. Everyone must learn to think about all aspects of their lives in terms of return on investment (what is commonly now called ROI).[99] Even government programs for the poor come to be centered on inculcating this neoliberal ethos.[100] The result is that self-governance replaces the government. It is the ultimate form of privatization.

Neoliberalism does not just produce economically minded citizens, it looks to them to be sources of capital production. Where workers' labor was once a factor in production, ordinary people's everyday activities are now commodified in ways that add to production, as when data mining of people's Internet use creates marketable information, or when people's consumption patterns create value based on popularity.[101] People are even encouraged to acquire more debt to invest in the development of their human capital (making education loans the largest source of debt in the entire economy) such that this borrowing becomes the basis for making the financial industry the largest source of profit for the entire economy. Neoliberalism is heavily invested in getting ordinary people to be not just factors in production but sources of capital themselves. Activating those on the bottom of the socioeconomic ladder to participate more extensively in investing in their own futures through acquiring debt, whether for schooling, buying a home, or other purposes, becomes an important source of economic growth in an economy led by the financial industry.[102]

Yet for those who fail at becoming on their own financially savvy neoliberal citizen-subjects who can develop and leverage their own human capital, the state works to inculcate market-compliant behavior via a panoply of incentives and penalties. And when that does not work, especially as the inequitable economy grows in ways that do not create economic opportunities for them, then coercive controls are imposed. The goal is to control and contain those left behind so as a disposable population they are less of a burden on the rest of society. Jodi Dean sees the trend toward neoliberalization of social and economic policy as buttressing the movement to a highly unequal society divided between those who are gaining from economic change and those who do not. Dean writes:

What will we see in 20 years (or earlier)? The amplification of the worst trends already present in our society: the super-rich sheltered in their gated communities and high-rises, defended by the military (inclusive of a militarized police) and their own private security forces. Private education would continue to educate their children. Private health care would ensure their health and longevity.

What about the rest of us? We will be free. Free to fight among our-selves—completely armed—for the scraps that remain. We will com-pete for scholarships—ostensibly proving the continuation of merit and opportunity. We will compete for grants for art, design, and various other sorts of contracts. We will work ever harder for ever less as public schools, roads, hospitals, and infrastructure declines. And when we resist, when we organize—the defense budget... will fund the drone warfare and surveil-lance used against us. Private prisons will provide housing.[103]

Dean is onto something that has implications for all Americans but espe-cially for social justice advocates and those in the helping professions who are tasked with working with the most marginalized in the transformed eco-nomic context. In other words, it is not just the economy and the political system that are undergoing a structural shift. In response to these broader economic and political changes, social welfare institutions are being adjusted accordingly. In the transformed context, we see a shift from redistributing resources to the economically disadvantaged to an emphasis on enforcing compliance to behavioral standards so that subordinate populations become less of a burden on society.

It is here at this neoliberal terminus that we find a transformed social work, depoliticized and refocused on managing disposable populations. Social work no longer stands outside power but now is more than ever thor-oughly assimilated to it. Across a wide variety of populations in need of var-ious forms of assistance and treatment, social work shifts to technologies of the state, forms of governmentality, practices associated with getting served populations to internalize an ethic of self-discipline and personal responsi-bility. The goal of this responsibilization is for subordinate populations to handle their own problems as best they can on their own, with the aim that they become less of a burden for the constrained state. As a result, they should become more willing to take up whatever limited positions in the globalizing economy that they are afforded. Social work increasingly com-prises forms of psychological services focused on helping realize the disci-plinary demands of the neoliberalizing state, which is now ever more dedi-cated to managing rather than serving disposable populations. When examining changes across a number of different areas of human service provision today, most striking are the parallel shifts in treatment toward a more disciplinary approach to managing service populations.[104] It is the end of social work as we knew it and the ascendancy of a neoliberal regime that disciplines subordinate populations to be market compliant regardless of the consequences.

PLAN B: THE NEOLIBERAL DISCIPLINARY REGIME

This disciplinary regime is not peripheral but actually the core of what I am calling neoliberalism. As critical as this aspect of neoliberalism is, it is, however, not really the preferred strategy of today's capitalists. Instead, neoliberalism is actually their "Plan B" for the state. Neoliberalism is not in this sense an ideology that prizes market fundamentalism and seeks a return to laissez-faire economics.[105] That would be Plan A. Yet Plan A has run afoul of Keynesian economics and its insistence that only the state is big enough to counteract market failure. Though often repudiated by the Right, Keynesianism has remained a point of contention since the Great Depression of the 1930s until now post–Great Recession. As a result, there remains a belief in the mass public generally that we need the welfare state to counter the capriciousness of the market and the adversity it creates for those who get marginalized. After the New Deal, after the Great Society, after years of getting accustomed to relying on Social Security, Medicare, and other entitlements, the positive policy feedback loop that policy analysts refer to has been enacted whereby over time these policies engendered their own support in the mass public. While certain programs such as welfare for the poor were vulnerable to being seen as handouts that encouraged a dependency on government that was unearned, the basic idea of the welfare state could not be simply wished away.[106] As a result, the proponents of neoliberalism cannot just sweep the welfare state away and return to a system of laissez-faire economics such as that which reigned in the nineteenth century and the age of the robber barons.

In other words, market fundamentalists could not ignore Marx's injunction that people cannot make history just as they please. Given the reality of the welfare state, the neoliberals cannot simply roll it back as Plan A would have them do. Instead, the Right must resort to Plan B. In other words: if you cannot eradicate the welfare state, the next best thing is to marketize it. Plan B for the marketeers involves not just trying to hollow out the welfare state as much as possible but also remaking the remaining welfare state programs to operate consonantly with market principles in service of more efficiently buttressing the market itself. From education vouchers to medical choice schemes to private investment accounts in lieu of social security, from welfare-to-work programs grounded in incentivizing taking low-wage work to the penalties and rewards in drug treatment programs, the programs of the welfare state are increasingly run structured according to strict market logic only to get clients also to be more market-compliant actors. The state increasingly contracts with for-profit providers who are incentivized to condition their clients to become more disciplined and docile, to internalize market logic so they will more willingly accept the verdict of the globalizing market and take whatever low-wage jobs, if available, they can find as their main source of economic salvation. Neoliberalized service provision features this sort of disciplinary work that providers impose on their workers who then must in turn impose it on their clients.

Nonetheless, neoliberalization's attempts at the marketization of state operations are still treated with suspicion among many groups. While the idea of choice is a powerful way of framing neoliberal programming as consistent with basic American values, there remains ambivalence about instruments for facilitating the freedom of choice. Witness the concerns that continue to be expressed about vouchers, whether in housing or other areas, but especially education.[107] Vouchers too often simply do not cover the cost of effective participation in the particular markets for which they are designed, leaving clients out in the cold and unable to access what they need. There is growing appreciation that other neoliberalizing policy efforts are just as problematic. Incentives for work still lead to poverty-inuring low-wage and insecure employment. Addicts are incentivized but still also very often remain poor, without work and often homeless. Reentry programs for ex-felons go the same way. Private accounts for Social Security retirement investments are likely to come up short as well. As more and more people are marginalized, as the lower tier grows, as people see they are left on the outside holding an empty bag, the willingness to go political, to take direct action, to rise from below will increase.

The cyclical turn is now shifting at this critical juncture away from neoliberalism as its pursuit of marketizing everything leads to growing economic inequality and diminished democratic decision making by the state. Witness the series of protests that spread across the country in 2012 as part of the Occupy Wall Street movement.[108] And now in the city where we saw Occupy emerge, a new mayor was swept into office in part with the support of a political party with ties to Occupy—the Working Families Party—and all the while promising to work to get beyond the neoliberal regime his predecessor put in place.[109] In spite of the concentrations of wealth among the elite, their ability to dominate the political process is not limitless. Further, with the mass protests in response to the killings of Michael Brown in Ferguson, Missouri, and Eric Garner in Staten Island, New York, the disciplinary dimensions of neoliberalism have confronted their greatest resistance yet. Policing to discipline the poor to be compliant with the neoliberal order in spite of their being marginalized by it has resulted in the growing illegitimacy of the state and its racialized use of police power. As neoliberalism pushes relentlessly toward opening up new markets by marketizing the state and civil society, it creates the need to increase discipline on those who do not fit in, cannot participate, or will not benefit from the increasingly marketized systems.[110] Neoliberalism's economic and political effects however produce their own resistance. Political mobilization by ordinary people is already having an effect with changes beginning to occur that include attacking those concentrations of wealth in tax policy and resisting the power of the state to police those marginalized. The economics of neoliberalism create its own political fallout.

Yes, just as proponents of market fundamentalism could not simply do away with the welfare state once it was erected, neither could the critics of the prevailing neoliberal disciplinary regime. Sometimes it seems that the response to the problems of neoliberal failure in social welfare provision is more neoliberalism. A good example of neoliberalism's persistence in this regard is the interest in social impact bonds as a meaningful response to the withering of the public sector. In response to budget cuts, policy entrepreneurs have hit on the idea to market social welfare programs to Wall Street investors with the promise of increased returns on the bonds they purchase should the program they invest in meet or exceed its benchmarks for program outcomes.[111] To paraphrase Jamie Peck and Nik Theodore, social impact bonds have become the latest example of a "fast-track global social policy" that quickly spreads from country to country in a globalized political economy where nations increasingly emulate each other in revising their social welfare programs to adjust to the changing conditions of the transformed global economy.[112] Social impact bonds have spread from New York City to Canada to the United Kingdom to Australia and beyond (see chapter 7).[113] Regardless of the value of social impact bonds as a way of financing social welfare programs, their emergence as a policy innovation that is being taken very seriously suggests that in spite of all the criticisms of neoliberal social welfare programming, the neoliberal approach very much remains the new normal when it comes to how to make and implement social welfare policy in the current era.[114]

As much as people have good reasons to wish away neoliberalism, the social welfare programs made in its image suggest it cannot simply be undone. Neoliberalism is the new normal; there is no going back in some simple swing to the left. Even if there is going to be a cyclical swing away from the disciplinary poverty management regime, reforms will to some degree likely reflect the neoliberal context from which they came. If there is to be something approximating Polanyi's double movement as a swing back against the undemocratic effects of neoliberal marketization, it must acknowledge the pervasiveness of neoliberalism, so as to work through it and not around it. Neoliberalism might not be "bulletproof," but it is deeply embedded in the very fabric of U.S. society today and its pervasive influence must be taken into account in pushing for political change.[115]

Ordinary capitalism has returned, with a neoliberal vengeance. The best responses recognize how quickly and pervasively it has embedded itself as an obdurate reality we ignore at our peril. Simply wishing to push it away to move to something better will not do. Instead, we must work through neoliberalism rather than try to blithely think we can work around it. Taking incremental steps that lay the foundation for more serious transformation over the long run is the road to a better future. This would not be a status quo incrementalism but instead a "radical incrementalism" (a topic I return to in chapter 8, the last).

2

MIDDLE-CLASS MELANCHOLIA

SELF-SUFFICIENCY AFTER THE DEMISE
OF CHRISTIANIZED CAPITALISM
(U.S. STYLE)

Today there is much talk that the ability to conform to the ideal of the self-sufficient self is in jeopardy in the United States.[1] The economic landscape has created a difficult terrain for ordinary Americans. The evaporation of decently paying manufacturing jobs, the declining influence of labor unions, the hollowing out of the welfare state, and the lag in economic regulation have now joined a shift to an economy where finance is the main source of profit.[2] These forces have combined to undermine the bedrock identity of the personally responsible, self-sufficient person that long ago was put on the cultural pedestal by the traditional Protestant work ethic. The risks of making it into and staying in the middle class are increasingly for people to handle on their own with less backup from the government, making middle-class status all that more tenuous.[3] The "fear of falling," as Barbara Ehrenreich called it, has become pervasive among ordinary people.[4] In particular, anxieties about taxes and debt, public and personal, weigh heavily on our individual and collective (un)conscious. The resulting political mood for the vast majority of Americans, those neither on the top nor the bottom, reflects what we can call "middle-class melancholia."[5]

Sigmund Freud famously distinguished melancholia from mourning when he wrote, "The analogy with mourning led us to conclude that [the patient] had suffered a loss in regard to an object; what he tells us points to a loss in regard to his ego."[6] Both mourning and melancholia reflect grief over a loss, usually of a loved one, a love object, a prized and valued attachment of some kind, or even an ideal. Yet while mourning is grieving over a loss external to oneself, melancholia grows out of a loss of self-regard, even if that comes from losing something or someone external to oneself. Melancholia, for Freud, reflects a disavowal of the loss incurred, where the person is internally at war with oneself, and is preoccupied with repudiating oneself as responsible for the external loss.

For Freud, melancholia was pathological compared with mourning, which he saw as a healthy response to loss. Ilit Ferber eloquently summarizes Freud's distinction of melancholia from mourning:

> In his 1917 essay "Mourning and Melancholy," Freud recognizes two mutually exclusive responses to loss—mourning [*Trauer*] and melancholia [*Melancholie*]. This sharp distinction between the two responses has long since become almost synonymous with the understanding of a normal versus a pathological reaction to loss, and the clear demarcation between them. At the outset of Freud's article the two responses would seem closely related, but the question of the acceptance and acknowledgement of the loss complicates the picture and draws them apart. Both Freud's mourner and melancholic begin with a basic denial of their loss and an unwillingness to recognize it. But soon enough, the mourner, who is reacting in a non-pathological manner, recognizes and responds to the *call of reality*, to let go of the lost-loved object and liberate libidinal desire. This is the point of divergence with the melancholic who remains sunken in his loss, unable to acknowledge and accept the need to cleave and in a self-destructive loyalty to the lost object, internalizes it into his ego, thus furthermore circumscribing the conflict related to the loss. The lost object continues to exist, but as part of the dejected subject, who can no longer clearly define the borders between his own subjectivity and the existence of the lost object within it. The structure of this melancholic response is conceived by Freud as an antithesis to the basic well-being of the ego, the survival of which is put at risk.[7]

Melancholia for Walter Benjamin was not necessarily pathological as much as it was a fundamental condition of human existence reflective of people's tragic sense of their mortality.[8] For Benjamin, melancholia and mourning were interrelated.[9] Extending Benjamin, Giorgio Agamben has noted that a close reading of Freud suggests that melancholia precedes the loss of something a person never actually possessed, in all cases whether it is a loved one, a status, or an ideal.[10] The lost object emanates from the imaginary, as in an imagined or idealized understanding that is being lost.

Melancholia therefore ultimately is about a sense of self relative to some idealized state of being. Elisabeth Anker characterizes in Freudian terms how the issue of identity emerges from the melancholic's handling of loss:

> For Freud, the process of identification begins out of an experience of losing something or someone that one has loved. This lost object can be a person, an abstract concept such as an ideal, or one's country. Identification is a way of managing this loss, and it requires relinquishing one's earlier desire to have what was loved and is now gone.... In identification, one substitutes oneself, part of one's ego, for the lost object.... Identification can be seen as a coping mechanism that constitutes subjectivity by its attempt to manage loss, an attempt to satisfy one's own desires when they are not satisfied by others.[11]

For Freud, the melancholic in the end endures a split sense of self where he comes to be obsessed with the idea that he was not worthy to be associated with what was loved (and is now lost).[12]

Middle-class melancholia is also very much an issue of identity. In the face of growing economic uncertainty, middle-class melancholia transforms material concerns over economic well-being into issues of identity. It reflects a self-loathing born from grief over loss of the ability to realize the personal responsibility ideal. Melancholia can be seen as an ongoing anxiety about what might come to pass concerning how one imagines his or her relationship to an ideal. Middle-class melancholia involves an ongoing anxiety about the sustainability of the self-sufficiency ideal (something that was never actually obtainable for many Americans) and whether a person can now even keep up the appearance of being financially secure (when in fact he or she under capitalism of necessity has to live a life that includes an always looming economic insecurity).

Middle-class existence was evanescent for many Americans for much of the country's history, but the middle-class ideal continued to be valorized as something worth striving for, as realistically feasible if not always realized in practice. For the middle class today, however, we increasingly hear that people worry whether even the self-sufficiency ideal is sustainable as something that is worth aspiring to, given it is decreasingly achievable via stable employment that made it the bedrock ideal of the capitalist economy of the post–World War II period. The melancholia that results from loss of the ability to attain the ideal adds anxiety to the growing concern about how more mundane things like taxes and debt affect the status of the middle class today.[13] Many people who had identified as middle class arguably come to simultaneously resent the ideal as cruel while still worrying about their ability to meet it. Middle-class melancholia ultimately involves of necessity a splitting of the self, as Freud suggests, that often takes the form of expressing self-loathing by demonizing today's actually existing indebted middle class, themselves included, when they give up the ideal and become preoccupied with financial maneuvering to sustain but the appearance of middle-class self-sufficiency.

Middle-class coping is a critical site for playing out anxieties about debt and taxes that are associated with the possibility of losing the ability to be seen as a personally responsible person who acts consistently with the self-sufficient ideal. Even though middle-class melancholia is more about the symbolic rather than the material conditions associated with the self-sufficiency ideal, it has palpable consequences for how people behave individually and collectively. And while they may not experience destitution like those in the social-economic strata below them, the economic shocks the middle class absorbs may be politically more consequential given their continued participation in the political process at relatively high rates compared with the working class and the poor. Middle-class melancholia may in fact become a significant fulcrum for coming political change.[14]

The actual experience of economic dislocation can compound the psychological destabilization. Not surprisingly, there is social science research demonstrating that experiencing economic shocks can heighten worries about one's economic future and these shocks can even affect policy attitudes.[15] Yet the real fact of the matter is that middle-class melancholia does not need such evidence for its activation because it is based on anxiety about what may happen regardless of whether it actually does. Middle-class melancholia, as I am conceiving of it, is activated irrespective of whether someone has actually experienced economic shocks. Middle-class melancholia is about affect more than effect. It is about the anxiety over continuing to make it in the changing economy and how that anxiety can affect how people see themselves and others in their class and irrespective of what their income and occupational status actually is.

We arrive at middle-class melancholia once the ideal of the self-sufficient self is called into question to the point that there arises among members of the middle class the necessity of resorting to a politics of self-loathing, where such things as politicking for more tax cuts and vilifying debt (both by people and the government) takes precedence in the name of maintaining appearances as upstanding middle-class citizen-subjects.[16] Middle-class melancholia is born of this impostor mentality that many in the middle class must maintain, pained as they are to have to resort to pantomiming the self-sufficient self, while violating the standard in their actual pecuniary practices (as when scheming as private actors who avoid paying their fair share of taxes). Middle-class melancholia encourages attempts at sustaining the idea that the ideal of the personally responsible, self-sufficient self can still be credibly enacted in practice but only by demonizing taxes and public and private debt because they are an embarrassing revelation that strips away the façade of middle-class status in the financialized economy.[17]

This is the psyche of many anxious members of the middle class today, especially those whose economic status has in one way or another caused them to confront economic "precarity." Guy Standing has suggested that a new class is emerging reflective of the transformed economy, which he calls "the Precariat."[18] For Standing, the precariat replaces Marx's proletariat as the new "dangerous class." Standing, however, emphasizes the precariat's diversity as opposed to the proletariat's homogeneity as a distinct stratum in the class system. The precariat includes homeowners who cannot pay their mortgages, as well as those who have been made homeless, the downwardly mobile professionals recently thrown out of the upper middle class, the long-term unemployed from the lower rungs of the laboring classes, students with massive amounts of education debt as well as people living off unpaid credit card balances, and a diversity of others struggling to survive in the changing economy. Their diversity implies variations in their concerns about their economic precarity; it also suggests the necessity of thinking in new ways about how they can be organized for political action to redress their grievances.[19]

While sustaining a middle-class identity has for much of the history of the post–World War II economy been a struggle for many Americans, the precarious nature of maintaining that identity has intensified over the last three-plus decades of economic change, where the economy grows but average incomes stagnate (see chapter 1). And post–Great Recession, stories abound about a marginal precarious workforce including "casualized" (i.e., temporary) laborers, especially so-called microearners who lack stable employment and work on assignment in what is called the "share economy" for a growing number of companies such as Uber, Lyft, and Task-Rabbit.[20] Whether they are ferreting travelers back and forth from the airport or taking on temporary child-care assignments, the small but nontrivial number of these workers sustain themselves by working from home, and going from one assignment to another at odd hours, often with low pay and without health insurance, sick leave, vacation, or retirement benefits. So the old precarity is now intensified or at least the myth of a broad middle class itself comes under a cloud of suspicion as no longer credible. The day laborer rather than the organization man becomes the archetype of the workforce as workers "downscale" their expectations and learn to get by with less. In the public imaginary, the evanescent ideal of the self-sufficient middle-class wage earner cannot but be looked on today from a melancholic perspective.

In what follows, I contrast the Tea Party and Occupy as critical movements that are disproportionately composed of people who identify as middle class and are responding to the rise of the self-sufficiency issue post–Great Recession. I examine how melancholia operates in each, especially regarding issues of debt and taxes. I rely on Tayyab Mahmud's argument about the centrality of the debt in the changing economy.[21] I demonstrate how debt preoccupations promote what Michel Foucault called "neoliberal governmentality," as the emerging orientation where people are expected to evaluate their self-worth in terms of their ability to leverage their own human capital to succeed in an increasingly market-centered society.[22] I analyze how neoliberal governmentality heightens the insistence that people adhere to the standard of the self-sufficient individual all the more intensely just at the moment it begins to fade away as a credible ideal. I conclude with a discussion of how to connect disparate forms of resistance to the debt economy in order promote political mobilization that can help people resist their subordination in the latest phase of ordinary capitalism. In an era when so much of American politics is focused on the idea of sustaining middle-class status as a stabile identity, middle-class melancholia looms large in casting a long shadow, for worse as well as better, over politics and the policy process.

Middle-Class Melancholia and Tea Party Doctrine

In an economy that makes ordinary people increasingly economically precarious, how do members of the middle class continue to imagine themselves as the standard bearers for the norm of the personally responsible citizen-subjects? Part of the answer is by practicing a middle-class melancholia that splits the self (between private debtor and public taxpayer), disavowing both dependence on assistance or the obligation to support it so as to sustain the commitment to the idealized, self-sufficient self. With this double disavowal comes a substitution: desire for the idealized self-sufficient self is replaced by the repetitive drive to enact lesser versions of it in the contemporary scene. In Freudian terms, the shift from mourning to melancholia involves a substitution where desire is given up and instead people settle into a preoccupation with the more fundamental instinctual drive without taking it to the level of pursuing fulfilling, self-affirming desire.[23]

The case of the Tea Party is instructive. The Tea Party has become a significant force in U.S. politics, as an elite-backed but nonetheless popular political movement. It has been found to be disproportionately older, white, and middle class in its members' identification (if not actual economic standing).[24] The Tea Party is most especially composed of people who are very concerned about whether government debt will lead to higher taxes for the middle class and above. It is a social movement that has achieved a significant presence in the Republican Party, pushing the party far to the right on these issues, while bringing new levels of desperate extremism into mainstream politics. Tea Partiers are most centrally concerned about the growing risks of downward mobility in the post–Great Recession restructured economy. As the economy loses the ability to ensure people the ability to realize the ideal of the self-sufficient self, those who have invested heavily in that ideal, psychically as well as politically and economically, become especially vulnerable to the anxiety that comes with having to try to sustain the realization of that ideal in their own lives by whatever means, including resisting tax increases to pay off the debts of people they see as not adhering to the ideal of the personally responsible, self-sufficient self.

The origins of the Tea Party as an idea has been traced to an outburst on television by CNN business reporter Rick Santelli over the Obama administration's proposals to bail out those homeowners whose homes were at that point "underwater" due to the bursting of the housing bubble. These homeowners bought their homes at much higher prices than they could get if they sold them at the time that the housing market went down taking the global economy with it. If they sold, they would not be able to pay off their mortgages in full, making them "underwater." The idea of the government stepping in and helping them restructure their mortgages infuriated Santelli, who on the air exploded in a tirade that included a call for a "Chicago Tea Party," evidently suggesting a reenactment of the original American Revolution Boston Tea Party action against taxes imposed by the British monarch but now in the president's hometown of Chicago.[25] Santelli was simultaneously suggesting that Obama was some kind of modern-day royal lording over the ordinary people and that people who would take such a bailout from the government were violating the implied standard about who is a responsible citizen-subject in our market-centered society. In other words, the government should not be imposing its will on us and we should be handling our economic investments on our own. Santelli's tirade against government aid to those who should be seen as people who must accept responsibility for the housing debts they have incurred might not have been the most eloquent or the most thought out, but it spoke deeply about the implied position of what would become the Tea Party movement. Therefore, from its inception, the Tea Party has been not so much a debtor class but a class of economically stratified people who share a number of economically conservative concerns including not having to assume obligation for other people's debt. As one popular Tea Party placard proclaims: "Give me liberty, not your debt"![26]

Yet there is a split in the Tea Party consciousness. For years, debt and taxes cut to the core of the practical workarounds many in the middle class have used for sustaining the identity of the personally responsible, self-sufficient self. For years, tax cuts, private debt, and public deficits have been relied on to keep up the appearance of that middle-class identity. Raising taxes to pay for other people's indebtedness becomes nothing less than scandalous for those suffering from middle-class melancholia. Theirs is a melancholy about how extra public burdens via taxation to bail out others (as well as payments on the public debt) will also threaten to reveal how they themselves have had to resort to various alternative means to keep up appearances as middle class.

This political-economic anxiety about avoiding public taxes while denying debt is compounded by demographic change in the electorate. At one level, this takes the form of seeing others as interlopers threatening to unmask the charade of keeping up middle-class appearances. The issue of public debt has been framed as borrowing money to pay for expensive social welfare programs for those who are not practicing personal responsibility and are not being self-sufficient. At another level, the anxiety stems from fear of being pushed aside politically. The electorate is increasingly younger, more racially and ethnically diverse, and composed of more people from the laboring classes below the Tea Partiers.[27] A growing anxiety beyond the Tea Party infiltrating the Republican Party overall is the concern that it is losing the ability to communicate its agenda to this changing electorate.[28] If not racist, Tea Party members have expressed high levels of anxiety about the changing racial composition of the electorate and its elected political leadership, starting with most especially the presidency of Barack Obama, the first African American elected to the highest office in the land. The Tea Party may appear to be celebrating capitalist individualism but on closer examination a better case is made that it serves as a crucible for political as well as economic anxieties of elements of the middle class. Given its concerns about how "other" people threaten to take away their idealized understanding of middle-class America, the Tea Party becomes nothing less than this country's National Front.

Yet in many ways we can say that the Tea Party has seen the enemy and they are them. For many people their status is liminal; they are at risk of both increased debt and taxation to cover their own growing need that comes with insufficient resources. To take one example, many participants in the Tea Party movement are older, white Americans who are recipients of Social Security; however, that reliance on the government must be repudiated in order to protect the cherished idealized self-sufficient self. Interviews with Tea Party participants show this disavowal can be difficult and even confusing:

> Yet while the Tea Party supporters are more conservative than Republicans on some social issues, they do not want to focus on those issues: about 8 in 10 say that they are more concerned with economic issues, as is the general public. When talking about the Tea Party movement, the largest

number of respondents said that the movement's goal should be reducing the size of government, more than cutting the budget deficit or lowering taxes. And nearly three-quarters of those who favor smaller government said they would prefer it even if it meant spending on domestic programs would be cut. But in follow-up interviews, Tea Party supporters said they did not want to cut Medicare or Social Security—the biggest domestic programs, suggesting instead a focus on "waste." Some defended being on Social Security while fighting big government by saying that since they had paid into the system, they deserved the benefits. Others could not explain the contradiction. "That's a conundrum, isn't it?" asked Jodine White, 62, of Rocklin, Calif. "I don't know what to say. Maybe I don't want smaller government. I guess I want smaller government and my Social Security." She added, "I didn't look at it from the perspective of losing things I need. I think I've changed my mind."[29]

As Suzanne Mettler reports: "At a gathering in Simpsonville, South Carolina, in August 2009, one man told Republican Representative Robert Inglis: 'Keep your government hands off my Medicare!' "[30] Tea Partiers are frequently, it seems, divided against themselves. They want to continue to be seen as conforming to the standards of personal responsibility and self-sufficiency that make for inclusion in the middle class but are opposed to the very programs that have helped people achieve middle-class status or maintain it in their later years. One way to resolve (or at least cover up) the contradiction is to suggest that government benefits are their own personal assets, as in "my" Medicare. In fact, programs like Social Security and Medicare are structured in ways that help perpetuate this divided self. Because people pay into the system for financing these programs they come to see their benefits as earned in contradistinction to welfare programs, which are seen as mere handouts.[31] The "insurance myth," as it has been frequently called, keeps alive the idea that these benefits are personal and private, that they are earned, that taking them does not mean you have added to the collective burden of society to support you in violation of the middle-class standard of the self-sufficient self.

This split consciousness is becoming more difficult to sustain. Arguably the charade is maintained today only by practicing a middle-class melancholia that splits the self (between private debtor and public taxpayer), disavowing both current dependence on assistance and the obligation to support it so as to sustain the self's commitment to the idealized, self-sufficient self. Under these conditions, we find a melancholia that involves not just anxiety about the inability to conform to the standard but also an unacknowledged giving up on the middle-class ideal itself. The economically precarious cannot but replace the ideal with an ersatz version. Part of this downscaled version involves a phobia regarding debt and taxes as both increasingly necessary and stigmatizing. This includes demonizing both personal indebtedness and the government's fiscal deficits when denied the ability to raise taxes to cover its debts. The private guilt over some people's inability to pay their debts becomes the public shame that we as a society likewise cannot balance our books.

Debt phobia continues even as the government imposes austerity on itself (which ends up holding back spending that could help reenergize the economy). Once the fear of debt takes hold it is out of proportion to the actual size of the debts incurred. What is critical here then are the psychic costs of giving up desire to realize the ideal of the self-sufficient self by engaging in productive activity and instead settling for the lesser preoccupation with getting tax breaks and benefits merely to maintain the appearances of being a self-sufficient self, even as these takings bankrupt the government and bring the issue of debt to the collective rather than the individual level. For Joseph Stiglitz, this shift from productive activity to gaming the tax system promotes a "rentier class" that is bound to become self-loathing if not explicitly melancholic:

> There is a strong intuitive case to be made for the idea that tax rates have encouraged rent-seeking at the expense of wealth creation. There is an intrinsic satisfaction in creating a new business, in expanding the horizons of our knowledge, and in helping others. By contrast, it is unpleasant to spend one's days fine-tuning dishonest and deceptive practices that siphon money off the poor, as was common in the financial sector before the 2007–8 financial crisis. I believe that a vast majority of Americans would, all things being equal, choose the former over the latter. But our tax system tilts the field. It increases the net returns from engaging in some of these intrinsically distasteful activities, and it has helped us become a rent-seeking society.[32]

The ultimate result politically is that this transferring of debt from the individual to the collective intensifies the charade of middle-class melancholia by putting it on a broader public stage and thereby making it all the more dramatically a subject for debate. The public shame of being complicit in helping the United States become a debtor society is added to the private guilt of those who have failed as self-sufficient selves.[33]

The reasons this split takes the form of melancholia taps deep emotional currents running through U.S. political culture historically. At its base, Tea Party melancholia is over the inability to continue to practice the Protestant ethic. Today, the "Evangelical-Capitalist Resonance Machine," as William Connolly has called it, animates Tea Partiers' melancholia.[34] It moralizes the preoccupation with addressing their economic insecurity as effectively as possible even if to the neglect of our collective well-being. The Tea Party's moralistic concern about the failure to be self-sufficient is simultaneously more and less intense than that that comes from their Christianity alone. Fred Block and Margaret Somers make this point when they tag the Tea Party outlook as a secular "market fundamentalism."[35] Block and Somers use "market fundamentalism" "because the term conveys the quasi-religious certainty expressed by contemporary advocates of market self-regulation. Moreover, [it]...emphasize[s] the affinity with religious fundamentalisms that rely on revelation or a claim to truth independent of the kind of empirical verification that is expected in the social sciences."[36]

This individualistic but moralistic mindset about the natural equilibrium of a self-regulating economy stretches back at least to Adam Smith. It creates the foundation myth that Karl Polanyi called the "economistic fallacy," that is, that autonomous individuals do not depend on anything else for their participation in a market system that is God-given, natural, self-regulating, and self-sustaining independent of the social and political institutions that brought them and it into being and make them possible.[37] The economistic fallacy of the autonomous individual participating in an autonomous market system has long predominated as an unquestioned conceit in the white-collar class, as C. Wright Mills called it. Mills traces its rise to the ascendency of market capitalism:

> The world of small entrepreneurs was self-balancing. Within it no central authority allocated materials and ordered men to specified tasks, and the course of its history was the unintended consequence of many scattered wills each acting freely. It is no wonder that men thought this so remarkable they called it a piece of Divine Providence, each man's hand being

guided as if by magic into a preordained and natural harmony. The science of economics, which sought to explain this extraordinary balance, which provided order through liberty without authority, has not yet entirely rid itself of the magic. The providential society did have its economic troubles. Its normal rhythm of slump and boom alternately frightened and exhilarated whole sections and classes of men. Yet it was not seized by cycles of mania and melancholia. The rhythm never threw the economy into the lower depths known intimately to twentieth-century men, and for long years there were no fearful wars or threats of wars. The main lines of its history were linear, not cyclical; technical and economic processes were still expanding, and the cycles that did occur seemed seasonal matters which did not darken the whole outlook of the epoch.[38]

It is this romanticized self-sufficient self of the providential society that now is the bemoaned lost object of a Tea Party trapped in unbalanced cycles of "mania and melancholia." At some level of consciousness (even if subconsciousness), the Tea Party engages in a middle-class melancholia much as Freud characterized melancholia, internalizing its loss as a loss of an idealized self. In splitting the self as it is experienced now from that idealized self, it disavows the self as experienced in the world today in the name of vouchsafing the unattainable idealized self. But then ultimately it forsakes the desire of the idealized self by substituting the mere repetitive drive enacting a lesser self as a neurotic response. The growing anxiety about debt coupled with infinite demands for lower taxes become the drive of a politics serving as a less than satisfying alternative long after the desire for pursuing the ideal self-sufficient self has gone away.[39] Post–Great Recession, the increasingly vulnerable, not-so-self-sufficient self, therefore, represents a shameful unmasking that must be covered up. The charade that comes with this cover-up must ultimately weigh heavily as cries of hypocrisy resound through public discourse and are likely to heighten the need to publicly denigrate others as even worse examples of failing to adhere to the moral standard of the personally responsible self-sufficient self.

A vicious cycle of denigration gives way to ritualized invocations of scapegoats. Middle-class melancholia begets a politics of demonization. The usual suspects are trotted out, the drug addicts, the welfare queens, and so on, to be symbolically hanged in the public square and to be literally cut off from needed public assistance. The result is a renewed moral panic leading to misguided state laws focused on disciplining the poor, especially those among the poor who cost money, such as welfare mothers who are accused of irresponsibly selling food stamps to buy drugs or not parenting their children properly or committing other acts that demonstrate they violate the moral code of the middle-class ideal of the self-sufficient self.[40] The moralistic character of these policies highlights how the anxiety about failing to conform to the idealized standard of the self-sufficient self is a question of identity more than of economics.

An aberrant but indicative event dramatizing how middle-class melancholia found expression in moralistic arguments about public debt occurred on the night of October 16, 2013, when the House of Representatives was voting to raise the debt ceiling and reopen the government after a seventeen-day shutdown that had been pushed by the Tea Party–led Republican majority in the House as a failed strategy to defund the Affordable Care Act (a.k.a. Obamacare) and to demand cuts in social welfare programs in exchange for raising the debt ceiling. As the votes were being tallied, a House stenographer, Diane Reidy, took the podium and proclaimed: "He will not be mocked…The greatest deception here is not 'one nation under God.' It never was. Had it been, it would not have been.… The Constitution would not have been written by Freemasons. They go against God. You cannot serve two masters. Praise be to God, Lord Jesus Christ." Reidy seemed to be suggesting that the House was divided over the debt ceiling not on economic grounds but on moral grounds. She was forcibly removed from the podium by the House parliamentarian, questioned by police, and then taken to a hospital to be evaluated as to her mental state.[41] This incident is seemingly inexplicable until we begin to appreciate how the Tea Partiers and others have come to see the issues of the debt in moralistic terms.

There is pervasive evidence available in public discourse that this insistence that we must be frugal and pay down our public debt reflects less an economic analysis than an argument that is grounded in moralistic arguments about personal responsibility. Yet it is more. The anxiety about debt reflects not just a moralistic orientation but one that reflects anxieties about class differences that are highly racialized. Among the Tea Party there is all too much talk about those "other" people who are trapped in poverty because they are not practicing personal responsibility and are dragging down the whole society, miring it in economic stagnation post–Great Recession.

Behind the concerns about not rewarding bad behavior, there is fear of the other and what that other represents about the future of the country. Christopher Parker and Matt Baretto write: "[P]eople are driven to support the Tea Party from the anxiety they feel as they perceive the America they know, the country they love, slipping away, threatened by the rapidly changing face of [what] they believe is the 'real' America: a heterosexual, Christian, middle-class, (mostly) male, white country."[42] The anxiety over losing "their" country to those "other" people results in a highly moralistic stance that buttresses political intransigence against almost any government intervention that would address the hardship of those on the bottom of the socio-economic hierarchy.

We might be tempted to say the intransigence against providing aid to those suffering the worst effects of the transformed economy is but indicative of a persistent and growing aversion on the political right to taking a Keynesian countercyclical approach to jump-starting the stagnant economy post–Great Recession. Yet even this aversion is consistently couched in public discourse more in moral than economic terms to the point of suggesting that it is un-Christian to take on more public debt, especially if it is to reward "other" people who are seen as not practicing personal responsibility and self-sufficiency. The metaphors used to denigrate debt created for purposes of aiding families in need are quite telling. The idea of the government helping families is frequently dismissed in terms of irresponsible household budgeting. The morally responsible family that lives within its means is the dominant metaphor that frames the intransigence as a moral issue fulfilling our promises to pay our debts and not impose burdens on anyone else (now or in the future).[43]

Rep. Paul Ryan (R-WI) is the leading proponent of slashing social welfare programs because they require too much debt. He has stirred controversy with his comments on the culture of poverty leading poor people to not work enough to improve their economic situation. In early 2014, when discussing his budget proposals to cut social welfare programs, he said: "One reason that we still have poverty in the United States is that a lot of poor people are born lazy."[44] Ryan's comments have been pointed to as examples of "dog-whistle politics," where racial references are made implicitly.[45]

The resistance to increasing government spending to stimulate the economy is therefore at its base a profoundly political stance not grounded in economic analysis at all. Instead, it is a moralistic argument reflective of deep anxieties about the changing demographics of the country. The resistance to

aiding the poor is expressed as opposing a morally irresponsible act that rewards bad behavior by "other" people who do not play by white, middle-
class rules of work and family. The fact that President Obama himself is not
white only further heightens the anxiety that nonwhites are taking over the
country and forcing whites to support their deviant social practices. (For
instance, in 2012 perennial presidential candidate and Tea Party favorite
Rick Santorum allegedly said he did not want to "make black people's lives
better by giving them somebody else's money.") In the end, the Tea Party's
argument about the relationship of the state to the market is a highly racialized and moralistic one reflective of deep anxiety about the social and cultural, as well as economic, precariousness of the white middle class in a
changing society. For the Tea Party, changing demographics, politics, and
economics combine to create a perfect storm of middle-class melancholia.

THE ETERNAL RETURN OF LEFT MELANCHOLIA

To be sure, melancholia is not a condition specific to the Right, let alone the
entrepreneurs of the middle class in the Tea Party. While not preoccupied
with the shame of keeping up appearances on behalf of the self-sufficient
self, the Left has its own problems with melancholia that revolve more
around issues of collective, rather than individual, action. In fact, it is arguably the case that the Left has been more vocal about the issue of melancholia in its ranks. "Left Melancholy," as Walter Benjamin first talked about
it, reflected disavowal of the futility of trying to sustain no longer viable
practices of political action that were inappropriate for the current era.[46] As
a result, leftists were reduced to antiquarian exercises aimed at maintaining
the purity of political thought in ways that led them away from staying focused on what strategic actions for revolutionary change would be viable
and appropriate in the current moment. Elisabeth Anker writes: "Left melancholy is akin to a process of reification, as habituated forms of leftist scrutiny drain the vitality and energetics of both the melancholic and the objects
he holds on to, vitality necessary for sustaining the critical push for freedom
in a dark and dangerous time. Diminishing revolutionary potential, left melancholy reflects the outward trappings that signify work for social change
while its animating core is inert, empty and lifeless."[47] As Benjamin noted of
Marx's analogy of revolutions as locomotives (given in chapter 1), perhaps
they are spearheaded by passengers applying the emergency brake.[48] There

is evidence that Benjamin's melancholic perspective haunts the progressive response to the political change today because it is arguably more often in resistance to change's negative trajectory.[49]

Left melancholy lays behind much of the criticism that the Occupy Wall Street movement has incurred from those you would think would be its supporters. Occupy Wall Street when it arose was at first seen as an exciting and healthy development in participatory democracy. It gave voice to people's discouragement with how the government was responding to the fallout from the Great Recession in ways that favored the investor class over everyone else. As economic hardship persisted well beyond the Great Recession, many began to wonder why there was no upsurge in protest beyond the crowds associated with Tea Party gatherings. Then, on September 17, 2011, protestors took over Zuccotti Park in lower Manhattan and Occupy Wall Street sprang to life. They were different than the Tea Party. They were diverse, young and old, students and the homeless, the unemployed from Wall Street as well as Main Street. Many were from the middle class concerned about their futures.[50] They and demonstrated in large numbers. As the protests spread to other cities, and then explicitly linked with protests already occurring around the globe, there emerged the mantra of "we are the 99 percent" that targeted the top "1 percent" who were benefiting at the expense of everyone else.[51] The message was refined; but more importantly there was now a movement. Finally, the people rose up as an organized force, as Occupy Wall Street, and they made their discontent visible for all to see, demanding justice in the face of the injustice of it all. Occupy was at times playful. It enacted creative, even theatrical, performances in protests all over the country, on college campuses, in city parks, at government centers. It performed its street theater in the name of openly and honestly highlighting the loss of economic opportunity that came with the rise of the debt economy.

Nonetheless, all this performing was quickly dismissed as not serious organizing for political change. In spite of Occupy answering the call and filling this need, the prevailing view, not just on the left, is that Occupy failed and it did so because it was not well organized. It was characterized as a disorganized eruption of passionate dissent that lacked grounding in systemic thought on its key issue of inequality, which also explains why the movement never developed an explicit public policy agenda and remains to this day at best an amorphous collection of protestors who could never make concerted demands for change on the government. Left melancholia about the loss of ability to sustain collective action overtook concerns about melancholia regarding the self-sufficiency ideal. Jodi Dean has written critically of how Occupy's porous, playful, and theatrical efforts at protest betrayed the long-standing approach on the left to build organized parties to contest power:

> And these massive events are more than just spectacles, more than momentary hints at the people's will, when they are strengthened by the specific achievements of specific, targeted campaigns. In many ways, this has already been a key component of Occupy. Yet, too much movement rhetoric denounces centralization and celebrates locality such that people lose confidence in anything but the local and the community-based.... Collective power isn't just coming together. It's sticking together. And sticking together requires a willingness to make sacrifices for the sake of others.... In sum, the Occupy movement demonstrates why something like a party is needed insofar as a party is an explicit assertion of collectivity, a structure of accountability, an acknowledgment of differential capacities, and a vehicle for solidarity.[52]

Dean sees the substitution of democracy for economic justice as its own melancholic practice. She asserts about the Left generally today but Occupy in particular:

> It sublimates revolutionary desire to democratic drive, to the repetitious practices offered up as democracy (whether representative, deliberative, or radical). Having already conceded to the inevitably of capitalism, it noticeably abandons "any striking power against the big bourgeoisie," to return to Benjamin's language. For such a Left, enjoyment comes from its withdrawal from responsibility, its sublimation of goals and responsibilities into the branching, fragmented practices of micropolitics, self-care, and issue awareness. Perpetually slighted, harmed, and undone, this Left remains stuck in repetition, unable to break out of the circuits of drive in which it is caught, unable because it enjoys them.... If this Left is rightly described as melancholic—and I agree with [Wendy] Brown that it is—then its melancholia derives from the real existing compromises and betrayals inextricable from its history, its accommodations with reality, whether of nationalist war, capitalist encirclement, or so-called market demands.[53]

Dean believes that Occupy frittered away the chance to create a sustained political movement aimed at overtaking state power and bending it toward the goals of social justice. She longs for a political party that will rise above the usual petty partisanship and stand for the people's collective wishes that their common interests be enacted via state action. Yet this critique of Occupy reenacts the melancholia that Brown finds in left critics of grassroots protest politics in the current era.[54] Left melancholia involves not just settling for reformist identity politics as a substitute for class-based radical mobilizing (as noted by Dean); it also involves nostalgically longing for one big movement organized along class lines in an era of more diversified forms of precarity (as noted by Brown). Much of the criticism of Occupy itself resonates with this sort of melancholia that bemoans the inability to continue to adhere to the classic standard for left anticapitalist organizing for revolutionary change.[55]

Their melancholia over the loss of traditional class-based organized political action led critics away from appreciating that Occupy was a contemporaneous success as a social movement that had as its role mobilizing the diverse members of the precariat, not the class-unified members of the proletariat. In the process, its job was to resist being co-opted into making public policy proposals that would only serve to undermine its main mission— to mobilize as many different people as possible by raising consciousness about the injustice of protecting the "1 percent" at the expense of ordinary people.[56] In other words, Occupy's critics conflated the different roles of protest and electoral politics for achieving political change today.

Some criticism of Occupy has been more focused but is still reflective of left melancholia. In a volume of essays by different social scientists who for the most part bemoan Occupy as a missed opportunity, David Laitin asserts: "My...proposals, though elaborated in the mathematics of incentives and not in the psychology of rage, are in the spirit of Occupy and would play an important complementary role to Occupy's symbolic protests in challenging an unacceptable status quo."[57] In other words, Occupy's passion needs the reason of objective social science so that it can have an explicit agenda with concrete proposals, or otherwise it will fizzle in the failure of overwrought emotionalism.

Occupy's critics often invoke an invidious comparison with the U.S. civil rights movement.[58] Yet the civil rights movement was a long-term project that itself had its ups and downs. The road from the Montgomery bus boycott to Selma was punctuated by the March on Washington with periods of inaction in between. Protests fizzled after the Montgomery boycott only to be reignited after the dramatic events at Selma. The lesson from the civil rights movement is not just that you need a sustained, committed, organized group with an explicit agenda. It is also that you have to be patient, wait for opportunities to protest, and be organized as protesters to take advantage of them when they come. All the same, it is important to remember that the core of such a movement is protest and mobilization and not lobbying or electoral campaigning.

The civil rights movement was led by a number of related groups, the Southern Christian Leadership Conference in particular. Yet the movement also relied heavily on the energy of youth, as embodied in the activism of the Student Nonviolent Coordinating Committee. These groups coalesced *not* around an explicit policy agenda so much as around mobilizing protesters to help raise consciousness about the injustice of racial apartheid in the United States. The two organizations also did not always agree on what to do when, and over time tensions developed between leaders such as Martin Luther King, Jr., and Stokely Carmichael (Kwame Ture). The movement was sustained by protests that increased the visibility of the issue, dramatized the injustice of segregation and racial discrimination, and eventually helped frame political discourse to the point that policy elites felt obligated to enact a series of civil rights laws.

In the debates about comparing Occupy favorably or unfavorably to the civil rights movement, an important point is context.[59] That was then and this is now. The two movements not only have different issues but different demographics, different locales, and perhaps, most importantly, take place at different times with different political climates. Occupy can never replicate the civil rights movement for all these reasons. Instead, Occupy needs to think about what it can do regarding the issues of economic injustice that animated it in the first place and have evolved since. Those who practice left melancholia experience what Jacques Derrida called "time out of joint."[60] As Anker seems to suggest, as implied in her comment quoted earlier, they continue to try to relive a lost past in ways that prevent them from being relevant to the times in which they live.[61] Occupy's role today, as compared to left movements of the past, I would argue, is increasingly to make visible the wide variety of people, young and old, single or with children, black and white, formerly middle class or persistently poor, who are being left by the wayside in a transformed economic system post the Great Recession—the "99 percent."

Occupy, Debt, and the Work of Mourning

Melancholia arguably afflicts Occupy and its critics regarding its effectiveness in giving voice to the concerns of various groups that compose the precariat. Yet its theatrics is also a sign that it actually created the opportunity to work through and leave behind the morbid preoccupations of melancholia. The exuberance of Occupy's demonstrations were dismissed by some as the extravagances of youth that ended up frittering away and eventually losing the opportunity to challenge corporate power in a more organized and sustained way. Nonetheless, the playfulness of many of the Occupy protests could be seen as manifestations of the healthier condition of honest mourning over the loss of economic opportunity in the debtor economy. Occupy owned its loss and paraded it proudly. Occupy protests were open demonstrations of mourning. Even with a fluid structure and an unspecified agenda, Occupy became an audible, and even often eloquent, voice crying out against economic injustice in the face of how Wall Street financiers had misbehaved in ways that took down the global economy and destroyed the livelihood of millions.[62] Occupy was not in denial about how ordinary people, the "99 percent," had been robbed of their economic futures by the privileged "1 percent." Occupy owned its loss, paraded it, demonstrated it, and openly announced it to the world.

Regardless of the youth of many of the demonstrators, Occupy was all about giving voice to how ordinary people had been made precarious; it was never in denial at least about that, but instead openly presented itself as representatives of the ordinary people who had been marginalized by external forces producing an extraordinary economic transformation. This is but one way in which it was a middle-class movement, not unlike the Tea Party. Yet Occupy did not for the most part express its loss in a melancholic way. It did not internalize the lost object of the self-sufficient self to make it a loss of self-regard that must be disavowed. The main message from Occupy about what was happening was not that it was an issue of loss of face or loss of ego. The growing indebtedness of ordinary citizens was not a reflection of their moral failings as deficient citizen-subjects who could not adhere to the standard of middle-class values of personal responsibility.

Instead, the Occupiers often playfully performed their "precariatization" by highlighting that the expectations put on them were increasingly impossible to meet in an economy that was growing ever more unfair. To be sure, the issue of debt was critical for Occupy but not as an object of melancholia. Instead Occupy was doing the work of mourning when it discussed debt.[63] Anker uses Freud again, this time to discuss the work of mourning post 9/11 about the loss of the ideal of the free, autonomous individual in ways that are relevant to the analysis here in distinguishing Occupy's response from that of the Tea Party post–Great Recession: "Other possibilities include sustaining the acknowledgement that loss engenders: that the object of desire is gone, that one's ideal is no longer tenable and perhaps was never viable. For Freud, this involves a mourning process that concludes by rerouting desire to a new, more tenable, more live object."[64]

Distinguishing Occupy's work of mourning from the Tea Party's melancholy is especially pertinent to their differences in dealing with issues of private and public debt. The debt issue is critical for it arguably is the specter that most ominously hangs over ordinary citizens' anxieties about their ability to thrive economically post the Great Recession. Tayyab Mahmud has incisively noted how Foucault's neoliberal governmentality operates through debt in the current era post–Great Recession.[65] While Foucault was by no means a fan of Freud, his neoliberal governmentality is arguably much like the Freud's superego that disciplines the ego in the melancholic personality. The superego of neoliberal governmentality instructs the ego to internalize the need to rationalize one's inability to be a self-sufficient entrepreneurial self who leverages human capital to succeed in a market-centered society or risk facing the strictures of the state's disciplinary regime.[66] In the face of growing appreciation of one's inability to realize this ideal, the self turns against itself, disavowing its desire and satisfying itself with substitutions such as pretending to be a capable, market-savvy actor by relying on recurring tax cuts and other allowances that prop up the image of the self-sufficient self that cannot be any longer sustained as a credible ideal.

For Mahmud, today the disciplining of the self-sufficient self is, however, not primarily enforced from either an internalized commitment or by the state's threats of punishment but more from the external force imposed by oppressive levels of debt needed to pantomime the performance of the self-sufficient self. For Freud, the result would be repression of a healthy ego; for Foucault the result is less repression than oppression where the ego knows more self-consciously its inability to act alternatively but cannot afford the risks associated with transgressing the disciplinary standards set for it.[67] Debt disciplined the people not by repressing their egoistic desires (it was not internalized); instead debt disciplined people as an external force that oppressed them by weighing them down with obligations they consciously would like very much to be without. Debt did not internalize, it did not repress; it was an external oppressive force.

Mahmud's main point, however, is that people have little choice regardless of how they see themselves since debt cycles have been critical to boosting the economy over the last few decades, as one debt-inflated bubble of growth burst only to be replaced by another. Without other sources for economic growth, the pattern has been to encourage incurring debt—credit card debt, mortgage debt, student debt, and medical debt in particular. Without debt, the ideal of the self-sufficient self could not be simulated. Yet periodically the debt bubble would burst, the economy would implode, and the shift to new forms of debt would need to be encouraged to recharge the hollowed-out economy. Economic growth in the postindustrial era, in the era where the financial industry would become the primary driver of U.S. economic growth, would increasingly come from soliciting debtors to borrow to bet on their future, to invest in their own human capital as the basis of their economic success. Yet that crushing debt would weigh heavily on homeowners with houses underwater, students with years of study but no degrees (or with degrees but no careers), patients without the means to cover the costs of their care, and most generally consumers who cannot repay the costs of their credit card purchases. The economy has come to depend on people incurring debts as bets on their economic futures, bets that increasingly must be written off as losses.[68] Debt not only is a questionable source of fuel for the economic system; it is a powerful way of disciplining subordinate populations who must preoccupy themselves with servicing that debt or risk being disqualified from competing for the limited economic opportunities that might come their way in the future. Credit scores operate much like felony records, marking who is to be included and excluded from mainstream society. As Andrew Ross notes:

> [T]he larger threat is to the workings of an operational democracy.
> A crushing debt burden stifles our capacity to think freely, act conscientiously
> and fulfill our democratic responsibilities. Too many young people now

feel their future has been foreclosed before they have entered full adulthood. And, given the creditors' goal of prolonging debt service to the grave, the burden of repayment is shifting disproportionately toward the elderly (many of whom now are routinely asked to cosign student loans). Democracies don't survive well without a functional middle class or a citizenry endowed with an optional political imagination, and the test of a humane one is how it treats seniors when they outlast their capacity to earn a living wage.[69]

Yet Mahmud sees Occupy as potentially offering an effective site for resisting the disciplinary regime of debt associated with the new economy:

> The crisis and the policy responses have also triggered resistance from below. From the Arab spring to Greek general strikes and from the Occupy Movement in the United States to mass demonstrations in London, new spaces and modes of resistance are being forged. However, the disciplinary function of debt is yet to find priority in the agendas of these movements. It is imperative that theory and praxis aimed at emancipatory transformation and global justice take account of the nature and magnitude of the contemporary crisis and the implications of policy responses on the offer. In particular, we must focus on new and refurbished disciplinary regimes that are reinforcing the discipline of debt on national policies to transfer all costs of the crisis to the working classes and the marginalized. Popular democratization of finance by managing finance as a public utility must be high on the agenda of popular movements. An urgent challenge is to explore agendas, coalitions, and organizational forms of resistive social movements suitable to pursue popular democratization of finance.[70]

Mahmud's concern has increasingly become a focus for those who had been active in Occupy, who over time have brought together various groups preoccupied with how their debt was weighing them down without offering them opportunity to be included in the changing economy.[71] And as the street protests have subsided, Occupiers have turned to the issues of debt, not in a melancholic act of disavowal in service of propping up the charade of self-sufficient self in the age of precarity but in a more honest form of mourning over the real losses incurred. Out of Occupy has emerged a variety of efforts to mobilize people to fight back against the debt economy.

For instance, noteworthy is the Rolling Jubilee and related initiatives to help people get out from under the debt they cannot cover.[72] These initiatives are not a melancholic cover-up of the role of debt in the pantomime of the self-sufficient self that neoliberal governmentality enforces, but instead a more honest and very public avowal of how incurring unrealistic debts has become a prerequisite for participating in society today. The jubilant rhetoric of the Rolling Jubilee indicates that its relationship to debt is nothing like the fraught, guilt-ridden self-denial associated with the Tea Party's attempt to resist working through its problematic relationship to the self-sufficient self in the era of neoliberal governmentality: "A bailout of the people by the people: Rolling Jubilee is a Strike Debt project that buys debt for pennies on the dollar, but instead of collecting it, abolishes it. Together we can liberate debtors at random through a campaign of mutual support, good will, and collective refusal. Debt resistance is just the beginning. Join us as we imagine and create a new world based on the common good, not Wall Street profits."[73]

Occupy openly embraces the reality of pervasive debt and seeks to deal with it forthrightly. In the process, it mourns the loss of the self-sufficient self-ideal rather than engaging in the melancholic anxiety about whether debt can substitute for acquired assets. It mourns but then it moves on from cries of protest to a rolling jubilee to strike the debt, from expressing grief over lost economic opportunity to fighting back against the debt economy, much like a jazz funeral—somber on the way out and jubilant on the way back.[74]

Both Occupy Wall Street and the Tea Party targeted debt, public and private, as the prime issue confronting us economically. Yet Occupy has questioned the external conditions that give rise to the problem of private debt, while the Tea Party has targeted as immoral public debt that actually could serve to boost the economy and make individuals more able to repay their private debts in the future.[75] As a result, even the arcane accounting issue of the debt ceiling for the federal government has become a way of shaming the government's leaders to accept cutbacks in basic social welfare programs that are still needed post the Great Recession. The Tea Party's approach to public debt is to treat it as a scandal that justifies shaming those who advocate it. Occupy's approach to private debt, however, is to see it as having been unfairly imposed and needing to be addressed as an external imposition. In the case of the Tea Party, debt becomes yet another source for the self-flagellation associated with melancholia, while for Occupy debt is from external sources that in no way should make people feel lesser selves.[76] Debt, more than taxes, has become the critical issue in the neoliberal economy. The Tea Party and Occupy approach debt in different ways reflective of their differences in grappling with middle-class melancholia.

CONCLUSION

After her failed vice presidential candidacy, Sarah Palin for a while talked in ways consistent with the Occupy movement.[77] She called out the banks for insisting on being saved by government before their toxic assets irreparably poisoned their profitability, while ordinary Americans financially drown because they were sunk in debt from mortgages that left them underwater. As a darling of the Tea Party, Palin was showing that the Tea Partiers had the potential to direct their ire at the leaders of the financial industry who have been promoting and profiting from the debt economy. Yet Palin would eventually focus primarily on what she called "crony capitalism," which made the problem seem largely the result of collusion between the government and corporate lobbyists. In the end, she even went so far as to accuse Occupy participants of being just more greedy and needy welfare recipients who wanted a bailout just like those bankers. Palin could have joined in the honest mourning of the passing away of the old economy that, while often very unfair to too many, still held out hope for a middle class that they could achieve a decent standard of living through stable employment. Yet Palin regressed to her disingenuous ways insisting that the middle class was just fine if it could be free of those freeloaders who wanted to live off government aid.[78]

Nevertheless, there are deep affinities between Occupy and the Tea Party as middle-class movements, as much as partisan politics makes these ties less than apparent. Both are concerned about how the transformed economy is one that puts in jeopardy the middle-class ideal of the self-sufficient self. Both respond in ways that point, even if furtively, toward how a neoliberal governmentality is insisting on an intensified program of "responsibilization" where people are expected to entrepreneurially leverage their own human capital and become that self-sufficient self just when the economy is making it all the more difficult to enact that ideal. Both recognize that debt is a dangerous resource that increasingly desperate people must rely on if they are to even begin to try to make it in the transformed economy.

While Freud saw melancholia as a pathological response to loss compared with the healthier grieving associated with mourning, Benjamin saw them as more related.[79] In the latter perspective, the differences between the responses of the Tea Party and Occupy are possibly more related than conventional politics is prepared to allow. In fact, the success of the Tea Party is in some respects a barometer of the failure of Occupy to effectively give voice to people's discontent today. In reference to the rise of rightist movements and the simultaneous decline of the Left in the United States and Europe post–Great Recession, Slavoj Žižek suggests: "Walter Benjamin's old thesis that behind every rise of fascism there is a failed revolution not only still holds today, but is perhaps more pertinent than ever."[80] The Tea Party fills the vacuum created by left melancholia. Yet it does so with its own politics of resentment. The Tea Party enacts a denial of middle-class melancholia that comes from insisting on a pantomime of self-sufficiency which ends up heightening the guilt over private debt and the shame of public debt. Occupy's concerns about debt are less obsessive. It offers a way forward, the melancholic criticisms from the Left notwithstanding. It engages in the work of mourning that more directly confronts how the debt economy works to keep people down. If the Tea Party could find a way to overcome its middle-class melancholia, it could join with those who had been active in Occupy in doing that important work of mourning so that a stronger populist uprising would result. Anything less is likely not to be enough as debt will continue to enforce its discipline, in the process shutting down the potential for political mobilization.

OCCUPY PRECARITY

CHALLENGING THE LIMITS OF COLLECTIVE AGENCY UNDER NEOLIBERALISM

We live in a time of protest.[1] We see it everywhere across the globe. Globalization begets its own resistance. And it is about time. Increasingly people throughout the developed world, but elsewhere as well, are becoming aware that the state is not there to protect them from the ravages of a runaway capitalist system. Instead a transformed state that disciplines them to be market compliant is emerging in its place. It is not just people of lesser-developed countries who are being exploited for the profit of transnational corporations. Those corporations have used their prior extraction of wealth to energize a global economy that regiments workers all over the world to take up subordinate positions in an economy that concentrates wealth at the top.[2] Most people would rather not be political, not risk losing what they already have, and not take their chances engaging in direct action. So when they do, we know something has happened to change the normal course of affairs. Once people come to see that there is less to lose by acting, they are ready to be mobilized. And that is a good thing since, as Frances Fox Piven and Richard Cloward once famously said: "A placid poor get nothing, but a turbulent poor sometimes get something."[3] Their point is that the historical record is clear that the only proven way to get real change is at those times when the people on the bottom rise up and say they are mad as hell and are not going to take it anymore. The global economic meltdown since the onset of the Great Recession in 2008 has created the crucible in which the new uprising has mushroomed. From the Occupy Wall Street movement to mass demonstrations in cities across the globe in reaction to inequitable economic policies, those marginalized and left to the wayside by the resultant global economic restructuring are finally fighting back.

The mass protests associated with the Occupy movement that began on September 17, 2011, with the occupation of Zuccotti Park near Wall Street were inspired in part by the protests of the Arab Spring and the European revolts against manufactured austerity. This massive upsurge in political protest has included a diversity of participants coming together to express their outrage at leaders of an ongoing economic transformation who continue to profit while the protestors and those they represent experience growing economic marginalization in a variety of different ways.

Judith Butler's Mary Flexner Lectures at Bryn Mawr College in December 2011 built on prior work to provide a critical perspective for theorizing the shape that the protests took, especially regarding how diverse groups of people can come together to act in concerted fashion.[4] Her approach points toward a coalitional politics grounded on diverse people's shared "precarity" given their economic marginality. Butler's focus on precarity enables us to highlight the importance of how people are subjectified in diverse ways that make it difficult to secure a stable place in any number of social fields.[5] This process of "subjectivation" in the current period has been insightfully anticipated by Michel Foucault's notion of "neoliberal governmentality," where people are enlisted to take up positions as self-disciplining citizen-subjects who can be responsible for using market logic for making personal choices in the name of enhancing their human capital or risk being subject to the punishments of the state's disciplinary regime.[6] In response, those at risk of marginalization, as deficient neoliberal citizen-subjects, come together as the diversely socially and economically dispossessed to act in concert as "the people" seeking redress for the marginalization and deprivation they endure under neoliberalism.[7]

In the wake of the terrorist attacks of September 11, 2001, Butler argued that precarity is a fundamental condition of life for all regardless of their differences.[8] More recently, she applied this perspective to analyze Occupy demonstrators as "bodies in alliance" against a common economic precarity.[9] Butler's theorizing of precarity has been characterized as an ethical turn away from political contestation toward a "mortalist humanism" that appeals to an ethical consensual concern for people's shared condition.[10] Yet Butler's turn to precarity in the case of Occupy itself reflects a profoundly political move enacted by movement actors themselves to bring together diverse groups uniting them around their shared economic marginalization. Precarity brings diverse bodies into alliance, if tenuously and contingently, in the name of representing a shared condition that needs to be challenged and contested through conflict with the powers that be. The representational performances of Occupy's public protests enact a politics of resistance, a politics of dissensus, central to political movements overall.[11]

"Precarity" as a unifying, as opposed to depoliticizing, force gains further traction when we consider Guy Standing's "Precariat" as a new class that can be counterposed to Marx's proletariat.[12] The precariat is, for Standing, a diverse group, occupying different positions in the class structure, from the poor and working class to the downwardly mobile middle class displaced from decently paying blue-collar manufacturing jobs and white- and pink-collar office work, to the better paid but now increasingly vulnerable professional class. The diversity of the precariat heightens our concern about how to practice a coalitional politics in the name of the differentially positioned, so as to integrate the newly dispossessed with those who have been for a long time systematically marginalized, middle-class professionals with the poor, whites with blacks, young with old, homeowners with the homeless, that is to say, how to ally those who share little but their increasing precarity in the current era. These challenges for Occupy resonate with the persistent political tensions in movements more generally: (1) how do they bring diverse people together to engage in collective action, and (2) how does a movement fit into the broader political landscape?

In this chapter, I suggest that Butler's perspective sheds important light on the conditions for effective collective political action today. I use Butler's focus on Occupy as "bodies in alliance" to underscore how it involves diverse individuals experiencing the subjectivation associated with neoliberal governmentality, where people come to be identified as failing to rely successfully on their human capital in a market-centered society. "Precarity" turns this subjection back on itself and thereby provides a basis for realizing the collective political agency of a diverse population that has been marginalized economically in different ways.[13] Much like the use of the word "homeless" to reference a shared lack among a diverse population, the use of "precarity" points to a position of marginality differentially experienced and uses it to highlight a shared condition for political effect.[14] Through public demonstrations, the participants of Occupy dramatize their shared condition by turning their shared subjection as deficient neoliberal subjects back at the state.

In what follows, I argue that "precarity" is not just a philosophical abstraction but an actually existing discursive practice operant in movement politics in recent years. Precarity turns out to have been relied on in European protests for some time, providing a basis for political mobilization.[15] "Precarity" is what Michael Shapiro calls an "action framework" constitutive of political action itself and not just a reflection of it.[16] Butler's turn to precarity therefore has direct relevance for understanding the challenges of Occupy, subsequent related protests, and the nature of movement politics more generally. I suggest that Butler's focus on precarity highlights how people's shared vulnerability becomes a basis for achieving political agency by way of public performances that serve to represent the common interests of those being variously marginalized by ongoing economic change.[17] I argue that this sort of politics of spectacle enacted via forms of street theater performs important work consistent with the role of protest movements in the broader political process. I conclude by suggesting that we can see this more clearly once we integrate Butler's theorizing with the work of Frances Fox Piven and Richard Cloward, so as to understand the political significance of Occupy as a protest movement to the political system overall.

THE POLITICS OF PRECARITY: COLLECTIVIZING INDIVIDUAL GRIEVANCES

Occupy confronted challenges in enacting effective representation of its diversity, including the diverse forms of economic precarity among its participants—students with debt, homeowners with debt, homeless people without a home of any kind, the unemployed professionals cast aside by either Wall Street or Main Street, and the growing number of unemployable made disposable by a neoliberalizing economy that expects people to trade on their human capital only to see a widening gap between haves and have-nots. Occupy encampments themselves varied, taking different forms in downtowns, city parks, and college campuses as well as involving different groups with different concerns. Diversity among participants in any one site had the potential to be both a source of strength and tension.[18]

For Butler, Occupy represents most strikingly a public venue and political space for diverse people articulating their connections via their shared precarity. Occupy enacts for Butler a representational politics when diverse people come together, appear publicly together, and form "bodies in alliance."[19] In particular, Butler sees the space of appearance as constitutive of appearing as such, where the background enables the foreground, where the public venue allows persons to be identified as bodies in alliance.[20] Butler asserts:

> Freedom does not come from me or from you; it can and does happen as a relation between us or, indeed, among us. So this is not a matter of finding the human dignity within each person, but rather of understanding the human as a relational and social being, one whose action depends upon equality and articulates the principle of equality.... The claim of equality is not only spoken or written, but is made precisely when bodies appear together or, rather, when, through their action, they bring the space of appearance into being.[21]

Diverse peoples unite as a people, as bodies in alliance, when representing in public a shared concern or condition. In her account of Occupy, Butler considers not only precarity as a shared condition for bodies to act in alliance but also how bodies in alliance enact their political agency collectively. Her concern is with the very precarity of precarity, how precarity is a tenuous, if important, basis for acting in concert. Butler appreciates the tensions between the individual grievance and the collective action, and she seeks to create ways that enable those tensions to stay in the foreground. Thus she attends to the ways that the private body in all its diversity that makes public action possible becomes a difference that gets neglected when we act in concert. As a result, she remains concerned with how collective action can do an injustice to individual concerns.[22]

For Butler, then, a key issue for Occupy is how difference and identity get imbricated in a politics of collective action.[23] She has suggested with John Muse that we can see this imbrication in the Occupiers' use of images, narratives, and numbers and the ways they get articulated one to the other.[24] One site for seeing this imbrication is the "We Are the 99 Percent" Tumblr website.[25] Here, we see starkly in serial fashion the iterative imbrication of the relationship of personal narratives to impersonal numbers, where individuals talk of the different ways they have been personally made more precarious in the current era, even as they join together under the impersonal statistic of the "we are the 99 percent."

In less than a year, the Occupy Wall Street slogan, "We are the 99 percent," became a commonplace in political discourse, likely affecting how presidential candidates were evaluated. A good case can be made that the 99 percent slogan provided the interpretive context for the public airing of Republican presidential candidate Mitt Romney's private comment to wealthy campaign donors that the "47 percent" of Americans who did not pay any taxes were voting for President Barack Obama out of a sense of entitlement, as victims for whom the government should care.[26] Exit polls would subsequently show that Obama was overwhelmingly seen as more empathetic than Romney to the plight of ordinary people.[27]

For Butler "We are the 99 percent" is a powerful slogan for a movement focused on a coalitional politics that brings together diverse people, bound only by their shared disdain for the state's failure to protect them and their individual and collective futures. In fact, it arguably was the critical discursive move for a movement that was wrought from a diffuse coalition of diverse actors. The web page Tumblr powerfully displays how diverse peoples can be united under this banner (see figure 3.1). It facilitates their coming together around their shared precarity. At the same time, it provides an opportunity to demonstrate the widely diverse ways in which different people experience the negative effects of the global economic meltdown. It further diversifies our understanding of how precarity can be variously experienced so as to make very different people can come to be seen as deficient neoliberal citizen-subjects incapable of effectively trading on their human capital to succeed in an increasingly market-centered society. We are all different but we are all not the 1 percent who profit from our increased economic marginalization.

Butler recognizes that individuals coalescing around an idea (such as their shared precarity) is not equivalent to mobilizing collectively for concerted political action. One way to address this distinction is to ask in what ways the actions of Occupiers constitute a form of agency. The Occupiers' agency is arguably something not of their own making, but in no small part structurally conditioned, producing participation in radical politics only by

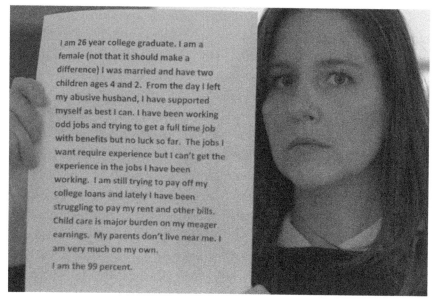

I am 26 year college graduate. I am a female (not that it should make a difference) I was married and have two children ages 4 and 2. From the day I left my abusive husband, I have supported myself as best I can. I have been working odd jobs and trying to get a full time job with benefits but no luck so far. The jobs I want require experience but I can't get the experience in the jobs I have been working. I am still trying to pay off my college loans and lately I have been struggling to pay my rent and other bills. Child care is major burden on my meager earnings. My parents don't live near me. I am very much on my own.

I am the 99 percent.

Figure 3.1 "We Are the 99 Percent."
Simulation of photos on the Tumblr website page "We Are the 99 Percent," http://wearethe99percent.tumblr.com/. Photo of Lindsay Meath taken by Emily Meath.

default. Depending on how the 99 percent narrate their precarity they may or may not be motivated toward collective political action. Jennifer Silva has insightfully highlighted how many of the young, working-class people suffering the effects of the Great Recession are trapped in what she calls a "neoliberal mood economy" where they articulate their responses as a personal challenge to be resilient in unfortunately deeply depoliticizing ways.[28]

Even among the Occupy participants, we find that many of them were new to movement politics and only radicalized because the failure of conventional avenues left them no other option. Their radicalization speaks of a different process of subjectivation in a neoliberal era when they have been enlisted or solicited as subjects by virtue of their place in the economic derailment and political dysfunction of the present—a process that seems to hold out the possibility of transformation to a deeply divided society of haves and have-nots.[29] The Occupiers' claim to stand for "the 99 percent" suggests that they represent all of us who increasingly feel we are on the outside looking in on a changing society. "Occupy" itself represents the idea that people should collectively reclaim as public the spaces that have produced our exclusion.

The imbrication of the personal individual in the impersonal collective as represented in protest actions raises the question of political agency.[30] Is the political agency of Occupiers found in their individual actions as conscious actors committed to change or in what they represent as a collective? These questions go to the heart of not just the issue of Occupy's future but the study of political behavior in general. For instance, much of conventional, mainstream, contemporary political science assumes that individuals can choose how to act and that researchers should focus on individual choices; the quintessential case is the American voter, but study of rebellious behavior should be equally subject to this characterization.[31] This orientation is at odds with a more critical, often leftist perspective that highlights the importance of social structures in constraining people's choices. The distinction between these two approaches, however, has been overdrawn. Karl Marx himself famously did not wholly favor structure over agency. As he wrote in "The Brumaire" (part of which is quoted in chapter 1):

> Men make their own history, but they do not make it as they please; they do not make it under self-selected circumstances, but under circumstances existing already, given and transmitted from the past. The tradition of all dead generations weighs like a nightmare on the brains of the living. And just as they seem to be occupied with revolutionizing themselves and things, creating something that did not exist before, precisely in such epochs of revolutionary crisis they anxiously conjure up the spirits of the past to their service, borrowing from them names, battle slogans, and costumes in order to present this new scene in world history in time-honored disguise and borrowed language.[32]

For Marx there was a dialectical tension between structure and agency that drives history forward; this insight was central to his philosophy of historical materialism and to its explanation of how social change, including revolutionary change, occurs. Agents of change carry the burden of history and act in response to its structural constraints but, within them, act to remake structural conditions that in turn shape how future agents subsequently produce further changes. People are not completely free to act, individually or collectively, but they are free to act in response to structured conditions in any one place and time. When they do, however, they may not always be actually working in service of their own ideals but instead unconsciously achieving other larger historically scripted ends via what Hegel, as noted earlier, called the "cunning of reason."[33]

From Marx's insight one might infer that Occupiers are merely acting out their frustrations in the face of their growing precarity wrought from historically embedded systematic processes of marginalization. Or are there varying degrees of conscious political calculation that promise a more strategic approach?

The coalition of the systematically marginalized has become a self-conscious movement challenging that system that is creating their shared precarity. The power of the "99 percent" slogan lies in no small part in its suggestion that, while we are the many who have suffered at the hands of the few, we are also a collective made up of individuals who can come together to solve our own problems when the state fails us. Perhaps it is only when the individual becomes part of the collective that political agency becomes manifest. Bodies must be in alliance before their political agency can be realized.

This centrality of the individual's relationship to the collective and vice versa has been made explicit in the "We Are the 99 Percent" Tumblr page. It is particularly noteworthy that the Tumblr page includes images accompanied by a note stating "I am the 99 percent." "I am the 99 percent." Not "We"! The I/we inversion is analogous to the word/image imbrication, serving in this case to humanize an impersonal statistic. The binaries of I/we, word/image, and narrative/number become reversible, so that we can slide back and forth as required to realize political agency. The Occupy movement is open for individuals to partake (divide and share) as needed for individual and collective effect. A movement builds by allowing participants to offer their unique stories in a common cause—a creative response suggesting that, even in our depersonalized and bureaucratized society, people find their place(s) and find their voices when they coalesce in collective action.

The collective becomes the site where individuals achieve agency via the relays between their personal stories and impersonal representations. It is also the site of the reverse—where the collective achieves agency via the uniting of diverse individuals acting and even performing as bodies in alliance. We see this imbrication of the personal and the impersonal in striking images of the European protests (see figure 3.2).

In speaking of the Russian punk rockers Pussy Riot, who were imprisoned for their antistate performances, Slavoj Žižek noted: "This is why they

Figure 3.2   "I Am a Profitable Person": Telefonica Strikers, Barcelona, Spain, November 2012.
AP Photo/Emilio Morenatti.

wear balaclavas: masks of de-individualization, of liberating anonymity. The message of their balaclavas is that it doesn't matter which of them got arrested—they're not individuals, they're an Idea. And this is why they are such a threat: it is easy to imprison individuals, but try to imprison an Idea."[34] Similarly, the anonymous European protestors depicted in figure 3.2 put aside their individual identities to act in concert anonymously in the name of a shared concern and a larger idea. So it is with "We are the 99 percent" protestors who take on the shared identity of an impersonal statistic.[35]

Deconstructing the personal narrative / impersonal number imbrication raises further issues of what it takes for people's (individual) actions to constitute forms of (collective) agency. This issue was brilliantly articulated by Carl Schmitt in 1928 in what amounts to a prescient critique of the yet-to-be Internet:

It is fully conceivable that one day through ingenious discoveries, every single person, without leaving his apartment, could continuously express his opinions on political questions through an apparatus and that all these opinions would be automatically registered by a central office, where one would only need to read them off. That would not be an especially intensive democracy, but it would provide proof that the state and the public were fully privatized. It would not be public opinion, for even the shared opinion of millions of private people produces no public opinion. The result is only a sum of private opinions. In this way, no common will arises, no *volonté générale*; only the sum of all individual wills, a *volonté de tous*, does.[36]

The implication of Schmitt's analysis is that if politics is ineliminably public and the public is more than the aggregation of private individuals, then political agency is only possible by interacting with others to express differences, articulate commonalities, and engage in concerted action to realize shared goals (or to learn to live with the unresolved differences). Political agency is contingent on participation in a public collective effort that involves thinking through what it is the people involved have in common and then trying to find ways to act collectively in the name of that commonality or to honor the remaining differences. The mere aggregation of individual opinions, or narratives, then is not nearly enough to constitute a public and serve as the basis for political action.[37]

For instance, the agency of the balaclava-wearing protesters ironically comes in their anonymity as part of a collective, where the process of deindividualization makes them a collective force that stands for an idea—in this case how they have all have been made precarious economically. Their political agency comes when they put aside their individual differences and stand for the precariat's great refusal to go along with the economic transformation and its manufactured austerity. They become a living example of a class "for itself," this time as a precariat as opposed to the proletariat.[38] They are Marx's "träger" as bearers or carriers of history, acquiring agency collectively by representing an idea.[39] It is this collective agency that enables the marginalized to be recognized as such.[40] Stressing their universally shared precarity in this way is not depoliticizing but instead emphasizes that those left behind in different ways by economic dislocation deserve to have their grievances heard and addressed.[41]

So it is then that the relays (as in connections) between texts and images, numbers and narratives, highlight the processes by which collective action can potentially address individual claims without doing an injustice to them. Coalitional politics arguably has not just its own ethics but a distinctive aesthetic as well (both of which can serve political purposes as part of a representational process). Jodi Dean suggests that the spectacle of the Occupy movement is more than street theater. For Dean, there is a politics of representation at the heart of Occupy. Dean writes:

> Those who construe Occupy as post- and anti-representation misread plurality as the negative limit to representation when they should instead recognize plurality as representation's positive condition. Occupy Wall Street is not actually the movement of 99 percent of the population of the United States (or the world) against the top 1 percent. It is a movement mobilizing itself around an occupied Wall Street in the name of the 99 percent. Asserting a division in relation to the fundamental antagonism Occupy makes appear, it represents the wrong of the gap between the rich and the rest of us. Critics of representation miss the way Occupy reinvents the politics of representation because their image of representation remains deeply tied to parliamentarianism. It's true that Occupy eschews mainstream electoral politics. It is also true that Occupy rejects the nested hierarchies that conventionally organize political associations. But neither of these facts eliminates representation. Rather, they point to a rejection of the current political and economic system because of its failure to represent adequately the people's will, a will that is itself divided and can only be represented divisively.[42]

Dean's argument about the representational politics of Occupy is consistent with Butler's focus on bodies in alliance coalescing around their shared precarity and enacted via a performative politics that generates political agency. Butler sees the performative dimensions of speech acts realizing agency when they involve a citationality where discursive practices get unmoored from originating contexts and get re-presented in ways that break with convention.[43] The transgressive, subversive, and disruptive politics of Occupy street demonstrations in the name of the "99 percent" involve not just recalculating who are the people in all their precarity; these are also performatives in service of a representational politics highlighting a shared condition not as an ethical argument as much as creating the basis for political action that merits meaningful responses.

In this way, Occupy's representational politics becomes a site for occupying (as in taking possession of) people's subjection as deficient neoliberal citizen-subjects who have failed to trade efficaciously on their human capital enough to succeed in a market-centered society.[44] Rather than accepting their precarity, people adopt this status as a source of their collective agency. They occupy precarity! They spit back their marginalization in the face of those who have marginalized them. By embracing this shared precarity, Occupy becomes a way of realizing a repoliticized subjectivity as the precariat acting for itself, representing the people as the "99 percent" and forging a collective force that needs to be recognized as a distinct political body. Much like the frontispiece of Thomas Hobbes's *Leviathan* where the king's body is composed of the bodies of his subjects, the subjectivity of the "99 percent" gets realized when diverse bodies in alliance represent their shared precarity via the politics of spectacle in protest demonstrations.[45]

Precarity: An Actually Existing Discursive Practice

We need to ask whether "precarity" is politically salient or just another academic conceit disconnected from political struggle, offering nothing of substance for those whose marginalization it characterizes. Is it another foreign term like "neoliberalism" that people in the United States are not prepared to use? "Neoliberalism," however, with time has proven itself a useful term for describing the juggernaut that seeks to marketize everything, especially state operations, and, more troubling, social welfare programs.[46] And like "neoliberalism," "precarity" points to something beyond marginalization in ways that underscore the growing uncertainties associated with the economic transformation currently under way. In fact, neoliberalism begets precarity, where the push to marketize everything and market volatility become pervasive problems people must constantly confront. Increasingly, people are expected to absorb more of the shocks of market volatility in a neoliberal society where everything more and more operates according to market logic.[47]

"Precarity" means more than income volatility. It adds to our ability to highlight a distinctive dimension of the transformation under way: how people are subjectified as citizens who must accept responsibility for handling the shocks of marketization.[48] "Responsibilization" is a term used to suggest this process whereby citizens are now to be expected to absorb more of the responsibility for handling the ups and downs of a more marketized society. Precarity is the fraught subjective condition that emerges out of responsibilization.

Yet there is a lingering concern that "precarity" is a term of art used by theorists and that it does not reflect how the people being described understand their plight. The discursive violence of imposing an alien term on the precariat is compounded when we consider that the term underscores vulnerability rather than the strength the precariat seeks to exercise in resisting its systematic marginalization in the changing economy. Like "the homeless," "the precariat" risks identifying a diverse population in terms of a lack, thereby reinscribing vulnerability and occluding shared strengths. The "strengths perspective" is often prized among social workers as a way of honoring the intelligence and abilities of clients rather than just seeing them as people with problems who cannot help themselves.[49] And just as "the homeless" masks a diversity of people with myriad conditions and challenges, so does "the precariat" risk lumping many different people differentially at risk of suffering the shocks of marketization.

Yet "precarity" only mistakenly seems to be an academic conceit from the U.S. perspective. The term comes from the front lines of political struggle in Europe, from the early protests over capital flight in the 1970s, which recurred with the intensified efforts to scale back social protections in the 1980s, and then ultimately returned (as it reappeared) in protests in the United States with the widening inequality between the have and the have-nots. Its latest appearance is once again in Europe in open defiance of the manufactured austerity that governments sought to impose after the Great Recession in the name of balancing budgets. As Andrew Robinson writes: "In addition to being a theoretical concept, precarity has been a focus for political organizing by social movements in Europe, such as Chainworkers, Intermittents du Spectacle and Precarias a la Deriva. These groups have organized a range of often attention-grabbing protests and actions, with their major mobilization being the Euromayday movement. In Italy, they have created their own patron saint, 'San Precario,' whose icons turn up on protests."[50]

Franco Barchiesi traces precarity to the autonomist school in the 1970s, noting that the theorists learned from the activists what to call their condition. Barchiesi thoughtfully observes:

> In his famous introduction to Begriffsgeschichte (or "history of concepts"), Reinhart Koselleck insists that concepts are not merely discursive constructs or static ideas but rather emanate and gain sense from political situations, social conditions, and historical trajectories. The conflicts that

shape such processes modify the meanings of words and deploy new terms to depict specific realities, entities, and problems. The ways concepts enter public debates respond in fact to forces that contend the definition of political possibilities in the present by pointing at desired futures whereas "this activity of temporal semantic construal simultaneously establishes the historical force contained within a statement." Modernity is for Koselleck therefore characterized by a use of concepts that does not merely systematize or describe an existing social order but historicize as change and "progress" the tensions between experiences and expectations so that "the moments of duration, change, and futurity contained in a concrete political situation are registered through their linguistic traces."[51]

So it turns out that "precarity" has its own historical trajectory. It was there on the front lines of resistance at the beginning of the long wave of economic change associated with neoliberalism in an age of globalization. It comes to us as an actually existing discursive practice used to highlight the tenuous positioning of citizens in the emerging neoliberal economic order. It is a concept of this moment in late modernity. It is not just a word for describing a contemporary condition; it is a politicized speech act constitutive of responses to conditions—Michael Shapiro's "action framework."[52] Consistent with Marx's thesis 11, the point of "precarity" is not to understand the world as much as to change it. We must occupy precarity, using it not just to make sense of how the new economy is destabilizing and profoundly unjust, but also to achieve collective political agency in spite of how we are differentially affected by it.

FROM WALL STREET TO MAIN STREET: ARTICULATING STREET POLITICS WITH CONVENTIONAL POLITICS

Occupy protests represent in striking terms the challenges of pursuing Butler's coalitional politics centered on highlighting the pervasive precarity associated with various subjectivities. There is a precarity to precarity; it has its own precariousness. I mentioned earlier making visible the processes in which collective action may incorporate individual claims. Nonetheless, the very fluidity and uncertainty of these articulations between individual and collective grievance is a source of concern for many who want the anarchic spectacle of the Occupy movement to be more than street theater that gestures in different ways without a sense of direction toward addressing common concerns.[53] Anticipating criticism from Butler and others who have emphasized the performative dimensions of Occupy, Dean writes: "In sum, the Occupy movement demonstrates why something like a party is needed insofar as a party is an explicit assertion of collectivity, a structure of accountability, an acknowledgment of differential capacities, and a vehicle for solidarity.... Leftists are justifiably anxious with regard to the party—a desire for collectivity is not the only desire for which parties have provided a form."[54] It seems then we have arrived at a Leninist moment in which the question of deliberate action presses against the effort to give voice to persistent suffering. The grievances voiced by Occupy may continue to go unaddressed unless there arises an explicit agenda for action to redress those grievances. It is not just those who are dismissive of Occupy and what it represents who are insisting that it be more organized.

Yet there are multiple dimensions to protest movements like Occupy. Between the performative dimensions of Occupy and the organized efforts to acquire political power and enact public change, there is the significant middle ground that the proponents of these other two dimensions miss. Too much emphasis on either the performative or the policy can lead us away from what Occupy has best offered. Some like Dean have overemphasized the need for a cadre-like party that takes the energy of the movement and channels it into an organization focused on acquiring state power and producing public policy change. Others at the other extreme have doubled down on the idea that Occupy Wall Street was not the failure that so many have proclaimed it because of, not in spite of, its performative dimensions.[55] Instead, such analyses argue that Occupy's value lay in no small part with it being an end in itself. While these writers concede that Occupy helped symbolize and frame the issue of growing inequality in a transformed economy, their argument goes that it most significantly created an opportunity for people to come together in public, to be as Butler says "bodies in alliance." In this way, Occupy did not just embody how the issue of inequality affected so many different people, it also created an opportunity for those people to be in alliance, to bond over their shared fate, to build community around their variegated forms of marginalization, and to create models for others to come together in ways that would enable this experience to become iterative, amendable to emulation, and ultimately transformative for people similarly affected. In this way, these writers argue that the critics of Occupy like Dean miss what was really significant about it when they criticize it as a failed political uprising that did not produce any material changes in public policy and political power.

Much of the criticism of Occupy as a failed effort to produce policy change is misplaced. Too many people have rashly dismissed Occupy as a spontaneous eruption that lacked focus, organization, a policy agenda, and a commitment to producing sustained political change.[56] It is important to understand the performative dimensions of protest politics and their significance for realizing the value Occupy has contributed to confronting the politics of inequality today. Yet somewhere between the internal dynamics of Occupy encampments as successful meeting places and the formation of an organized and sustained political organization dedicated to producing tangible political and policy change is where I find the sweet spot of Occupy. In other words, one side in this debate veers too far in the direction of overvalorizing the performative value of Occupy as an end in itself just as much as the critics go too far in dismissing Occupy for failing to achieve substantive political and public policy restructurings. Instead, I would look to a middle ground to understand what is significant about the Occupy movement.

In other words, too much can be made of Butler's arguments. It is admirable that Occupy participants learned about each other, especially how regardless of their differences they were bonded together by their shared plight. Yet to emphasize this as the most significant dimension of Occupy is I suspect only to add ammunition for those on the left who hope that something like Occupy never occurs again. The Occupy encampments, in town centers and parks, at universities and city halls, were remarkable demonstrations of community and cooperation among those who shared concern about their marginalization in the transformed economy. Students, the unemployed, the unemployable joined with the homeless and others to show how they could become a collective force in spite of their diversity. Yet it is not clear that their encampments are easily replicable and to what effect.

I do, however, reject the idea that simply because they maintained an open, porous, anarchistic form they failed to become an organized and systematic force for political and policy change. Both extremes miss the central and main dimension of protest movements like Occupy. The primary role of a protest movement like Occupy lies in this third dimension between community building and political party organizing. The third dimension emphasizes that the primary role of protest movements is to heighten awareness of an issue and to frame understanding of it in a politically poignant way. Occupy's slogan about how it represented the "99 percent" was astoundingly successful, isolating the "1 percent" and making them vulnerable for significant political pushback that continues today even after President Obama was reelected on the promise of raising taxes on the wealthy, a promise he was able to deliver on after the 2012 election in spite of unprecedented gridlock born of extreme political polarization between Democrats and Republicans in the U.S. Congress. In fact, the emphasis on dicing up the population by percentages most likely helped create the context for evaluating Mitt Romney's infamous "47 percent" comment that in all likelihood proved key to subverting his presidential ambitions and sending him down to defeat in the 2012 election. Romney suggested in a profoundly confused way that 47 percent of the public were dependent on handouts from the government, making them beholden to President Obama and therefore unlikely to vote for Romney as someone who would oppose their welfare dependency. What is important here is not Romney's confusion about who gets what from the government and what effect it has on them politically, but the effectiveness of Occupy in fulfilling its key role as a protest movement in framing the issue of our time. It is this (third) dimension of Occupy as a protest movement that needs emphasizing over and above how it worked to create opportunities to enact community or how it failed to create a permanent political organization for change.

In fact, the limitations of Occupy are actually its strengths, at least if they are not overemphasized to the point that just showing up for protests is an end in itself. If we put Butler's emphasis on the performative dimensions of protests like Occupy in conversation with the best thinking of political scientists, we can see that the issue is not understanding Occupy in isolation but articulating the relationships of the movement to the political parties it seeks to connect to. The real question is not choosing one or another form of protest politics but instead the relationship of protest politics to electoral politics. There is a long-standing debate on the relationship between protest politics and the conventional political process, including elections, interest group lobbying, and public policymaking and implementation.[57] The issue recurs across a number of topic areas.[58] It arises as a critical focus when discussing political action by marginalized groups.[59]

The specific issue of the relationship of protest politics to electoral politics has been perhaps been best addressed by Frances Fox Piven and Richard

Cloward.[60] Piven and Cloward, scholars who were not shy about also being activists, serve as a critical resource for understanding what Occupy should be doing now.[61] For Piven and Cloward, there was an important division of labor between protest politics and conventional party-electoral politics. In fact, there was a dialectical relationship between them. Protest politics helped widen the discourse, highlighting grievances neglected by the electoral process, and elections provided the most effective way for the marginalized to influence the policy process once politicians saw that if they did not respond more disruptive actions would be likely.[62]

Piven sees Occupy as having effectively articulated a relationship to the electoral process. As the 2012 presidential election approached, she wrote:

> [It is said that] electoral politics and movements proceed on separate tracks, and we have to choose one track or the other. This is a false dilemma. Elections and movements do not proceed on separate tracks....Moreover, when protest movements do emerge, the price of appeasement can rise dramatically. Protest movements raise the sharp and divisive issues that vague rhetoric is intended to obscure and avoid, and the urgency and militancy of the movement—with its marches, rallies, strikes and sit-ins— breaks the monopoly on political communication otherwise held by politicians and the media....Movements work against politicians because they galvanize and polarize voters and threaten to cleave the majorities and wealthy backers that politicians work to hold together. But that doesn't mean that movements are not involved with electoral politics. To the contrary, the great victories that have been won in the past were won precisely because politicians were driven to make choices in the form of policy concessions that would win back some voters, even at the cost of losing others.[63]

Protest politics is not an alternative to electoral politics; they work synergistically.[64] It is a point often forgotten. Piven and Cloward's radicalism has sometimes been used by others only to confuse the issue. They never expected protest movements to endure to the point that they completed the project of radical transformation. They were but part of the process. Failing to appreciate this, critics took umbrage when Piven and Cloward moved from focusing their activist scholarship on the welfare rights movement to their successful drive to get the motor voter law enacted that required government agencies to register citizens to vote.[65] Yet this kind of criticism fundamentally misunderstood the synergistic view of protest and electoral politics. Protests like Occupy with its slogan of "We are the 99 percent" can widen political discourse, open up electoral campaigns to consider submerged issues, pose the threat that elections will be affected if protestors' concerns are not taken seriously. At the same time, candidates who call for the public to be engaged, like President Barak Obama has, can encourage political activism beyond elections. As a result, protests can make electoral campaigns more robust and electoral campaigns can mobilize the people to make claims beyond voting for particular candidates. As the anniversary of Occupy approached, Piven wrote:

> A movement forceful enough to change the course of history must accomplish two great tasks. [Beyond being disruptive, it is] communicative. The movement must use its distinctive repertoire of drama and disturbance, of crowds and marches and banners and chants, to raise the issues that are being papered over by normal politics, for the obvious reason that normal politics is inevitably dominated by money and propaganda.
>
> On this, Occupy has already made substantial headway. The slogans that assert we are the 99 percent, they are the 1 percent, named the historic increase in inequality in the United States during the past few decades as the main issue, and the movement dramaturgy of encampments and masks and general assemblies and twinkling fingers helped to give the message heft and appeal, even to the media that had at first simply disparaged the movement. To be sure, there were lots of complaints that Occupy had failed to issue its own policy proposals—which I think it was wise not to, since to do so would have ensnared the activists in endless disputes about particulars. But that is quibbling. It is far more important that we can see the influence of the movement's main issue—extreme inequality—on the speeches at the Democratic convention, for example.[66]

Given this analysis, we can see that the widening of political discourse wrought by Occupy's "we are the 99 percent" arguably was part of a winning formula that helped Obama get reelected by insisting that the wealthy had to pay their "fair share" to help fund government programs needed to assist people in a time of economic malaise.[67] From Butler's perspective, the transgressive, performative politics of Occupy is the source of its agency by allowing different people to articulate connections as bodies in alliance, without extinguishing their diversity while acting in concert. In this way, people's subjection becomes its own source of realizing a newly repoliticized subjectivity. For others, this is in fact the limitation of street politics more generally: it is a rudderless politics of spectacle. Yet once we place Occupy and protest politics more generally in a broader context, as Piven and Cloward have done for us, we can see that there is a place and role for protest politics to be just that: protests that give voice to discontent. The dynamic relationship between protest politics and electoral politics allows protest politics to serve an important function in the overall political landscape. Protests that effectively present people's shared precarity offer a call to action that actors in the conventional political process ignore at their peril.

CONCLUSION

Integrating Judith Butler's philosophical arguments about Occupy as composed of diverse bodies in alliance contesting shared precarity with the empirical analyses of Frances Fox Piven and Richard Cloward about the dynamic relationship between protest movements and elections strengthens both as forms of political inquiry that promise more effective political action. We come to better understand why Occupy did what it did and what it has to offer as part of the struggle for political change.

Neoliberalism begets precarity, and in multiple forms. We live in an age of precarity for the young as well as the old, the educated and the dropouts, the housed and the homeless. A diversity of people are coalescing around their shared marginalization in the face of the changing economy that radically widens the gap between haves and have-nots. A coalition of the dispossessed has come to represent the people's shared precarity. As a movement, Occupy has widened political discourse and beaten back criticisms against class warfare. Because it is a movement built from coalitions, its performativity makes for an openness that invites in a diversity of people, experiencing precarity in different ways, and does so in a way that realizes their shared political agency. Its coalitional character allows for a revitalization that can sustain the protests, branching off to address specific issues. Its status as temporary is not a weakness but a feature of its particular role in the dynamics of political change. It has already done much; it can do more. In the process, we see better not just why Occupy's coalitional politics makes sense given the challenges of activating diverse groups of people, but also why a focus on giving voice to disparate concerns among the marginalized enables the movement to widen political discourse. People come together by repoliticizing their subjection as failed neoliberal citizen-subjects; their shared precarity becomes the basis for their becoming a new class—that is, the precariat. They make not a banal ethical appeal but spit back their subjection to the powers that be and achieve collective political agency in the process. As a result, Occupy performs important representational politics even as it resists offering an explicit public policy agenda. It ends up playing its part in the larger political process where those concerns get registered in elections, as we have seen, and in the public policymaking process, where its full effect remain to be seen.

THE DEEP SEMIOTIC STRUCTURE
OF DESERVINGNESS

DISCOURSE AND IDENTITY
IN NEOLIBERAL WELFARE POLICY

Part of the battle over the problem of inequality today is not just a question of the movement, as in Occupy; it is also about the message, as in the framing narratives we use to understand and respond to that growing inequality. The politics of inequality has a deeply culturally embedded subtext that people employ, consciously or not, for making sense of the gross inequalities occurring today. In this sense, just as the subconscious for Freud was not entirely hidden, and was a "sub-" conscious as much as an "un-" conscious, the basis for our interpretations of social inequalities is ironically "hidden in plain sight."[1] We therefore need to examine how unarticulated understandings of ourselves and others influence our judgments about inequality, what causes it, and what we should do about it. In particular, we need to understand how the narratives influence how we judge people, their social positions, and whether they are deserving of where they have ended up in the social-economic pecking order. To paraphrase an oft-repeated refrain among contemporary social theorists, we need to understand that "the discourse spoke us as much as we spoke it."[2] We need to ask what is the role of discourse in perpetuating the subordination of marginal populations in our society.

This focus on discourse highlights that there are key categories for discussing welfare policy that actually go beyond the well-established if implicit racial subtext that frequently informs the demonization of the poor in the United States historically and even—in fact especially—today. Study of historical texts of welfare policy has convinced me that most white Americans have always been skeptical about providing public assistance to the poor regardless of their color.[3] When it comes to providing public assistance to needy families, it is clear: we are not Sweden. The most fundamental aspect of welfare policy discourse in the United States is that it works to reinscribe an invidious distinction between those who have "earned" benefits and those who are getting "handouts."[4] There exists what I call a "deep semiotic structure of deservingness" embedded in welfare policy discourse.

A semiotic approach is most appropriate for interrogating a socially significant dichotomy such as the one the divides the population into those who earned their benefits and those who are seen as surviving on handouts.[5] Semiotics is the study of signs. Semiotics focuses on signs as opposed to symbols or signals (the other two of the three main ways of communicating via discourse). Signals, like traffic signals, are limited in the interpretations they allow: red is stop, green is go. Symbols are at the other extreme and are the most porous and open to interpretation. Signs are in between, not as prismatic as symbols but more open to interpretation than signals. Semiotics focuses on how signs operate to create fundamental distinctions that structure the ways we interpret the world, as when welfare policy discourse reinscribes a tendentious divide between the deserving and undeserving poor. The semiotic approach to the study of social phenomena starts with the assumption that the culture of any society is at its base grounded in an interpretive grid or a structure of intelligibility that informs the discourses we use to express our understandings of ourselves, our relationships to each other, and the world around us. The interpretive grid or structure of intelligibility comprises interrelated binary distinctions that operate as codes communicating fundamental distinctions about what is natural and cultural, good and bad, moral and immoral, rational and emotional, and so on. Therefore, semiotics emphasizes the ways deeply sedimented binaries or dichotomies serve as the basic codes for structuring the making of meaning in any particular social order. For Jack Balkin in *Cultural Software: A Theory of Ideology*, these binary codes operate as "cultural software" that provides a set of "nested oppositions," trading on each other in a form of intertextuality to create hierarchies that privilege one side of a particular binary at the expense of the other. These codes are not epiphenomenal but central in providing the basis for narratives we use to make sense of social relations writ large.

Semiotics falls between structuralism and poststructuralism. Structuralism emphasizes deeply embedded patterns, such as the underlying order of binaries that inform our thinking. Poststructuralism opens the door to the free play of signifiers. The semiotic approach to culture enables us to go beyond a structural analysis of the means by which society is organized, in ways that constrain social choices and actions, to show that implicit in these structural conditions there is an interpretive grid that informs, mediates, and constitutes our social relations. For instance, Jeffrey Alexander, in writing about election campaigns in the United States, has effectively highlighted the power of the underlying coded binaries that form the basis of a culture:

> Difference is a semiotic truism, but it is also one of the major strategies of politics. As campaigns work the binaries, they try to simplify the meaning of every issue that comes up, bringing it into semiotic alignment, on one side or the other of the great divide. Everything must be made clean or dirty, and, whenever possible, the newly pure and polluted folded into the narrative arc of historical transformation. This spinning machine comes to an end on 4th November, when the act of voting allows a purging catharsis, a spitting out of the negative, and a transformation of the individual into the collective will. Until that day, politics is about creating difference, not overcoming it. The principal strategy for protecting the purity of your candidate's image is to categorize the other candidate in polluted ways. If we are to be coded as clean and democratic, he must be made dirty in the litany of tried and true, antidemocratic themes. If we are to be narrated as heroic, he must become a villain.[6]

As for elections, so it is for social welfare policy. Since the Social Security Act of 1935, the United States has had a two-tier system of distributing cash benefits.[7] The top tier consists of the nationally administered social insurance programs, including, most prominently, Social Security retirement benefits for the elderly; the bottom tier comprises the state-administered public assistance programs for the poor, including what is commonly called "welfare," in particular the Temporary Assistance for Needy Families (TANF) program. The top-tier programs are federally funded, with benefits that adjust to the cost of living, and recipients are generally not stigmatized for receiving their benefits, but rather characterized as deserving, often on the assumption that they earned those benefits by virtue of participation in the labor force by either themselves or the head of their family. Bottom-tier programs are funded in part or whole by states, with low benefits that are not adjusted for the cost of living, and recipients are often stigmatized as undeserving because they did not earn their benefits through work. For years, this tiered system has operated to reinscribe an invidious distinction between recipients of the different programs.

In the literature on public policy, the theory of policy feedback suggests that policies do not just reflect politics but also circle back to affect our political attitudes and behaviors.[8] This is a good way to characterize how the tiered system of social provision has worked to reinscribe this long-standing distinction between the deserving and undeserving poor. The poor who get welfare are undeserving because they are not like the elderly who earned their benefits by working. Prior research I have collaborated on concluded that even after welfare reform forced TANF recipients to work they still were seen as undeserving in the eyes of many citizens, perhaps because requiring them to work only reinforced the assumption that they had not been working before they were required to do so.[9] The assumption is, unfortunately, often wrong, since welfare recipients for years have frequently been combining welfare and wages.[10] Yet facts rarely have affected the extent to which people allow unexamined stereotypes to influence their attitude toward those "other" people who are allegedly not playing by white, middle-class rules. Welfare recipients, both white and nonwhite, frequently do not conform to stereotype. Yet that does not matter, since it seems that the tiered system of social provision feeds back and reinforces mass attitudes about the poor. The very design of the welfare state helps to perpetuate what seems to me to be a long-standing semiotic structure of deservingness.[11]

HOW IT WORKS

Public discourse on welfare is polluted with distortions and deceptions that arise from the efforts of those keen to repudiate the need to fund public assistance programs. No matter how we use statistics to debunk popular myths associated with poverty and welfare, people keep insisting that the welfare poor are those underserving "other" people who are not playing by the white, middle-class rules of work and family. The 1996 welfare reform law came to be seen as successful simply because its enactment was followed by the on-going decline in the number of welfare recipients (which actually had started with an uptick in the economy in the early 1990s). No amount of empirical research that highlighted the real conditions of the poor and the need for social assistance seemed to matter. In search of the role dominant narratives have played in the now largely successful campaign to repudiate public as-sistance, there is a need to unearth the mechanisms by which the deeply embed-ded invidious distinction between the deserving and undeserving has been reiterated repeatedly. As part of this process, I would argue it is important to focus on the relationship of narrative to discourse more seriously than pre-viously (and in ways that lead to semiotics).

Looking at narrative as distinct from discourse involves learning to "read between the lines."[12] I say "read between the lines" because discourse has come to mean the unsaid more than the said: it is that unsaid underlying structure of intelligibility that creates a referential context for deriving meaning from what is said. As Barry Laga clarifies, "by 'discourse,' I mean not only the way we use language, but also the assumptions, attitudes, values, beliefs, and hierarchies that are attached to [the] way language is used. [The] task is to show how a text functions within a discourse or show how a text attempts to negotiate among competing discourses."[13] Just as Jacques Lacan could effectively suggest that the unconscious is structured like a language, discourse is in significant part like the unconscious, hidden in plain sight, available to be referenced, even if not explicitly so.[14]

In this rendering, discourse is different from narrative. Narratives are the surface textual representations of actions and events, while discourse is the underlying interpretive context for making sense of those surface narratives. Consciously or not, we inevitably rely on the underlying discourse for inter-preting the implicit understandings that are only suggested by the explicit, surface narratives. Just as we rely on implicit understandings to interpret nonverbal cues, we rely on the structure of intelligibility associated with any discourse to connect the dots in any narrative. Narratives are potent with meaning in ways that only discourse can reveal. To focus on the explicit narrative at the expense of the implicit discourse is, metaphorically speaking, to miss the forest for the trees.

An example of the relationship of the unsaid discourse to the said narrative comes from film. In criticizing reviews of Stanley Kubrick's film *Barry Lyndon*, Michael Klein distinguishes between discourse and narrative:

> There seems to be an expectation, virtually prescriptive, that the core of the film should reside in the narrative, in the sequence of events and point of view of the main characters. However Kubrick's modernist perspective is somewhat different. While the events do shape the characters' lives, they are relatively neutral, incomplete signs. The characters are devoid of self-consciousness. The total configuration of visual and aural signs (including the music and the voiceover), that is the discourse, defines and determines our response to and comprehension of the events.... The discourse is ironic and analytic (places the characters and events in a larger perspective); it also engages our sympathy (defines value and meaning). A discourse is a configuration of [s]igns...that over-determines the narrative.[15]

When examining the underlying discourse, we see that even the tried-and-true distinctions regarding what is natural versus cultural, or what is reason versus emotion, or even male versus female, practice their own intertexuality: each claims to refer to a real binary, but in fact its ability to reference the real world is infinitely deferred, and these distinctions only end up referring to other distinctions. It is like finding out that behind the curtain there is no real Wizard of Oz, just some old man. The foundation is actually made of sand; the cat chases its tail; any attempt to get to the origin of it all is frustrated by the continuous reference to another distinction. When we try to explain a distinction between two words, we must use other distinctions to clarify. We never get to ground that distinction in a definitive way in the world of objective material reality, whether it is to distinguish what is natural from what is cultural, what is rational from what is emotional, or even what is essentially male from what is female (even if the last distinction suggests we can come close—i.e., do genitalia really define the difference between male and female?). There is no terra firma on which we can base our use of words to reference real things objectively understood. The alleged fundamental distinctions regarding what is real refer not to objective reality but instead only to each other, one binary to the next endlessly, never quite getting to anchor their particular distinctions in the material world. Our access to the real world is ineliminably intertextual.

In this sense, everything is intertextual. Take something centrally related to the topic of the underserving poor. Consider the historically privileged citizen-subject of Western, liberal political discourse—the rational, autonomous, self-sufficient male. He actually emerges out of the intertextuality of nested oppositions that suggests that women are more emotional than men because they are more tied to humans' biological nature due to their childbearing capacities. The relevance for critiquing welfare policy discourse is acute. For instance, this kind of demystification helps question the dichotomy of structure and agency that lies problematically at the base of the still-hegemonic, Western, liberal-capitalist political discourse that assumes at its foundation the independent, self-sufficient, autonomous citizen-subject—for example, a male breadwinner—who is therefore to be privileged over those subjectivities that imply dependency and an inability to act for oneself on one's own terms—for example, a female welfare recipient.

Questioning the implied subjectivities of all policy discourses is in fact political work that is critical. At the center of the imaginaries of most policy discourses is the implied subject of that policy: the policy identity assumed to be reflective of the citizen-subject who is the target of that policy, be he or she citizen, taxpayer, worker, voter, business owner, homeowner, welfare recipient, retiree, illegal immigrant, ex-con, terrorist, green consumer, hedge fund manager, and so on. The implied subject position so defined by any one particular public policy is the quintessential example of how policy discourse operates by creating an unsaid, assumed reference point to which the ostensible metaphors of the surface narrative of any policy gesture (see table 4.1).

Table 4.1   Discourse, Narrative, and Metaphors.

Surface Level:

Narrative (often including a story of how policy problem and its solution came to be)
Framing Metaphors (always present in any policy narrative referencing an underlying discourse for making sense of the narrative and its story)

Underlying Structure:

Discourse (comprised of critical distinctions for making sense of particular policy-narratives)
Subjectivities (key distinctions that reference why some identities are to be privileged in a policy narrative)

Heuristically, it can be argued that there is value in suggesting that there are levels of policy discourse, much like the idea that there are levels of consciousness. On the surface, there are key framing metaphors embedded in any policy narrative that point to an underlying discourse that provides reference points for making meaning from the framing metaphors and the ostensible narratives with which they are associated. As Deborah Stone has insightfully noted, policy narratives often tell politically convenient "just so" stories, often championed most effectively by the most powerful groups active in the public policy process, that suggest why it makes sense to see a policy and its problem of concern a particular way.[16] The policy narrative and the story it provides inevitably include framing metaphors that suggest that the saga told about a policy, its problem, and the people associated with dealing with it are analogous to other situations and characters. The context for interpreting these metaphors is that underlying structure of intelligibility, or what I am calling here the discourse, which itself relies on key binary distinctions for privileging certain practices and people.

The policy narrative and its framing metaphors rely on that discourse for implying that there is a certain type of identified citizen-subject who is assumed to be the focus of concern (either as a problem person or praiseworthy person, as, for example, in the case of welfare policy in the United States today, where such a protagonist is cited as either a demonized "welfare mother" or a "personally responsible mother," the latter designating, ironically for welfare reform, a "working mother" who assigns paid employment outside the home her top priority).[17] Frank Fischer has written:

> Employing literary and rhetorical devices for symbolic representation, policy stories are tools of political persuasion. As strategies for depicting problems and interests, discursive devices such as synecdoches (which represent the whole by one of its parts) or metaphors (which make implied comparisons) are pervasive throughout policy stories. Such linguistic constructions are designed and introduced to convince an audience of the necessity of a political or policy action; they help identify the responsible culprits and the virtuous saviors capable of leading us to high ground.[18]

The semiotic approach highlights that there is an underlying cultural interpretive grid in any society that provides the basis for the implied subjectivities of any public policy. This structure gives rise to basic distinctions in policy discourse that we rely on to make sense of people's identities, as good or bad, in or out, deserving or undeserving. Related questions begin to form: Who are these imagined personas that inhabit any particular policy discourse? How do they get created? How do they get to act? What kind of agency do they have? What is their power over us? And how can we engage them in ways that are democratic and that enable people to work toward a more socially just set of public arrangements? These are questions that a revitalized form of discourse analysis provokes. As Fischer suggests, the inquiry into the discursive construction of policy identities has the potential to make a distinctive, democratizing contribution to public policy analysis. More than conventional approaches, semiotic policy analysis offers the opportunity to interrogate those assumptions about identity that are embedded in the analysis and making of public policy, thereby enabling the questionable distinctions that privilege some identities at the expense of others to be rethought and resisted. Public policy analysis can benefit from the emphasis on how discourse constructs identity.

The model provided in table 4.1 gives insight into how every policy has its "other"—its unsaid, implied citizen-subject that makes us assume that the policy is logically related to real people when in fact that other is an artifact of the policy discourse that personifies its political biases. Social welfare policy in the contemporary postindustrial United States has been shown to participate in the construction and maintenance of identity in ways that affect not just the allocation of public benefits but also economic opportunities outside the state.[19] Yet the discourse of this policy is a well-established black art. Mired in old, invidious distinctions, welfare policy discourse today helps to re-create the problems of yesterday.

THE DEEP SEMIOTIC STRUCTURE OF DESERVINGNESS

History teaches us that there is a deep semiotic structure of deservingness undergirding contemporary welfare policy discourse in the United States. It is deeply embedded in the nation's roots, stretching back over two centuries. This discourse is anchored in the contrast between two central subjectivities: the deserving autonomous, self-sufficient individual and the undeserving dependent (see table 4.2).

Table 4.2 Welfare Discourse, Narratives, and Metaphors.

Surface Level:

The Welfare Dependency Narrative (including stories of how relying on welfare is an addiction, means you are a bad mother, makes you a bad role model, etc.)

Dependency, Personal Responsibility, self-sufficiency as key Welfare Policy Metaphors (these framing metaphors suggest that accepting welfare is to be understood by referencing an underlying discourse that connects welfare reliance to other denigrated practices)

Underlying Structure:

Welfare Reform Discourse (comprised of critical distinctions for making sense of welfare reform narratives: active/passive, independent/dependent, work/care, etc.)

Subjectivities (identities to be privileged in the welfare reform narrative: the self-sufficient, autonomous subject)

These two central subjectivities not only anchor how we approach thinking about the public realm generally but also serve to create a basis for questioning whether to extend aid to the needy. We can see this in the debates about welfare that have historically informed welfare policy discourse in the United States. From before the time Thomas Malthus wrote his infamous *Essays on the Principles of Population* in 1798 in England to after Charles Murray reiterated those arguments in *Losing Ground* in 1984 in the United States, social welfare policy discourse has been dominated by what Albert Hirschman has called the "perversity thesis."[20] In Malthus's hands, the perversity thesis combined classical liberal economic theory with Christian morality to suggest that, contrary to the apparent reality that offering financial aid to the "poor" was a kind and charitable act of assistance, such intervention actually undermined the natural order of things and corrupted the individuals who accepted such succor, so that they lost the ability to practice self-discipline and exercise personal responsibility.

The theory held that helping poor people in this way actually had perverse effects because the poor are different from other people and lack the ability for self-discipline when it comes to issues of work and family: the poor are lazy and promiscuous. If you give them financial assistance, they will just squander it, and if you persist in helping them, they will just take society down with them. The perversity thesis has proven resilient even in the face of secularization. For well over two centuries, at varying times and to varying degrees, much success has come to the perversity thesis and its cousin, the "futility thesis," which maintains that "the poor" will always be with us no matter what we do.

This success testifies to the power of discourse. Arguments like the perversity thesis can be persuasive independent of historical circumstances. The facts of "welfare dependency" at any time seem far less significant than the enduring power of the perversity thesis to appeal to ingrained moralisms in Western, liberal-capitalist societies about public aid corrupting the individual and undermining the self-discipline assumed to be central in the making of the autonomous, self-sufficient, liberal citizen-subject. To accept welfare is therefore often characterized as "welfare dependency" because it is associated with undermining the autonomy and independence associated with the model type of citizen-subject we all need to become if we are to take on the subject position in the liberal public sphere. If we are all dependents, then who will be able to fulfill the role of the independent citizen free to act on his or her own accord in the public sphere, politically, socially, economically, and so on? The entire edifice of the liberal, democratic, capitalist order is built on the assumption that there are free consenting individuals who enter into economic, social, and political contracts and other arrangements. Any behaviors that suggest that we are not free or independent, but instead beholden to others, or dependent, undermine the plausibility of this assumed subjectivity and pose a risk to that order that must be resisted.

The history of welfare dependency as a meme for public policymaking attests to its enduring role in reinscribing the dichotomy between who was seen as adhering to the dominant standards of work and family in our society and who was not.[21] Welfare, in the form of cash assistance provided by the state to low-income families, has admittedly never been popular but it has proven a necessity for tending to families who cannot provide for themselves. Nonetheless, especially in a market-centered society such as the United States, welfare has historically been provided, most often reluctantly and always with great suspicion. The dominant cultural bias has been that the people receiving aid do not really need it or will become accustomed to receiving it to the point that they will lose motivation to seek work, which has always in the United States been prized as the primary way that families should support themselves.

The historical roots of the opposition to what came to be called welfare dependency stretch back to Europe and prohibitions in the early modern period against giving alms by parishioners of the church for fear of encouraging indolence (as was the case in England with the enactment of the Statute of Labourers, 1349–50). Categorizing the poor as to their deservingness followed suit, such as designating "sturdy beggars" as prohibited from seeking aid. Over the centuries, many different schemes of categorization have been deployed to indicate who is deserving of aid and who is not. The primary preoccupation has been to ensure that those who could be working do not substitute public aid as an alternative.

Arguably, the most significant public exchange on the issue arose in the late 1700s in the debate on population in England. That debate was focused on whether the long-established Elizabethan Poor Law dating back to 1563 encouraged the poor to propagate beyond their means. This debate provided a prominent venue for Malthus to publish his essays on population and promulgate his philosophy that aid to the poor was ironically detrimental to their well-being and also dangerous for the security of society overall. Malthus feared that aid would lead to growing numbers of the poor whom society could not support. He believed in fact that such aid violated the natural order of things and was not only unscientific according to economic theory but also un-Christian according to religious tenets regarding what God had created for man and how he was expected to live in society. In the end, Malthus's combination of economic science and Christian theology won the debate on population and the Poor Law was reformed in the early 1830s. The 1834 Report on the Poor Law reflected his thinking. The reforms made welfare less readily available and restructured the provision of aid to ensure that work was always seen as the preferable alternative.

At the time, the Speenhamland Rate, as it was called for the village in Berkshire County from which it originated, was repealed. Developed in response to the economic downturn of 1795, the rate set a standard for supplementing the wages of workers who were paid below a minimal amount. It came to be adopted by a group of southern counties in England but soon took on wider significance in the debate over population and its focus on welfare dependency. The Speenhamland Rate was actually an early form of a guaranteed basic income. Yet in the public debate about the Old Poor Law, it was widely repudiated and not just for encouraging the poor to work less than they needed to in order to support their growing families. Opponents also argued that it depressed wages by allowing employers to assume that they did not need to raise the pay of workers knowing their incomes would be supplemented to bring them up the minimal level set by the rate. Based on the 1834 report, the reforms as enacted explicitly installed the principle of "less eligibility," which required that welfare should always be provided in amounts and under conditions that were inferior to the lowest-paying jobs. The principle of less eligibility was designed to incentivize work to the point of making it attractive to take whatever jobs the economy provided no matter how poorly they paid and no matter how horrible the conditions. Welfare dependency was the scourge resulting from the Old Poor Law of 1563 that the New Poor Law of 1834 explicitly attacked. The principle of less eligibility led to the repeal of not just Speenhamland but also all forms of what was called "outdoor relief," which was cash aid provided to families in their homes. In place of these forms of assistance, a national system of poorhouses was established where those in need were required to live and work under harsh conditions in exchange for food and shelter. This system made it highly unlikely that even the worst of the lowest-paying jobs would not be preferable to receiving the "indoor relief" offered by the poorhouse.

The British preoccupation with welfare dependency was imported to the United States and came to be infused into the systems of social provision.[22] Yet over time, a cyclical pattern of alternating emphasis on indoor and outdoor relief emerged with the fluctuations in the economy and political unrest among the poor. In particular, when times were dire economically and people were desperate, outdoor relief became more readily available as an alternative to overcrowding in the poorhouse. By the 1880s, however, concern over the dangers of welfare dependency led even the leaders of the charitable sector to push back against extending outdoor relief to the needy. The Charitable Organization Societies promoted scientific charity and argued that the systematic provision of aid to the poor should promote their self-sufficiency rather than dependence on the government and the charitable sector. The local societies units in a number of states successfully got outdoor relief programs curtailed and as a result the population of the poorhouses began to grow once again. Another development, however, made this cyclical shift even more troubling. The number of children in orphanages also began to grow as single mothers, but also sometimes two-parent families, living in destitution would increasingly turn their children over to the orphanages on the grounds that they could not support them. Many children in orphanages were not strictly speaking orphans but were better described as abandoned children (though this went unspoken). Immigrant children from struggling families came to be a growing proportion of the orphaned population housed in these facilities.

The growing concern about creating a generation of abandoned children led to a movement for mothers' pensions, which was essentially outdoor relief for mothers so they could keep their children and not place them in the overflowing orphanages. In the first two decades of the twentieth century, states followed each other in adopting mothers' pensions programs. They were most often administered locally at the county level, resulting in great variation and unevenness in coverage and benefits. Yet just about everywhere African American mothers were denied aid partly based on the racist thinking that they were more appropriately mothers who could be working as domestics and servants and aid to them did not fit their role as "different" kinds of mothers who did not stay home to care for their children.[23] Mothers' pensions were nativistic in that they were championed as a way to help white families raise children to become good Christian Americans. Part of the campaign of mothers' pensions was to beat back "race death" and promote "white republican motherhood." Nativistic, patriotic, and racist as well as feminist, mothers' pensions represented a diverse set of interests. Even so, this form of outdoor relief most often did not reach even most white mothers who needed aid and when it did the aid was meager at best. The scourge of welfare dependency cast a long pall over even this dramatic shift in welfare policy.

With the Great Depression of the 1930s, President Franklin Delano Roosevelt got a heavily Democratic Congress to support his Social Security Act, which included Title IV programs to aid the poor.[24] Prominent among these programs was Aid to Dependent Children, which essentially created a federal structure for mothers' pensions. State programs that were consistent with national standards would receive funding from the federal government to cover much of their costs. The law emerged from Roosevelt's Committee on Economic Security which was headed by Frances Perkins, a social worker who was the first female secretary of labor. The committee designed the program to continue to discourage welfare dependency, limiting aid in most cases to families without a male breadwinner present and allowing states to set benefits and eligibility standards that were consistent with local labor markets. The principle of less eligibility lived on even with these dramatic reforms. And Roosevelt himself publicly proclaimed that once the economy recovered Aid to Dependent Children would wither away.

The program eventually came to be called Aid to Families with Dependent Children to recognize the need to support the parents as well as the children. By the mid-1960s, in the wake of the civil rights movement, the welfare rights movement arose, organizing around research that revealed that only about half of all families eligible for welfare were receiving it. Protests, demonstrations, litigation, and even a campaign for a guaranteed basic income led to liberalization by the federal government and the states in response in the hopes of mollifying the poor. The "welfare explosion," as it came to be called, resulted in massive increases in the number of families receiving welfare across all states between 1964 and 1972. Growth among low-income African American families was the most dramatic, leading to welfare increasingly being seen as a "black program" for those "other" people who were not playing by white, middle-class rules of work and family. In response, a guaranteed income was proposed by President Richard Nixon, of all people, but was twice defeated in the early 1970s by a divided Congress. Concerns about welfare dependency were part of the reluctance to do away with the now universally unpopular welfare system.

The Aid to Families with Dependent Children program was finally abolished in 1996 when dramatic reform legislation replaced it with Temporary Assistance for Needy Families.[25] The TANF program time-limited welfare so that no family could receive federal aid for more than five years. It imposed work requirements including having recipients sign "individual responsibility plans" that had them take steps to move from welfare to work. Recipients had to complete thirty to forty hours a week in work-related activities including community service and paid employment in order to continue to receive any aid. The TANF program gave each state a block grant with wide discretion on how to use the funds. By 2000, less than half of all the block-grant funding went to cash assistance and most went to welfare-to-work services designed to get recipients to make "rapid attachment" to the workforce and as much as possible practice a "work first" philosophy in deciding how to handle their economic destitution. Strict sanctions that reduced cash benefits were imposed for recipients who failed to comply with these rules as structured variously by states and localities. For-profit providers contracted to administer the system's key programs became popular in most states and they often took a business-minded approach to move recipients off welfare as quickly and as cheaply as possible in order to maximize their profits. By 2005, the number of recipients had declined by more than 60 percent since the inception of the reform initiatives starting in the mid-1990s (see figure 4.1).

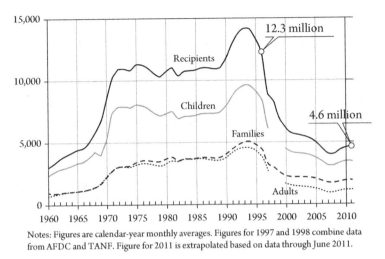

Notes: Figures are calendar-year monthly averages. Figures for 1997 and 1998 combine data from AFDC and TANF. Figure for 2011 is extrapolated based on data through June 2011.

Figure 4.1 Welfare Caseloads, 1960–2011 (in thousands).
Administration for Children and Families, TANF caseload data, 2011, as reproduced at http://www.familyfacts.org/charts/305/welfare-caseloads-have-declined-since-the-1996-welfare-reform.

With the TANF program welfare dependency came to be seen as analogous to other dependencies, such as chemical dependencies. It was treated as akin to an affliction or addiction. It was something from which one had to be weaned. Welfare programming became highly medicalized, with clients treated for their limitations and barriers that prevented them from practicing good behavioral health that would lead them down the road to recovery as a self-sufficient citizen. Welfare reform combined economic and medical reasoning to discipline the poor to accept the verdict of the globalizing labor market and take whatever low-wage jobs were provided even if that left them as poor as they had ever been. This outlook still predominates in welfare policy discourse nearly twenty years after the reform law was enacted.

Given this history, we can say that from the perspective of discourse analysis, the facts of welfare dependency in this sense have been always already there, ready to be materialized in quotidian practices of welfare administration that treat welfare recipients in self-fulfilling, denigrating ways. All it takes evidently according to the historical record is a less than active imagination willing to interpret welfare participation unreflectively, as if it were without question a sign of personal deficiency. Sadly, as we have seen, the modern history of the Western world, especially in the United States and England, is replete with such instances of underutilized imagination, placing whatever facts that were offered about welfare use in terms of this argument about an unchanging underlying moral order. And the facts of welfare dependency are less than apparent.

Our most recent history demonstrates this clearly. In the effort to celebrate the reductions in welfare recipients in the first years after welfare reform was enacted in 1996, the proponents of welfare reform were spouting interpretations of these numbers in self-serving ways, to make the policy seem to be the success it was not. Their interpretations implicitly traded on the assumption that welfare receipt was inherently bad and reducing the rolls in any way possible was an unalloyed good. The discourse framed welfare reform as an inevitable success, irrespective of what happened to the people who got kicked off public assistance. In fact, prior to welfare reform, as people championed the need to time-limit the receipt of public assistance, no amount of facts rebutting the myths of welfare dependency could dissuade them from whipping up a moral panic over welfare receipt. Pointing out factual misstatements did no good whatsoever in undermining the ideological juggernaut the conservative, right-wing cultural warriors had developed to impugn the already sullied image of welfare recipients as malingerers and no-counts, that is, promiscuous women lazily living off welfare.[26]

Racial bias figured prominently in the narratives that circulated among welfare reform supporters and highlighted how deeply embedded racialized definitions of who is deserving permeated policy discourse. The gender bias of the discourse was equally stunning, overlooking that the overwhelming majority of recipients of cash assistance to poor families are single mothers who are trying to handle both breadwinning and caregiving responsibilities on their own. The mere recitation of factual evidence about contemporary welfare recipients was to prove woefully inadequate in the face of an argument that had endured at least since the eighteenth century and had convinced people to ignore empirical information in order to appreciate the underlying "natural order of things." And in the Western, liberal political imaginary, the underlying natural order of things was assumed to be one in which the privileged citizen-subject was the autonomous, self-sufficient, male head of a family. It was as if extending aid to black, single mothers jeopardized the perpetuation of the natural order of things and needed to be resisted.

Therefore, dependency discourse in the United States is, arguably, paradigmatic of discourse in general. It provides an exemplar of how discourse operates to make itself real. Like all discourse, it interprets symptoms to be signs of some preexisting, underlying condition that it, retroactively, identifies as always already having been there, often for reasons attributable to the characteristics or traits of some implied type of person associated with a particular identity, that is, a subjectivity. In this way, it can be said that all discourses, welfare policy or otherwise, have their "others." In semiotic fashion, discourse implies identities, both a privileged identity and an "othered," denigrated identity. In the case of welfare policy discourse, from Malthus on, dependency discourse with its perversity thesis imputes a preexisting set of pathological behaviors in a timeless way to "the poor" as an othered group comprising distinctive types of people who then in their otherness give rise to the poverty and welfare dependency that we see before us in the contemporary scene. And once we accept as real this narrated discourse of implied identities, we organize our affairs, including public policies, to address the deficiencies in the denigrated identity to the point that people so identified have almost no choice but to either capitulate to being treated on those terms or risk being marginalized further as deviants of a more difficult sort.

From Medicalization to Neoliberalization

One prominent narrative about welfare dependency in recent years, as mentioned above, depicts it as akin to other dependencies, such as a chemical dependency. Welfare discourse has in fact increasingly become medicalized. As result, welfare receipt has come to be seen as like a sickness. The age-old perversity thesis was reincarnated in highly technocratic ways, now retrofitted for the new forms of governance that rely heavily on a medicalized discourse to characterize the welfare poor as a deficient population in need of treatment. It is an example of the process of intertextuality at work. Contemporary welfare policy discourse understands reliance on public assistance in highly medicalized terms by borrowing metaphors from other service domains that end up imputing the causes of poverty and reliance to the individual and her or his personal deficiencies.

Medicalization is, arguably, the main way that welfare policy discourse today creates a stage for enacting what Michel Foucault called "neoliberal governmentality," where the state is in the business of disciplining the poor to become self-disciplined citizen-subjects who will be less of a burden on the rest of us in spite of the persistent poverty they endure.[27] Neoliberal governmentality is premised on the idea that all of social life, public and private, in civil society as well as in the state and the market, should be seen as a venue for developing and deploying one's personal human capital so as to perform as a social actor consistent with market logic. This hypertrophy of market logic to become the common-sense basis for making all social choices requires that people become disciplined citizen-subjects who internalize market rationality as their social ethic. For low-income people who lack ability to perform effectively in this manner or who simply resist the orientation, there is the emerging danger that they will be seen as in need of behavioral modification in the form of what is called behavioral health and related services offering treatment to overcome whatever personal limitations prevent them from practicing neoliberal governmentality.[28] Social welfare policy increasingly is oriented toward combining medical and economic logics in service of disciplining clients to act consistently with neoliberal governmentality and thereby reduce the burdens of the state in assisting people to live otherwise. In the process, what emerges is an economistic-therapeutic-managerial discourse for treating subordinate populations in an age of neoliberalization.[29] The goal is to reinscribe the neoliberal cardinal principle that all people in the social order need to take personal responsibility for the choices they make.[30] The goal is to produce disciplined citizen-subjects who are capable of effectively making rational choices for improving their life chances, leaving aside and even rationalizing the fact that low-income individuals and subordinated populations are really given nothing more than an empty gesture when asked to choose between the lesser of two evils. These forced, false choices invariably leave the poor just as they are, poor still. This is the pervasive reality of the fraudulent nature of the choice system neoliberalism puts in place, whether it is about choosing a social welfare service provider, charter school, or low-wage job.

By the 1990s, this discourse's preoccupation with getting the poor to accept responsibility for their bad choices had become ascendant in welfare policy discourse and had helped frame "welfare dependency" as the problem that needed attention rather than poverty.[31] This amounted to nothing less than an aphasic shift, where welfare discourse operates to impair our ability to put into words the trauma of poverty, and we use euphemistic substitutes such as "welfare dependency" to paper over our complicity in perpetuating other people's destitution, while simultaneously shifting the blame away from the structure of society to the individual behavior of those who are forced to live in poverty.[32] With this old aphasic shift taking new form, welfare dependency becomes the center of our discursive terrain dealing with how, in the contemporary parlance of our therapeutic culture, to "treat" recipients for their diseased condition of dependence on welfare. Welfare use beyond the shortest periods of time as a form of transitional aid, as, say, when a single mother relies on welfare while working through a divorce, is now considered abuse. In other words, welfare use beyond a few months is now welfare abuse, signaling the need to undergo treatment to overcome one's dependency on welfare. The dependency metaphor operates like a metonymy in which a contiguous reference point is emphasized rather than the original object of concern. The poverty that precedes welfare dependency is ignored, and instead we are asked to focus on the reliance on welfare.

This semiotic shift is, arguably, most convenient for the rich and powerful in the United States, who increasingly need to deflect attention from the lack of upward mobility afforded to the lower classes in the ossifying and deeply unequal class structure that has emerged with the changing economy associated with globalization, and the proliferation of low-wage jobs as the only recourse to subsistence for many. Dependency becomes a displacement for talking about the underlying structural poverty of that economy, which our liberal, individualistic, agentistic political discourse cannot effectively address. So "welfare use," "welfare receipt," and the especially verboten "welfare taking" are all being replaced by "welfare dependency." As a result, reliance on welfare is articulated as a sign that a single mother suffers from "welfare dependency," which, like other dependencies, is something from which the client needs to be weaned with an appropriate therapeutic treatment. Under welfare reform, all applicants for assistance are screened, diagnosed, assessed, and referred for the appropriate treatment to accelerate the process by which they can overcome their vulnerability to being dependent on welfare.

Medicalization represents modernity's preference for science over religion, expressed in the growing propensity to conceive myriad personal problems in medicalized terms. Yet that revised outlook comes with a price: welfare dependency is defined as the product of an individual's behavior, more than the inequities in the social structure or political economy. In this way, medicalization suggests that upward mobility is still possible. The poor are not fated to be poor; they can be cured of their ills and thereby activated to advance economically. This convenient displacement story, redirecting focus away from the structural embeddedness of persistent poverty in the changing economy, serves the political interests of powerful groups invested in not having to attack those structural roots of contemporary poverty. By highlighting that the poor can be cured of their dependency on welfare, medicalizing implies that mobility is still possible, when in fact it is less than likely.

One manifestation of how medicalization implies mobility is the proliferation of "barriers" talk in welfare policy implementation.[33] A major preoccupation in welfare reform as a new form of governance is assisting recipients to overcome "barriers to self-sufficiency." "Barriers," contrary to the term's ostensible meaning, is most often construed under welfare reform as personal problems. Racial and sexual discrimination in the workplace or the lack of decently paying jobs is not usually acknowledged in state welfare programs as a barrier to moving from welfare to work. Instead, barriers are most often discussed as personal problems arising from internal issues specific to the individual rather than as external conditions in society that are blocking one's advancement. As a result, more and more programming under welfare reform is concentrated on what are seen as the related conditions that give rise to welfare dependency, be they mental health issues, behavioral problems, or addictions. In the masculinized discourse of welfare reform, even children risk being referred to as barriers to work. The goal is to get single mothers to be comfortable being the breadwinner for their families, even if it means cutting back on their commitments to their children. Yet the idea of instilling a commitment to taking paid employment is couched in the terms of liberal political discourse. Self-esteem classes as well as psychological counseling have become common features of welfare-to-work programs as ways of engendering the self-confidence needed for participants to become the autonomous, self-sufficient actors assumed by liberal political discourse.[34]

Over time, this issue enacts its own neoliberal self-fulfilling prophecy. As more and more of the welfare population exits under welfare-to-work programs that require recipients to make "rapid attachment" to paid employment in the labor force, the remaining population is increasingly made up of recipients who have indeed incurred certain personal problems at high rates. For instance, it is estimated that "a growing share of [those individuals receiving] Temporary Assistance for Needy Families, which offers cash support to low-income single caregivers, is composed of individuals with mental illness, as new work requirements result in faster exits of those without mental health conditions."[35] The rate of depression among TANF recipients grew in the post–welfare reform era. This, ironically, reinforces the medicalized character of welfare dependency as if it were a real phenomenon that was always already there in the first place, as if most recipients were always suffering from the illness of welfare dependency and its related medicalized conditions. Just like any good discourse, "welfare dependency" then becomes its own self-fulfilling prophecy, making itself real by manufacturing the reality that, it claims, preexisted it. Reliance on welfare comes to be seen less as an economic problem and more as a mental health issue.

Yet medicalization has not changed fundamental attitudes about welfare, which remain ambivalent at best. Most Americans still do not in principle oppose government assistance for low-income families and in fact continue to believe that we have a collective obligation to help the poor. For instance, from the 1980s through 2009, 60 to 70 percent of Americans indicated they supported government assistance for the poor and believed government had a responsibility to guarantee every citizen food to eat and a place to sleep.[36] At the same time, most Americans also continued to believe that those in need should receive assistance only if they maintain a commitment to personal responsibility and a work ethic. The campaign against welfare dependency was successful not because it changed this mix of attitudes.

Instead, its success was in reframing the issue to focus on welfare dependency as a problem that needed immediate treatment. The problem of dependency came to be seen as a major source of society's economic as well as social and cultural ills. It increasingly was framed as creating a significant drain on the economy even as it encouraged out-of-wedlock births, single parent families, and a decline in the work ethic. The dependency frame saw public assistance not as a hard-won protection *for* poor workers and their families; instead, it viewed welfare as a policy imposed *against* workers' values as well as their bank accounts.

RACE, GENDER, AND THE NEOLIBERAL CRISIS NARRATIVE

Welfare has for a long time been depicted in the mass media using highly misleading racial terms and imagery. As a result, the public tends to exaggerate the extent to which blacks receive public assistance and is critical of welfare as a program for poor blacks, who are seen as "other" people not like most white middle-class families and who do not adhere to work and family values. Racial resentments and old stereotypes spawn growing hostility toward welfare.[37]

The reframing of the welfare issue as a problem of dependency concentrated in a black underclass has involved the policy equivalent of a gestalt switch by which the same facts came to be seen through a new lens, leading to a different interpretation. In an earlier era, liberals had framed "troubling" behaviors among the poor as products of poverty and used images of social disorganization, especially among poor blacks, as evidence for the necessity of extending aid. The conservative campaign against welfare dependency, however, reframed these same behaviors as products of "permissive" social programs that failed to limit program usage, require work, or demand functional behavior. "Long-term dependency" became a key phrase in welfare debates, usually treated as part of a broader syndrome of underclass pathologies that included drug use, violence, crime, teen pregnancy, single motherhood, and even poverty itself. Gradually, permissiveness and dependency displaced poverty and structural barriers to advancement as the central problems that drew attention from those designing welfare policy.

The discursive turn to dependency had important political consequences. First, welfare dependency and its effects on the poor set the agenda for poverty research in the 1980s and 1990s. To distinguish myths from realities, researchers expended great effort identifying the typical duration of participation spells and the individual-level correlates of long-term program usage. Structural questions received less attention as defenders responded to critics in a debate that focused on work effort, program usage, and poor people's behaviors. Second, as dependency came to be seen as a cause of intergenerational poverty, it became a kind of synecdoche, a single part used to represent the whole tangle of problems associated with the poor. To fight dependency was, in essence, to fight a kind of substance abuse that led to unrestrained sexuality, drug problems, violent crime, civic irresponsibility, and even poverty itself.

As a synecdoche for diverse social ills, dependency became the basis for a powerful crisis narrative in the 1980s and 1990s. Critics spoke of a "crisis of dependency," often in conjunction with fellow travelers such as the "teen pregnancy crisis" and the "underclass crisis." As Murray Edelman argues, such crisis language evokes perceptions of threat, conveys the need for immediate and extraordinary action, and suggests that "now is not the time" to air dissent or seek deliberation.[38] Claims about the prevalence of long-term program usage were often overblown, and images of wholesale social disintegration depended on highly selective readings of poor people's attitudes and behaviors. But by applying the label "crisis," critics turned ambiguous trends among the poor (many of which also existed in the rest of society) into a fearsome threat to the values of "middle America."

Just as the "drug crisis" seemed to require a tough, incarceration-minded war on drugs, the crisis of dependency called for nothing short of an assault on permissiveness. In this environment, poverty advocates who tried to direct attention toward issues other than dependency were seen as fiddling while Rome burned. Long-term program usage was viewed as a major social problem requiring a bold solution; it called for extraordinary measures, not tepid liberal palliatives. The only suitable response was to attack dependency at its root by imposing a new regime of welfare rules designed to dissuade and limit program usage, enforce work, and curb unwanted behaviors. In 1996, that is exactly what welfare reform did.

This reframing of welfare dependency as a manifestation of the pathologies of the poor, and most especially black, underclass created the political climate that led to President Bill Clinton joining with a Republican Congress to "end welfare as we know it." The result was ending of the political impasse to finally enact the reform law in 1996 that abolished the sixty-one-year-old Aid to Families with Dependent Children program, which had come to be an entitlement that citizens had a right to receive once determined to be eligible. In its place, states receive block grants under the TANF program, which could be used to provide cash assistance as the earlier program did, but they had to meet quotas in moving recipients into paid employment. The rolls plummeted with work requirements, time limits, caps on benefits, and sanctions for not complying with contracts that promised to take steps to leave welfare for work.

The purging of the welfare rolls that had started in the early 1990s with waivers allowing states to experiment with some of these new restrictions accelerated after 1996 until the economy slowed in 2001. As a result, it has come to pass that President Clinton's promise to "end welfare as we know it" has proven to be more than political rhetoric. And while welfare reform was widely heralded as a success for this reason alone, it has resulted in most single mothers leaving to become mired in poverty. These hardships have been most frequently visited on black single mothers, who are also likeliest to be forced off welfare by sanctions and to have to cycle back on if they have limited-time eligibility remaining.

Welfare was thus retrenched in no small part because of the way welfare dependency discourse had reframed this policy in gendered and racialized ways in a crisis narrative that portrayed welfare use as a pathology that had to be treated therapeutically. Borrowing metaphors from allied arenas of service provision laid the basis for a veritable medicalization of welfare dependency as a personal pathology that required individualized treatment as much as any other behavioral problem. With such a reframing, it became all the more difficult to see reliance on welfare as a product of structural problems in the economy or society. Public opinion was not so much changed as mobilized to support the retrenchment of welfare as the primary means by which we as a society could attack not just the scourge of welfare dependency but the cluster of pathological behaviors with which it was associated.

Therefore, the crisis narrative framed the dominant understandings of the welfare poor as wholly "other." In fact, it has made the welfare poor not just other but now a medicalized other in need of treatment for the disease of welfare dependency. With the medicalized discourse of welfare dependency firmly entrenched today in public deliberations about welfare use, welfare reform increasingly has turned into the social policy equivalent of a twelve-step program. Rather than a program to redistribute needed income to poor families with children, it has become a behavioral modification regime centered on getting the parents of these children to become self-disciplined so that they in turn will become self-sufficient according to ascendant work and family values. Increasingly, this behavioral modification regime is implemented via public-private partnerships in which state and local governments contract with private, often for-profit, providers to move single mothers with children off welfare and into jobs and marriages.

The medicalized discourse of dependency logically calls forth new forms of governance that can practice the neoliberal governmentality needed for regimenting low-income parents into the low-wage labor markets of the globalizing economy. The net result is that poverty is displaced as the persistent underlying problem that it is, and welfare policy comes to be focused ever more on reducing welfare dependency as an end in itself. The medicalized discourse of welfare dependency may, as noted, have made reliance on welfare the social policy equivalent of an addiction, thereby making welfare recipients out to be "sick" rather than "bad."[39] Yet this discursive shift did not exonerate the poor. The medicalization of welfare dependency simply reinforced the belief that most welfare recipients were passive dependents who were idle when they could have been working; and it further reinforced the idea that offering the poor aid only perversely encouraged the bad habit of idleness. In fact, in today's medicalized parlance, offering aid was characterized as "sick," as Newt Gingrich and others noted in the years just before welfare reform was adopted by the United States Congress in 1996.[40]

From this perspective, it became that much easier to believe that if welfare recipients were treated for their condition, they could be taught how to do what is right, and then they could take their place in the workforce and begin to work their way to self-sufficiency, if not quite out of poverty. Indeed, although the rolls have declined and the labor force participation rate and earnings of former adult welfare recipients were for a time up, the underlying poverty that afflicts their families persists. The "welfare poor" have been replaced by the "working poor." And the metonymy of dependency as a product of individual choice continues to leave us in denial about the structural causes of poverty in our economic system.

The Persistence of the Semiotic Structure of Deservingness

Today's welfare system trades on a long-running, deeply entrenched discourse that ends up operating in ways to make itself real by becoming its own self-fulfilling prophecy. The neoliberal governmentality associated with contemporary welfare policies has been aptly described as "a political project that endeavors to create a social reality that it suggests already exists."[41] In fact, poverty governance today assumes that welfare recipients are already market actors even before they start taking paid employment. As a result, the different dimensions of their lives, from mental health issues to child-rearing responsibilities, are termed "barriers" to work that must be overcome. This reconstruction is but one element of a broader rewriting of identity that is well captured by the exhortations of a welfare "job club" instructor observed by Anna Korteweg: "No one in this room has been out of work, the way we're going to write your resume. You're working in the house, you're a taxi driver, a budget planner, you volunteer at your children's school, you're a food preparer. You're self-employed, you're not receiving the income but you're working all the time. You have been successfully and diligently working daily."[42] Welfare policy discourse repositions single mothers on welfare as protoworkers who are to prove their worth to society by taking paid employment under almost any conditions and regardless of how poor the pay is. They are to be regimented into the bottom of a globalizing economy of declining wages. There, they learn to be the compliant members of that subordinate caste. Their inclusive exclusion is executed when we come to see them as no longer the "welfare poor" but now the "working poor."

In fact, the deep semiotic structure of deservingness undergirds much of contemporary U.S. politics in these transitional times. Witness the Tea Party's success in recent years in attacking the efforts of the Obama administration to aid those disadvantaged by the Great Recession or those who find even when the economy is growing that they cannot afford health insurance. The Tea Partiers have been obsessed with demonizing the unemployed and the uninsured as undeserving dependents sucking at the teat of government.[43] The Tea Party activists tie the Obama administration's attempt to aid the disadvantaged with the paranoid delusions of Glenn Beck that Barack Obama is an acolyte of Frances Fox Piven and Richard Cloward, who is bent on aiding the undeserving poor just to bankrupt America and force the country to adopt a communist form of government. As one sign read in front of the U.S. Supreme Court when the Court considered the constitutionality of the Affordable Care Act requirement to buy health insurance, "no Obamarx Care or Cloward and Piven spending."[44] The very idea of aiding those who are not working or working at jobs that do not provide health insurance is not just treated suspiciously as aiding the undeserving but is assumed to be a communist plot to undermine the American way of life where each person pulls his or her own weight.

As the United States watched the breathtaking return since the 2012 presidential campaign to the victim-blaming discourse trained on the welfare poor, it was difficult not to become convinced that there is nothing less than an abidingly deep semiotic structure of deservingness that undergirds almost all of U.S. political discourse at a most fundamental level. This is not some marginal facet of U.S. politics; it is at its structural core. It is the source for the resonance of the "dog-whistles" (as the use of code words is now called when implying who is in and who is out). It is a source of tremendous political power, but it is held in reserve, only available to be reinvoked as needed to push people's preexisting prejudicial buttons, to score political points, by whipping up hysteria, to in the end mollify people's concerns by finding ready-made scapegoats for our economic travails and cultural anxieties.[45] In other words, the deep semiotic structure of deservingness gets reenacted again and again to reinscribe hierarchies of privilege and subordi-nation. It does so through a diabolical relationship between discourse and identity where words demonize people just for being poor.

This relationship between discourse and identity is older than our founding fathers, but its own origin story defers grounding our understandings of de-servingness in the real world of real people and their real life circumstances. Instead, nothing more than its self-referentiality provides the basis for how we decide that "they" are not like "us," and that the "poor" need to learn to act "middle class." Symbolic shadowboxing becomes how policy discourse continually pummels the poor. Rust never sleeps and neither does the deep semiotic structure of deservingness.

THE END OF SOCIAL WORK

IMPLEMENTING NEOLIBERAL PATERNALISM
(WITH BASHA SILVERMAN)

The deeply embedded structure of deservingness operating at the base of market-centered societies gets applied differently with the neoliberalization of the welfare state. Over the last few decades, human services have been transformed, not just in the United States, but also in other countries where pressure grows to emulate the United States in a globalizing world.[1] Commentary abounds among diverse researchers.[2] In fact, this transformation is not limited to a select set of specialties or modalities of treatment, but covers multiple areas of social service practice. Neoliberal organization reforms, such as devolution, privatization, and performance management, have been joined with paternalist policy tools, including sanctions, that is, financial penalties, for noncompliant clients, to create a flexible but disciplinary approach to managing the populations being served.[3] What we can call "neoliberal" paternalism represents a significant movement to marketize the operations of social service organizations more generally so that they inculcate in clients rationally responsible behavior that leads them to be market compliant, and thus less dependent on the shrinking human services and more willing to accept the positions slotted for them on the bottom of the socioeconomic order.[4] Organizations are being disciplined so that they can be held accountable for disciplining their clients in this more market-focused environment. Neoliberal paternalism is transforming the human services into a disciplinary regime for managing poverty populations in the face of state austerity and market dysfunction.

This transformed environment is bound to be debilitating for new entrants into the human services workforce. The human services morph into policing agencies in order to get their clients to accept the verdict of the market and not rely as much on the state. At a minimum, the ideal of altruistic service to those in need is that much more difficult to sustain under these conditions. Today, students in the allied helping professions often energetically enter their fields following the ideals and values set by the powerful change agents who came before them, only to become disillusioned by the transformed organizational environment and new ways of working with clients. In our experience, students are increasingly questioning their role in the helping professions with a discerning critique about the disconnect between their altruistic intentions and the neoliberal paternalist organization where they intern or work currently. In particular, given these experiences, students often worry that the opportunities for professional discretion to help clients in a number of related areas of service, either as front-line workers or program administrators, are arguably today diminished.[5]

In the analysis that follows, we contrast existing research on the negative consequences of neoliberal paternalism for welfare-to-work programs with initial considerations from reports about how similar changes are occurring in an entirely different field of practice—drug treatment. These distinctively different areas of human service provision demonstrate the wide reach of neoliberal paternalism in transforming human service policy implementation writ large. The analysis contrasts welfare-to-work in Florida with drug treatment in Delaware. With two very different states and two very different areas of service provision, we suggest the broad impact of neoliberal paternalism in transforming the human services today. We find striking parallels involving: (1) deskilling in staffing patterns associated with relying on former clients as caseworkers, along with (2) marketizing of administrative operations stemming from the institution of neoliberal organizational reforms, and (3) disciplining of clients via paternalist policy tools. These findings provide evidence of the transformation of the work environment whereby the human services today must not only discipline their clients but also their staff and do so in ways that call into question their ability to act consistently with the most altruistic ideals of the helping professions.

DISCIPLINING THE POOR: WELFARE-TO-WORK

Our case study of welfare-to-work comes from Florida—frequently mentioned in hearings in Congress as an innovator regarding welfare policy implementation.[6] Florida's Welfare Transition (WT) program is designed to move welfare recipients into paid employment and is integrated into the workforce system administered by twenty-four regional workforce boards under the Workforce Investment Act of 1997. The research we report on drew from field interviews with front-line case managers in four purposively selected regions of the state. As our Florida case suggests, U.S. welfare policy today reflects the emergence of a neoliberal-paternalist regime of poverty governance.[7] It is characterized both by neoliberal organizational reforms, such as devolution, privatization, and performance management systems for holding accountable contract agencies and by paternalist policy tools, such as financial sanctions, used to discipline the poor to become market-compliant actors willing to take the low-wage jobs emerging in a globalizing economy. Florida combines both in a way that has made it a leader in implementing the neoliberal disciplinary regime.

These changes in organization and policy were a long time in coming. From the penultimate moment of the welfare rights movement in the early 1970s until the passage of welfare reform legislation in the mid-1990s, the number of welfare recipients stabilized at relatively high levels (even as benefits declined), and recipient families came to have essentially entitlement rights to assistance, albeit modest and often attached to moral censure, under the federal Aid to Families with Dependent Children program. While opposition to growing welfare rolls built over this period, gridlock over how to address the welfare issue did not break until passage of the federal Personal Responsibility and Work Opportunity Reconciliation Act of 1996. The reform law actually formalized reforms that had been developing in the states, codifying them in the Temporary Assistance for Needy Families (TANF) program. As described in chapter 4, TANF ushered in time limits for the receipt of cash aid, accompanied by work and behavioral requirements, as well as sanctions that impose financial penalties for failure to comply with these requirements.

Welfare policies have long been entwined with multiple purposes, among the most important of which have been to return to the roots of social service work and instill or restore morality in the poor so as to assimilate marginal groups into mainstream behaviors and institutions.[8] Further, as Richard Cloward and Frances Fox Piven contend, welfare policy has historically served to "regulate the poor," effectively undermining their potential as a political or economic threat.[9] Others have noted that welfare served to regulate gender relations by stigmatizing single mothers receiving aid.[10] The stigmatization of welfare recipients as undeserving people who need to be treated suspiciously has not only deterred many welfare recipients from applying for public assistance but also communicated to the "working poor" more generally that they should do whatever they can to avoid falling into the censorious category of the "welfare poor." Welfare reform in the 1990s, however, accentuated the disciplinary dimensions of welfare policy in dramatic ways.

During the debates leading up to the passage of reform legislation, President Bill Clinton rather infamously touted his determination to "end welfare as we know it." His success in this aim can be judged by at least three indicators. First, and most obviously, as noted before, the number of welfare recipients has plummeted under reform: a 72 percent decline in the number of welfare recipients from 1996 to 2008. Second, by 2001, also as previously noted, more than half of the federal TANF funding to for noncash services, rather than for direct cash assistance to families in need.[11]

Yet the most profound changes associated with welfare reform occur at the deeper level of its underlying logic.[12] Welfare reform is more than reducing the number of recipients and shifting expenditures from cash assistance to work-support services. These trends reflect a much more fundamental neoliberal-paternalist restructuring of public assistance that involves both the neoliberal organizational reforms and paternalist policy tools to create a system of disciplining service providers so that they can be held accountable for disciplining clients.[13] It is a disciplinary regime that marketizes human service provision in order to promote market-compliant clients who are willing to take low-wage jobs even if those jobs leave them profoundly poor.

The shift to a more disciplinary approach to managing the welfare poor was facilitated by a concerted campaign by conservative political leaders to replace poverty with welfare dependency as the primary problem to be attacked.[14] Welfare reform became not only about a "new paternalism" associated with teaching the poor what to do, but about labeling the poor as sick and in need of treatment.[15] As described in chapter 4, in the run-up to welfare reform, welfare dependency came to be seen as similar to a chemical or drug dependency; clients needed to be treated for their addiction and weaned from its source. At the height of the reform campaign, then Speaker of the U.S. House of Representatives Newt Gingrich based his support of welfare reform on his oft-repeated and highly vituperative argument that a "sick society" encouraged further sickness with its failed antipoverty policies.[16]

With this heightened rhetoric about welfare dependency, the importation of behavioral-health models of treatment and associated organizational and staffing patterns came to be seen as not only plausible but desirable. As a result, welfare reform has remade the delivery of welfare-to-work services along lines that parallel addiction recovery programs (see drug treatment example below). Welfare agencies have instituted services that are the social welfare policy equivalent of a twelve-step program: individuals learn in the new "work-first" regime to be "active" participants in the labor force rather than "passive" recipients of welfare.[17]

Such a view of welfare dependency has led to the importation of a "recovery model" into welfare reform, one aspect of which is the staffing of welfare-to-work contract agencies with "recovered" former welfare recipients. While former recipients have been relied on in the past, several studies of welfare reform have in recent years noted that the agencies studied had undergone change such that now about one-third of the case managers are former recipients.[18] This proportion indicates numbers that go beyond mere tokenism.[19] One of the virtues of the recovery model is that it is consistent with long-standing calls for a representative bureaucracy (RB)[20] that can practice cultural competence (CC) concerning the unique needs of its clients:[21] a culturally competent bureaucracy is one "having the knowledge, skills, and values to work effectively with diverse populations and to adapt institutional policies and professional practices to meet the unique needs of client populations."[22] A representative bureaucracy that draws from the community it is serving is seen as furthering the ability of an agency to practice cultural competency in ways that are sensitive to community members' distinctive concerns and problems.[23] In other words, RB = CC. The recovery model holds out hope that a more representative bureaucracy will be more sensitive to the ways in which its welfare clients are approaching the unique challenges that have brought them to the agency's doorstep.

Yet there are ironies in this way of moving toward realizing the RB = CC formula. Former recipients, as indigenous workers from the community, under the medicalized version of welfare are seen as former addicts in recovery. If welfare is seen as a dangerously addictive substance, then the implementation of a disciplinary treatment regime is a logical next step. The decentralized service delivery systems and private providers that so characterize welfare reform are fertile ground for the importation of medical models of dependency treatment. The use of performance management systems is also entirely consistent with the need to track measureable outcomes resulting from the provision of services or the application of treatment to clients. Under this scheme, case management is a routinized and deskilled position focused largely on monitoring client adherence to program rules and disciplining them when they are out of compliance. There is, in fact, evidence that with the shift to a more decentralized, privatized system of provision, local contract agencies have gone ahead and moved to a more deskilled welfare-to-work case management by replacing civil servants, social workers, and other professionals with former welfare recipients.[24] In the process, a form of community self-surveillance is put in place that Cathy Cohen calls "advanced marginalization," where some members of a subordinate group get to achieve a modicum of upward social-economic mobility by taking on responsibilities for monitoring and disciplining other members of that subordinate community.[25]

While this staffing pattern may at times be relied on for less controversial reasons as a simple cost-saving measure consonant with the business model, it is also entirely consistent with a recovery model philosophy that puts forth former recipients as behavioral role models. These former recipients are frequently referred to in the literature as "success stories."[26] Yet the recovery model suggests they are hired for another reason. The recovery model is grounded in the philosophy that underpins the twelve-step program of Alcoholics Anonymous and its predecessors, which over time has spread to other areas of drug treatment and mental health services, along with the core conviction that clients must be willing to support one another in overcoming their addictions.[27]

Government programs now run more like businesses, and the application of the business model to welfare involves getting case managers and their clients to internalize the business ethic as well. Policy changes emphasize case managers using disciplinary cost-saving techniques to get clients to move from welfare to paid employment as quickly as possible regardless of whether they and their children improve their well-being.

Florida's WT program is designed to integrate welfare recipients into the workforce. To that end, Florida has actually closed welfare offices across the state, requiring applicants to sign up online, using public libraries for Internet access if necessary. Once approved by the Department of Children and Families, applicants must report to a local one-stop center that is run by a contract agency on behalf of a regional workforce board. The twenty-four workforce regions are governed a combination of public officials, private employers, and citizen and worker representatives sit on the local regional workforce board to decide local policies for implementing federal and state programs including the WT welfare-to-work requirements. The boards most often contract with for-profit providers to run one-stop centers where case managers monitor the progress of clients moving from welfare to work. Essentially Florida has abolished welfare and integrated it into the work-force system.

In the Florida WT program, local devolution and privatization emerged alongside one of the nation's leading systems of performance management. Each year, a state board negotiates with each regional board to establish region-specific performance goals. Goal-adjusted performance measures are then used to determine state-level evaluations of the regions and service providers. Provider "pay points" are tied directly to statewide performance goals, which local contracts often specify in distinctive ways. There is wide variation among states, which have autonomy over how they arrange service provision. The Florida case is important analytically, because of the extraordinary extent to which it has elaborated contracting and performance arrangements, not because it is typical of all states. The Florida case reveals aspects of this new performance regime that may be more difficult to discern elsewhere. Case managers interviewed consistently invoked a dichotomy that distinguished a repudiated old approach as "social work" to be replaced by a much more preferred "business model."

Performance in the WT program is tracked on a monthly basis and focused squarely on goals related to work promotion. Results are reported at regular intervals in a competitive format via "the red and green report"—so called because it uses colors to indicate the rankings of the twenty-four regions: red for the bottom six, green for the top six, and white for the twelve in between. Rankings on the red and green report have significant material consequences. Green scores can qualify a region for substantial funding supplements, while red scores can result in the termination of a local service provider's contract. Between these extremes, providers typically lose pay points and draw unwanted scrutiny when their performance falls below expectations.

Proponents of neoliberal organizational reform predict that local organizations will respond to this system by innovating in ways that advance statewide goals and improve client services. Devolution will provide the *freedoms* they need to experiment with promising new approaches. Performance feedback will provide the *evidence* they need to learn from their own experiments and the best practices of others. Performance-based competition will create *incentives* for local organizations to make use of this information and adopt program improvements that work.

Studies have suggested several reasons why organizations may deviate from this script in "rationally perverse" ways. Performance indicators provide ambiguous cues that, in practice, get "selected, interpreted, and used by actors in different ways consistent with their institutional interests,"[28] Positive innovations may fail to emerge because managers do not have the authority to make changes, access learning forums, or devise effective strategies for reforming the organizational status quo. Performance "tunnel vision" can divert attention from important-but-unmeasured operations and lead managers to innovate in ways that subvert program goals.[29] To boost their numbers, providers may engage in "creaming" practices, focusing their services on less-disadvantaged clients who can be moved above performance thresholds with less investment.[30]

The Florida field research confirms the primacy of neoliberal preoccupation with performance outcome measurement as an organizing principle for WT implementation. Regional personnel working for private contract agencies must expect to be held accountable for their outcomes. They scrutinize performance reports and keep a close eye on other regions. Most express a strong desire to improve performance through evidence-based reforms. Indeed, local officials routinely describe performance numbers as the heart of the business model that organizes service provision in the WT program. In a contract-centered system such as Florida's, where performance is exchanged for payments, performance management becomes inseparable from, and is ultimately a form of, revenue management for the for-profit and nonprofit entities that invest in service provision. As one program manager put it, "If we make it [the performance standard] we get paid. Then if we don't, we get zero."[31]

With state officials stressing the need for every region to "make its bogey" (i.e., meet its benchmarks), regional personnel rely heavily on performance measures as guides for action. Interviews with case managers indicated that performance anxiety is a pervasive feature of organizational culture in the WT program. The expressed anxieties about performance measurement suggest that its effects on implementation deviate considerably from the optimistic predictions of the proponents of these measurements schemes. Consider, first, the double-edged nature of performance competition and its relation to trust. In theory, competition should encourage regional managers to learn from one another's experiments. Yet it also encourages them to view other regions as competitors who have a stake in outperforming them. Field visits quickly showed that the latter dynamic tends to undermine the former. Policy learning and diffusion require a modicum of trust, and this trust can be undermined by highly competitive performance systems. Echoing others who were interviewed, one local manager said that regions try to maintain an edge by guarding their best ideas as "trade secrets" and, in the same interview, asked not to tell other regions about new techniques being tried at her one-stop facility. Another indicated that high-stakes evaluations undermine learning by fostering suspicions of cheating: "They can't tell you their 'best practices' because their practice is cheating [to win the] competitive game." In these and other ways, competition works at cross-purposes with policy learning. It encourages local actors to distrust the numbers that other regions produce, the best practices they recommend, and the wisdom of sharing their own positive innovations.

Policy learning also founders on a second dynamic that flows from the discursive tensions between devolution and performance management. Statewide performance reports and efforts to publicize best practices function as parts of a discourse of generalization, suggesting that "what works there can work here too." By contrast, the discourse that justifies local devolution and problem solving trumpets the idea that communities have radically different needs, populations, and capacities. Not surprisingly, these two mindsets clash in the consciousness of the local manager. When presented with success stories from elsewhere, local officials cited a litany of traits that distinguish the region of origin from their own. Managers in rural regions often cited resource differences in this regard. The broader tension, however, is between a discourse that denigrates "one size fits all" ideas by celebrating local uniqueness and a discourse that treats localities as comparable and seeks to generalize innovations across them. Local officials interviewed generally rejected the practice of interregional performance competition, saying it did not make sense to compare different regions that operate under different circumstances.

In addition to these problems, three other dynamics flow from the fact that local managers hold discretion over how to respond to performance incentives. Proponents predict that performance pressures will encourage local actors to select more effective and efficient program strategies. At the street level, however, managers often select one strategy over another for a more practical reason: from an organizational perspective, it is simply an easier path to pursue. The best-known form of this response, documented by many studies, is for organizations to count the same old things in brand new ways.[32] Efforts to improve poverty and employment outcomes are usually seen as arduous campaigns with uncertain consequences for performance numbers. In the short run, strategies of "creaming" suffice; it is far easier to change how one counts existing conditions. Thus, local officials report that "people game the numbers all the time" by classifying in creative ways. To illustrate, one regional official interviewed related that a client took her pastor to church on Sunday and the case manager arranged to have the pastor say it was community service. The manager could then count this service as a work-related activity under the WT program, when in fact it was what the client was already doing as a church parishioner unrelated to job searching and paid employment.

In this environment, case managers are under constant pressure to get their clients to stay in compliance with welfare-to-work rules and if the clients fail to do so they are penalized with sanctions that reduce their benefits. This preoccupation with monitoring clients for compliance represents a change in the role of the case manager as part of the administrative transformation of welfare policy implementation. The rise of neoliberal paternalism in fact is associated with a shift in the nature of casework, marked by the passage of federal welfare reform in 1996.[33] The prime directives for TANF case managers today are to convey and enforce work expectations and to advance and enable transitions to employment. Efforts to promote family and child well-being are downplayed in this frame, but they are not entirely abandoned. Under neoliberal paternalism, they are assimilated into efforts to promote work based on the idea that "work first" will put clients on the most reliable path toward achieving a self-sufficient, stable, and healthy family.

Thus, case managers today initiate their relationships with new clients by screening them for work readiness and delivering an "orientation" to describe work expectations and penalties for noncompliance. In parallel with individualized drug treatment plans, welfare-to-work case managers then develop "individual responsibility plans"—or "contracts of mutual responsibility"—to specify the steps that each client will take in order to move from welfare to work. These rites of passage establish a relationship in which the case manager's primary tasks are to facilitate, monitor, and enforce the completion of required work activities. In celebratory portrayals of the new system, case managers are described as being deeply involved in their clients' development, as "authority figures as well as helpmates."[34]

In Florida, this ethos is expressed by the neoliberal relabeling of caseworkers as "career counselors." The label evokes images of a well-trained professional who draws on diverse resources to advise and assist entrepreneurial job seekers. In practice, however, few aspects of welfare case management today fit this template. None of the more than sixty case managers we interviewed in four workforce regions we studied had a social work degree of any kind. Many did, however, have management degrees from Strayer, DeVry, Capella, or other vocationally oriented schools that line the strip malls in cities around Florida (and across the country). About a third of the case managers were also former recipients who qualified for their jobs by virtue of their experience with the system. Under the business model of service provision, the relationship between client and case manager is rooted in an employment metaphor: the client has signed a "contract" to do a job and should approach the program as if it were a job.

The case manager's job is now to enforce that contract, often using the threat of sanctions to gain compliance. Case managers spend most of their time enforcing compliance to individual responsibility plans and very little time counseling clients.[35] The change is palpable. One former recipient case manager in Florida stressed in a most poignantly metaphorically way that welfare in Florida is no longer a social service. She suggested it was now herding cattle instead of tending sheep; while a shepherd takes care of the sheep, a cattle herder just runs the herd through a pen in an insensitive fashion.

The shift from tending sheep to herding cattle at one level is not necessarily that significant since both can be interpreted as dehumanizing. Yet the desensitization implied by this way of characterizing the shift is noteworthy in itself. It also points to another problem with performance measurement. The preoccupation with numbers emphasizes meeting benchmarks as the primary goal irrespective of whether the client is actually helped. In the public management literature, this is the problem of suboptimization.[36] Simon Guilfoyle refers to suboptimization as analogous to synecdoche, in which a part stands in for the whole. Suboptimization occurs when a measure of one particular outcome of service provision implies that other dimensions, usually less measureable, if no less important, have also been met. Suboptimization is rife in human services where the intended outcomes almost always include difficult-to-measure subjective states of being, including improvements in overall well-being. Suboptimization results when outcome goals are achieved in name only and the full spirit of the goal is lost or forgotten in the process. Meeting performance benchmark targets can misleadingly imply that the overall goal has been met when in fact only an indirect indicator implies that is the case. Welfare-to-work targets might be met but all that has really happened is that we have moved clients from the "welfare poor" to the "working poor" with no real improvements in their overall well-being.

Yet suboptimization's deleterious effects go further. They can produce an instrumentalization, a veritable means-ends inversion, where the performance measurement benchmark or target becomes the end in itself. Under these conditions, human service professionals are encouraged to forget about the overall goals of their program and focus exclusively on meeting the designated benchmarks. Once this happens, it is likely that all work with clients is converted into activities associated with meeting the target irrespective of whether the broader goal is achieved. Once an agency puts in place a performance measurement system it risks creating an instrumentalization that changes the very work that human service workers do. With all the debate about "high-stakes testing" under neoliberal education reform, the threat of performance measurement to change how work is done is most popularly discussed in the mainstream media as the "teach to the test" effect, where school teachers teach students only what they need to know to improve their test scores even if this means their overall learning is not really enhanced (because critical thinking skills and other important forms of learning are neglected).

Under these conditions, case management gets deskilled and is routinized; it becomes reactive and clerical. It focuses primarily on documenting client activity hours and entering the results into the one stop service tracking data system. Indeed, managers at several levels argued that the data-entry fields of the tracking system function, in daily organizational routines, as the real policy on the ground. Interviews with the case managers indicated that the people on the front lines see the computer screens as the policy. Given their marginal status, either as former recipients or otherwise, case managers are less likely to risk challenging the disciplinary regime on behalf of their clients. They are likely to follow the computer as if it is a program manager.

The automated nature of case workers' obligations to monitor and discipline clients comes through in the interviews. When asked to describe their workday, case managers consistently report that they begin by logging on to the information system so they can address the slew of new alerts that arrives each morning. The alerts focus on two kinds of actions: documenting work participation hours for clients and pursuing disciplinary actions when such documentation is lacking. From this point forward, the daily round consists mostly of efforts to do one or the other, punctuated by face-to-face meetings with clients that often focus on the same two issues. Case managers spend most of the day either seeking documentation for work-related activities (a key performance indicator) or taking the next steps in the sanction process such as sending out a "'pre-penalty'" warning letter, requesting a sanction, or working to bring a sanctioned client back into compliance. In short, performance and sanctioning are two sides of a single coin in the work life of the case manager and, together, they stand at the center of the job.

The resulting stress felt by case managers can be traced partly to their belief that performance numbers matter for job security and trajectory. WT case managers make modest wages in a job with few guarantees. They often struggle to make ends meet and, as a result, tend to view performance through the prism of their own anxieties as breadwinners. In a system of for-profit contracting, most are keenly aware that performance numbers drive profits, and declining profits could lead their current employer to downsize the staff or even to sell the operation to another company whose retention of old employees is uncertain. At a less absolute level, most expect that if they produce weak numbers, they will be subjected to greater supervision in a way that will make their work more stressful and harder to do.

Buffeted by performance pressures and lacking the tools to respond to client needs, case managers experienced their workdays as a series of frustrations and disappointments. The results of all this performance anxiety is not better outcomes for clients. The Florida study found that most clients remained poor after leaving welfare and sanctioned clients fared the worst of all.[37] To turn a phrase, the preoccupation with discipline just made the worse off worser. And these negative results were not evenly distributed across racial groups, with African Americans faring the worst.

Florida might be a leader in implementing the neoliberal disciplinary regime, but that also means it leads in corruption associated with such a parceling out of the state's welfare operations. Scandal has wracked the system from its inception and continues today. In July 2011 it was reported that "[Florida] Governor Rick Scott today confirmed that the U.S. Department of Labor has launched an investigation into Florida's 24 regional workforce boards to determine if they have been improperly awarding contracts to companies controlled by board members or their relatives."[38] Scott himself previously was able to propose and sign into law legislation requiring all welfare recipients to undergo drug testing (even though he came under attack for possible conflicts of interest since he had been the primary investor in the largest drug testing company in the state, which was now under his wife's control). The corruptions of privatization aside, the neoliberal disciplinary welfare-to-work regime in Florida represents an elaborate shift to get the poor to accept more responsibility for their poverty without providing the necessary support for them to do anything about it. It is a new regime that imposes strict performance outcome monitoring, deskills the case management associated with the program, routinizes client treatment, puts the focus almost exclusively on disciplining clients in the name of program compliance, and does so in ways that do not lead to improved well-being for those clients and in ways that track closely by race. It represents a stark example of neoliberal failure. It is the end of social service work on this end of the human service work continuum.

NEOLIBERAL-PATERNALIST DRUG TREATMENT

Drug treatment delivery is also characterized both by neoliberal organizational reforms, such as devolution, privatization, and performance management systems to manage spending and funding eligibility, and by paternalist policy tools, such as financial penalties, imposed to hold clients accountable. This reflects an undeniable similarity to the practical concerns identified in the welfare study already outlined. Here we draw attention to another area of human service work where attracting a talented, trained, and passionate workforce is paramount to ensuring high-quality care, but the field is transforming in ways that will not only deny such persons access to these jobs but will also rob them of their ability to creatively apply their craft, jeopardizing client care. The examination that follows does not include a rigorous evaluation or generalizable conclusions. However, it has been included to highlight how widespread and potentially dangerous the use of disciplinary practice in social services settings can be for the agencies, workers, and clients within these spheres.

While drug treatment is often privatized, practice is heavily constrained by public policy and regulatory guidelines. Following a neoliberal marketized approach, the federal government has provided guidance to states to ensure efficiency, with recommendations for the utilization of measurable evidence-based practices; it is the responsibility of each state to ensure that these recommendations are implemented and measured. In 1999, the National Institute on Drug Abuse published a guide entitled *Principles of Drug Addiction Treatment* describing twelve "efficacious scientifically based treatment approaches."[39] In 2006, the Institute of Medicine's report *Improving the Quality of Health Care for Mental and Substance-Use Conditions* identified a critical need for quality and measurement improvement of health-care provisions in both mental health and drug treatment.[40] The report acknowledged the importance of permitting states to redesign their grant-based financing systems but recommended that they do so incrementally. This process would include adding specific goal-oriented performance measures. As a result, performance measurement contracts have become commonplace, with a specific neoliberal focus on the use of incentives or rewards.

Drug treatment's relationship to the health insurance system has undoubtedly provided a conduit for innovations in medicine to seep into its practices. The broader medical field has in fact adopted similar practices, such as Medicaid programs incentivizing primary care providers who assist their patients in illness management by awarding end of year bonuses when costs (even as projected) of expensive chronic illnesses can be reduced. This system of reinforcement has been referred to by Thomas McLellan and associates as "provider contingencies."[41]

The use of incentives and rewards is not new to the field. According to Stephen Higgins and Nancy Petry, "contingency management," a treatment model where patients receive rewards based on their behavior, such as adherence to program rules and achieving treatment goals, with desired behavior reinforced with incentives and patients sometimes even punished for noncompliance, has become one of the most popular treatment strategies applied in drug treatment.[42] What is new is its application to treatment providers, where funding sources are now using this system of behavior modification with the agencies they contract with. The neoliberalization process extends contingency management to incentivizing providers to act more like private for-profit agencies in competition with each other. These requirements, mandated by the funding sources, extinguish opportunities for creative and responsive management. Trained social service professionals are restrained, compelled to deliver services as prescribed, and involuntarily consumed by neoliberal forces beyond their control.

Many states have adopted the use of performance incentives to improve service provider behavior in general; however, only a few states report using financial incentives.[43] More broadly referred to as "purchasing levers," incentives are viewed as successful delivery strategies for "value-based financing" of drug treatment that maximizes the states purchasing power to ensure high-quality services. These purchasing-lever strategies can include contract requirements that mandate the utilization of evidence-based practices by linking them to financial performance incentives.[44] According to a report produced in 2003 by Join Together, a policy panel at the Boston University School of Public Health, "the panel's primary recommendation is that purchasers of treatment services should reward results—an idea that is very consistent with other leading edge efforts to improve the quality of health care for other diseases."[45]

In Delaware drug treatment providers are typically licensed, funded, and monitored by a single state agency within the Department of Health and Social Services known as the Division of Substance Abuse and Mental Health. Using both state and federal funds, the division contracts with private agencies to provide direct service while maintaining responsibility for training, technical assistance, and outcome oversight to ensure that funds are used efficiently. In this context, Delaware is among the leading-edge states in neoliberalizing drug treatment. In response to federal pressures to attain fiscal accountability and improved clinical management, the Department of Health and Social Services took a cue from the state's Department of Transportation, whose contracts included provisions for financial rewards for work completed ahead of schedule as well as penalties for failing to meet deadlines. McLellan et al. note: "That same thinking was applied to the purchase of the addiction treatment services in Delaware."[46]

Historically, drug treatment provider contracts in Delaware had been based on cost reimbursement or fee for service and were calculated based on the costs associated with the specified level of treatment. While the department was committed to the adoption of evidence-based practices, there was no way to enforce their implementation or hold providers accountable for improving client outcomes. In 2001, Delaware changed its payment process to conduct an experiment with outpatient treatment providers by creating performance-based contracts whereby providers became eligible for financial incentives and subject to financial penalties. While there was flexibility built into the contracts, this new performance measurement system was designed to alter the managerial practices of providers by including significant financial incentives for meeting or exceeding target areas and financial penalties for failing to meet them. According to Jack Kemp, a leader in neoliberalizing drug treatment administration in Delaware, "this approach was adopted to test whether or not 'financial incentives' for better 'program performance' might offer the conditions under which the adoption of new evidence-based therapies might be feasible and indeed a good business investment."[47]

In Delaware, a new set of managerial tools was not only suggested but required for the implementation of performance measurement and evidence based practices. The department's effort to improve accountability and effectiveness included "behavioral contingencies" in the performance contracts based on the provider's ability to attract, retain, and "graduate" outpatient drug treatment patients. The funds would then be tied to the agreed-on indicators.[48]

McLellan and associates conclude that within this neoliberalized contracting system, Delaware became a trailblazer in the movement toward a performance management accountability system. Programs are now rewarded for achieving three goals. (1) Increased client admission and engagement. If the program meets 90 percent of its utilization goal, it is rewarded 100 percent of the contract amount. If less than 90 percent is achieved, deductions to the contract amount are made accordingly. (2) Active participation. This is dictated by the specified number of sessions and varies based on the stage of treatment. Incentive payments or bonuses are made for exceeding this goal with a maximum of 5 percent over target. (3) Program completion. This includes graduation, abstinence, and achievement of treatment goals. An additional financial incentive is paid for each "graduation" with a maximum limit in each contract.[49] Problems of creaming and suboptimizing potentially lurk in these changes in Delaware's drug treatment regime just as they have been realized in Florida's welfare-to-work system.

The neoliberalization process was furthered by private funding. From 2006 to 2009, the State of Delaware took part in the Robert Wood Johnson Foundation's Advancing Recovery: State/Provider Partnerships for Quality Addiction Care national initiative (http://www.advancingrecovery.net/Home/Home.aspx). This initiative represents cooperation among the Network for the Improvement of Addiction Treatment, the Treatment Research Institute, and the foundation. The goal was to restructure existing administrative and clinical systems for drug treatment to produce more successful outcomes. The initiative provided funding to local programs for technical assistance to improve their systems, remove barriers to treatment entry, and increase retention. The project promoted the use of evidence-based practices through innovative partnerships between drug treatment providers and the state to foster the sharing of business model strategies. Delaware was one of six state-provider partnerships that participated in a learning network that provided tools to improve the delivery of addiction treatment.

These new conditions led to innovations being treated more like trade secrets of the for-profit "business model" than just use of community resources. The external changes led to obvious internal modifications to traditional service delivery. With increased pressure from funding agencies for greater accountability, there is a rising demand for program use of evidence-based practices. As a result, treatment strategies now emphasize achieving the specific outcomes related to performance measures. While drug treatment clients have always been held personally accountable for their choices, even once "addiction" was determined a "chronic disease," there is now pressure on the agencies and their staff to push clients to meet benchmarks on the road to recovery via personal agreements (or contracts).

With competition for funding ever rising, drug treatment providers must establish in their applications that they have the ability to implement their proposed plans. This includes the mention of the latest buzzwords related to the empirical research and assurance that their agency personnel have been appropriately trained in the next greatest life-changing model being popu-larized. This can lead to funding awards and contracts that pigeonhole the agency and the staff into using the one specified practice they proposed to execute.

This is extremely problematic for several reasons. With the threat of suf-fering financial penalties for underperformance, employees must be trained in the new model. First, forced training attendance results in lost time that could otherwise be used to manage high client caseloads. Second, brief "basics-only" trainings often omit details necessary to effectively apply the models to practice. Third, training is expensive and often offered only one time over one or two days. Finally, money is rarely invested in follow-up training, such as supervision to ensure the practice is properly implemented. When an agency is contracted to use a specific practice, this inevitably puts pressure on and causes anxiety in personnel who are forced to implement it regardless of their preparation to do so.

Just as our case study of welfare-to-work in Florida highlights how neolib-eral paternalism has encouraged the medicalization of welfare dependency, our analysis of secondary sources in Delaware shows the "welfarization" of drug treatment. Drug treatment providers in Delaware are routinely required to apply the associated prescriptions and proscriptions of an evidence-based practice for all clients served within a given program. Counselors are hand-cuffed to the stipulated intervention models, their time is measured, and their sessions are nearly scripted. This practice robs the clinical staff of their professional discretion and forces them to work within the limits of power and control already established by the funder. When an agency selects new practices, there are changes in service delivery patterns, program designs, and paperwork that inevitably create a great deal of confusion and anxiety among the staff. They are taught to be "client centered" while simultaneously expected to deliver one form of intervention (as if it is one size fits all). This could have devastating effects on the client. Alternatively, when a clinician becomes wedded to one model, and that model fails, the clinician blames the client, labeling the client "noncompliant" or "resistant to treatment."[50] This result is analogous to the welfare worker pathologizing a client's social circumstances.

When a clinician realizes that the "one size (meant) to fit all" evidence-based practices may not work for a particular client, he or she becomes concerned about being penalized for not utilizing the practice. This concern can lead to falsifying of records, forcing an outcome, or at least documenting one when it is not really there. Further, when the counselors want to explore more of their client's environmental obstacles, there is no time in the session that is designed to be clinically focused, thus diminishing the human service worker's ability and power to affect the client's environment or circumstances that stand in the way.

The parallels with welfare-to-work extend to staffing and workload issues. Today, drug treatment providers are faced with a myriad of personnel issues in general such as an insufficient workforce to meet the increasing demands for drug treatment, an increased utilization of medically assisted therapies, challenges related to the stigma associated with addiction, and the shift to mostly public funding. When agencies are under pressure to perform with limited resources, they respond as all businesses do—they need to get the most bang for their buck. While the delivery of evidence-based, life-saving interventions would seem like something worth investing dollars, time, and resources to support the most qualified clinicians, an agency under economic pressure must make tough decisions.

In addition to the enormous burden on the staff to operate within the new financial constraints associated with a system of rewards and penalties without sufficient resources to manage the ever-increasing demand as mentioned, there is equal pressure on the provider to hire and train qualified staff while still saving money. When it makes the best sense to hire the most highly trained and experienced, but it costs less to get a lesser credentialed or newly minted clinician, the decision is made. As long as clinicians have the minimum credentials necessary for billing, they are hired. This practice of skimping on workforce quality can have devastating effects on client care, staff morale, and agency practices.

The complexities of staffing in neoliberal paternalist drug treatment are demonstrated in the movement to "behavioral health." There has been greater awareness and understanding, albeit many questions still exist, around the idea that chemically dependent clients are often simultaneously suffering from an additional mental illness such as anxiety or depression. There is a great deal of emphasis on treating clients with what is referred to as "co-occurring disorders" or "dual diagnosis." The field is increasingly concerned with its reputation and perceived competence to treat more complex populations. Rather than fighting stigma, the field has taken an alternative position by strategically rebranding itself as "behavioral health" to position providers' eligibility for funding and reimbursement by Medicaid and private insurers. Administrators are working hard to repackage themselves as "behavioral health providers," using marketing efforts similar to those used by corporate America to shed their old reputations that limited their options as the field makes way and prepares itself for health-care reform. Morphing the name and the services is seen as necessary to stay in "business." With health-care reform, parity for mental health and substance abuse treatment, and increased emphasis on qualifying as experts in "behavioral health" drug treatment, agencies are laboring to make it appear as if they are treating clients more holistically, offering more services in one place, and hiring more qualified staff.

Staffing challenges reflect the history of drug treatment. It began as a self-help campaign, born out of the twelve-step movement and tenet that there is great value in "one alcoholic helping another."[51] Former users began working in the field as drug counselors with little training, only life experience. Academia still lags behind; majors such as psychology, counseling, human services, and social work often include one class or even worse only one week that covers addiction-specific material. While researchers continue to try and explain addiction and find a cure (treatment) by looking at medications to curb cravings or reverse one's desire, the personnel in the field today are often underqualified to meet the outcome-oriented expectations of the neoliberal regime. They are often without the tools and resources to meet the real needs of their clients while trying to game the system to get the level of care and treatment dosages that are reimbursable.

The behavioral health approach intensifies these tensions, especially given the complexity of problems confronting clients. Referred to as "once-were" drug treatment centers, they are growing but also changing as they follow the money trail, all in the name of providing more "holistic" services. They are adding more in-house programs to create "one-stop shopping." These programs can include vocational rehabilitation, primary care, family planning, and dentistry. On its face removing obstacles to improving health outcomes is the obvious answer, but this can be dangerous to the clients as well. By offering all services under one roof, there is a risk of sending unwarranted further stigmatizing messages, such as "this treatment center is the only place where they belong." This type of practice and messaging only affirms notions of deviance and being the other.

All the while, contract agency personnel are stretched beyond the breaking point. Meeting the bottom line is the driving force in drug treatment today.

Service providers are guilty of creating categories that determine whether someone deserves treatment based on that "bottom line." Administrators determine who is eligible for services based on the likelihood the contract agency will be reimbursed for providing those services. In the nonprofit sector, clients are rarely denied treatment and waiting lists are discouraged. Drug treatment administrators are likely to ensure easy access and admission for the uninsured because the state pays for them in full.

Among for-profit drug treatment providers a similar type of cherry picking happens but for-profit providers are often most interested in the retention of privately insured clients. For example, when a third party payer is known to authorize a longer stay in treatment, the treatment provider may adjust its practices to best accommodate a client with that insurance. This could include kinder treatment and relaxed enforcement of the rules in an effort to keep the client happy and less likely to leave treatment. There is great financial interest in retaining those clients for the duration of their recommended length of stay. This type of discursive practice also exists in the reverse; clients are discharged immediately when coverage is denied regardless of whether their symptoms persist.

Another progressive development being subverted by neoliberal implementation in Delaware is the renewed emphasis on prevention. Prevention programming relies heavily on "street outreach" that has been historically implemented using a peer-led approach. In fact, the most widely utilized evidence-based practice designed for street outreach is the model of the National Institute on Drug Abuse known as the indigenous leader outreach model.[52] In practice, drug treatment programs hire former drug users from the targeted community to engage active drug users and offer information and referrals for treatment. This "recovery model" of staffing that relies on former clients, as behavioral role models, has become increasingly popular and has been imported into welfare-to-work and other areas of social service provision. And while it has the potential to improve agency staff and client collaboration, it also offers the prospect of promoting a more effective disciplinary regime via self-policing by target populations. (See welfare section.)

Yet the major problem with utilizing the indigenous leader outreach model is not so much with the theory; instead, it is with its application in a neoliberalized environment. As drug treatment is changing to meet the demands of the market, it is becoming even more important for agencies to implement the most cost-efficient versions of the model. With more pressure to justify expenses comes a new labeling, credentialing, and even legitimizing the "outreach worker" and forcing new qualifications that are still easier to obtain than any academic degree. In Delaware, eligibility for prevention dollars has been limited to providers who employ individuals who are credentialed as certified prevention specialists. This forced certification for personnel with limited training requires staff to apply (and pay a fee), obtain a range of continuing education credits, and incur recertification costs to maintain the credential. This has produced a disgruntled group of outreach workers and, needless to say, has negatively affected their performance without any evidence of improvement.

The certification requirements are further evidence that deskilling not only reduces costs of operations, it does so in ways that require legitimizing rationalizations like new superficial credentials for undertrained staff. These requirements only serve to undermine the whole idea of employing indigenous workers. The community-based workforce becomes more reluctant partners in an effort to rationalize a more cost-efficient approach to providing services.

A final example is the new behavioral contracts adopted in relation to individualized treatment plans for clients. Such a plan is an agreement between a caseworker and a client that reflects a strong parallel with the disciplinary practice to enforce personal responsibility in welfare-to-work programs through what are called individual responsibility plans. In Delaware, drug treatment behavioral contracts are included in individualized treatment plans to specify an agreed-on set of practices or behaviors with clearly defined elements such as length of treatment, how behavior change will be measured, and reinforcements and penalties for adhering or not adhering to the agreement. There is some research to support the notion that these contracts are effective techniques to reduce problem behavior among clients in drug treatment.[53] The contract is commonly used in clinical social work practice to document agreed-on boundaries between the client and the clinician as well as to outline specific treatment goals. In drug treatment, clients are often required to sign contracts that stipulate the agency rules and expectations.[54]

The use of contracts, however, can undermine prior understandings in the drug treatment community to treat clients as partners working with clinicians to achieve recovery.[55] Contracts are also often used to withhold privileges or even put time limits and expectations for change that are in fact not client driven. These contracts are used to not only regulate the clients but produce the outcomes that are expected of the providers. In this context, the clients are empowered to act but in ways that are limiting and confining. Furthermore, the contract erroneously projects the idea that there is a shared understanding and agreed-on arrangement. While clients are often provided an opportunity, or "appeal" process, to bring their concerns to the administration if they want to reverse a decision made by the clinical administration regarding a rule or expectation outlined in their contract, this process only intensifies the adversarial tensions introduced with enforcing behavioral contracts. The emphasis on cost-efficiency inevitably makes individualized treatment plans neither individualized nor much about treatment. They are more about enforcement. Deskilled workers, using routinized, manualized procedures to treat clients, facing excessively high caseloads, are in no position to individualize treatment effectively. One-size-fits-all programming is more likely, as we have mentioned regarding several other aspects of the neoliberalization of drug treatment in Delaware. Clients end up agreeing to contract requirements they do not understand or cannot remember and counselors end up having to enforce contracts but having little time to do anything else. Under neoliberalism, the structural roots of the drug crisis are long forgotten and treatment of individuals to get them to practice personal responsibility becomes paramount. In practice, the shift toward individualized treatment itself falls prey to the market insistences of neoliberalism and clients suffer the consequences. With this sort of treatment regime in place, we are inclined to suggest that the disciplinary neoliberal regime comes to drug treatment as much as by default as by explicit intention.

CONCLUSION

The parallels between welfare-to-work in Florida and drug treatment in Delaware are suggestive of the ongoing shift toward a disciplinary regime of poverty management across the board in the human services today. Two widely different areas of human service provision in two very different states are changing in ways that reflect the broad reach of neoliberal paternalism. Neoliberal organizational reforms and paternalist policy tools appear in both and are changing who are the front-line workers, how organizational expectations affect their work, and how policy tools shape their treatment of clients. At the core of these developments are innovations that put the emphasis on routinized practices for screening, diagnosing, and treating clients in ways consonant with the overriding objective of the neoliberal paternalist disciplinary regime to enforce personal responsibility cost-efficiently. Whether this brave new world of human services policy implementation will lead to better outcomes for clients is an urgent question in need of increased attention. While recent research suggests that front-line workers often do not endorse the philosophy that undergirds these changes,[56] we would argue that this is perhaps besides the point. Front-line workers today operate in a disciplinary regime whose dictates they transgress at their peril. While there may be opportunities for subversive actions to help clients, participating in this "moral underground," as Lisa Dodson calls it, is a risky venture in the disciplinary regime of neoliberal paternalism.[57] Here, in the ordinary everyday of the moral underground, caseworkers operating under the neoliberal regime have some possibilities for a transgressive politics, incremental to be sure, but potentially radical overall, if isolated instances can be consolidated as part of a larger campaign to keep client needs paramount.[58] Yet as it is right now, it is our conclusion that the emerging neoliberal-paternalist panopticon of human service policy implementation makes the transgressive use of caseworker discretion more challenging today.

SCHOOLING THE
CORPORATIZED CITIZEN

FROM GRADE SCHOOL
THROUGH COLLEGE

The ongoing neoliberalization of social welfare policy is not limited to pro-grams for the most marginalized. Neoliberalization represents more than a shift from redistributing income to disciplining subordinated populations to be market compliant. Instead, the neoliberalization of social policy is dif-fused across policies, extending beyond those concentrated on the poor to policies serving the wider population. Education policy represents a critical example of how neoliberalization's reach extends not only across the policy continuum but also to both ends of the conventional political spectrum.[1] For instance, the No Child Left Behind (NCLB) legislation relies on a per-formance measurement scheme grounded in high-stakes testing of students to impose accountability on networks of public and private schools; and it has often benefited from bipartisan support. Local school districts increasingly rely on for-profit charter schools, which are given greater latitude in how to educate public school students in a more decentralized system. In other words, we see the same neoliberal organizational reforms that are now common-place in programs for the poor: devolution, privatization, and performance management.[2] In addition, education reforms offer the same policy tools of neoliberal changes we see in the wide array of programs focused on subordi-nate populations, from welfare-to-work to drug treatment programs. Today, sanctions and subsidies are becoming more prevalent in education systems, whether in the form of vouchers that subsidize public school students attend-ing private schools or zero tolerance rules to discipline students once they attend the school of their choice.

Further, the neoliberalization of education policy is by no means finished. In recent years, education's neoliberalization has extended beyond the school-house to produce a fundamental transformation of higher education.[3] The neoliberalization of education knows no bounds, reaching from kindergarten to graduate study. It is embedded in the market logic that informs education policy reforms. It is reflected in the performance measurement schemes that are increasingly deployed to hold accountable students, instructors, and schools. It is manifest in the for-profit corporations that increasingly dot the educa-tion landscape. Education is being neoliberalized right before our eyes.

In this chapter, I look at three troubling dimensions of the neoliberaliza-tion of education: market distortions, performance measurement perversi-ties, and the growing inequality in outcomes due to neoliberalizing reforms. I show how these are occurring on different levels of education simultane-ously. In the process, I demonstrate how these changes are associated with the broader movement to neoliberalize the welfare state overall.

THE CONTINUUM OF STATE POLICY

The case of education reform points to how neoliberalism represents nothing less than a regime-wide transformation of the state. We can see this transfor-mation as traversing the continuum of domestic policy across the welfare state. The idea of state policy existing on a continuum is put to good use by Pierre Bourdieu. Bourdieu has noted that the state is riven with conflict and that it is better to characterize it as a "bureaucratic field."[4] Bourdieu suggests that within this bureaucratic field there is a continuum of domestic policy, with the left hand of the state providing aid and the right hand of the state imposing discipline. Yet for Löic Wacquant, there has been a joining of the left and right hands of the state in recent years as policies have become more punitive, emphasizing punishing the poor for their failure to conform to social and legal norms, especially regarding work and family.[5] Social welfare and criminal justice policies, for instance, have become more alike, aiding and disciplining the poor simultaneously so that they will be less likely to engage in deviant social practices. Neoliberalism is spreading punishment across domestic policies in the name of disciplining the poor to become personally responsible, market-compliant actors.[6]

Yet neoliberalization involves more than punishment in the name of disciplining the poor. The marketization of social welfare policies actually has been the most noteworthy development under neoliberalism. In policy after policy, there has been a dramatic shift to relying on private providers, where clients are turned into consumers who get to make choices, and both are held accountable via performance measurement systems that indicate whether market-based objectives have been met. Examples include: welfare reform where private providers now dominate in placing clients in jobs, managed-care systems for regulating the private provision of publicly funded health care, Section 8 vouchers for subsidizing low-income families' participation in private housing markets, and education vouchers that subsidize parents' placing their children in private charter schools (where students must score sufficiently high on standardized tests for the schools to continue to participate in the privatized public education system in that locality).

Neoliberalism involves both carrots and sticks; it is about discipline more than just punishment.[7] Public policies across the social welfare continuum are undergoing a fundamental transformation as they are being neoliberalized to shift to imposing discipline to achieve market compliance by all actors in the system, service providers as well as clients. From income redistribution programs such as public assistance for the poor to criminal justice policies such as the system of mass incarceration that has arisen in the era of the war on drugs, social welfare policies are becoming more alike as they feature a strong disciplinary approach grounded in marketized operations. Increasingly, for-profit providers are required to demonstrate they can meet performance standards. Clients must manage to make do with whatever limited opportunities the economy provides. Education is located at the center of the public policy continuum, being neither an income redistribution program nor a component of the prison system. It therefore provides an excellent site for examining neoliberalism's marketizing effects on social welfare policies.

The Pretext for Reform: Crisis Narratives
of at-Risk Youth

As in other areas of social welfare policy, the introduction of neoliberal reforms to education did not occur automatically. Instead, reforms came about as a result of a sustained campaign created a sense of crisis that framed the problem as one best addressed by marketization. Deborah Stone, Murray Edelman, and others have highlighted how crisis narratives are commonplace in the public policymaking process.[8] For Stone, policy problems are inevitably narrated in a way that gives them an implied trajectory such that the preferred solutions of the narrators are suggested as the logical response. In this way, policy solutions do not so much come after a problem is recognized; instead, they are the pretext for framing an understanding of the problem in a politically selective way that implies the framers' already preferred solution is the best response. The narrative is a just-so storyline that just happens to fit with the preferred solution being seen as appropriate for the problem given how it has been framed in discourse. For Edelman, crisis narratives are intended to first activate the mass population to be concerned about a situation as a problem that urgently needs solving and then in a second phase deactivate the public by reassuring people that the government just happens to have on hand a ready-made solution. In the process, the state, the existing structure of power, and the prevailing hierarchy of vested interests get relegitimized. Crisis narratives help to consolidate established power relations more than destabilize them.

The campaign to introduce neoliberal reforms in education finds its origins in a long wave of crisis mongering about the declining international competitiveness of U.S. public school students stretching back at least to the much discussed report *A Nation at Risk: The Imperative for Educational Reform* from President Ronald Reagan's National Commission on Excellence in Education.[9] *A Nation at Risk* was released in 1983 and greatly accelerated debate about the need to restructure U.S. education policy. The introduction of the report indicated:

The Commission's charter directed it to pay particular attention to teenage youth, and we have done so largely by focusing on high schools. Selective attention was given to the formative years spent in elementary schools, to higher education, and to vocational and technical programs. We refer those interested in the need for similar reform in higher education to the recent report of the American Council on Education, *To Strengthen the Quality of Higher Education.*[10]

At the time, reform of higher education along the same neoliberal lines as elementary and secondary education was not a topic of widespread public discussion. Yet that would change and today the neoliberalization of higher education is more widely appreciated.[11] In any case, the report focused primarily on restructuring public secondary education.

The primary focus on secondary education stemmed from the directive that there was special concern about teenagers who were "at risk" of not being able to translate their education into marketable skills that would make them employable in a globalizing economy.[12] The report made this point explicit in suggesting that students and the nation were both "at risk" in this particular economically oriented way:

> The risk is not only that the Japanese make automobiles more efficiently than Americans and have government subsidies for development and export. It is not just that the South Koreans recently built the world's most efficient steel mill, or that American machine tools, once the pride of the world, are being displaced by German products. It is also that these developments signify a redistribution of trained capability throughout the globe. Knowledge, learning, information, and skilled intelligence are the new raw materials of international commerce and are today spreading throughout the world as vigorously as miracle drugs, synthetic fertilizers, and blue jeans did earlier. If only to keep and improve on the slim competitive edge we still retain in world markets, we must dedicate ourselves to the reform of our educational system for the benefit of all—old and young alike, affluent and poor, majority and minority. Learning is the indispensable investment required for success in the "information age" we are entering.[13]

The focus on teenage students suggested the urgent need to improve their education to become more successful in labor markets that were increasingly sensitive to global pressures. The point suggested that all kinds of students were being let down in this way by the failures of the existing education system to help them acquire the human capital for a changing economy. The report concluded: "the Federal Government, in cooperation with States and localities, should help meet the needs of key groups of students such as the gifted and talented, the socioeconomically disadvantaged, minority including language minority students, and the handicapped. In combination these groups include both national resources and the Nation's youth who are most *at risk*" (italics added).[14]

As Garnet Kindevater and Joe Soss have insightfully noted:

> "At-risk youth" is just the most recent arrival in a long history of stigmatizing labels applied to groups deemed to be deviant, deficient, and in need of reform. From this perspective, the "crisis of youth at-risk" is a construction (in the sense Murray Edelman elaborates) that advances an invidious process of "othering" and justifies extraordinary state inventions. Valuable as this perspective may be, it obscures a crucial point: The "at-risk" youth has yet to behave in any way or have any kind of experience that presents the state with a problem it might deem a crisis. Rather, the population of at-risk youth is defined by—and "the crisis of youth at risk" is produced through—a teleological imaginary in which the state *anticipates* a catastrophic future. The at-risk youth is not a perpetrator of acts but rather a bearer of probabilities.[15]

A Nation at Risk offered a crisis narrative about the need for education reform. That narrative traded on the emerging social work trope of "at-risk youth."[16] It served to create concern about problems that had a calculable probability of happening to the young students who might become unemployable and to the country that might then start to lose out in global economic competition. As a classic crisis narrative, the story of students and country as being "at risk" helped frame the problem before it actually had fully materialized in practice and accelerated the push to transform the U.S. educational system. And in classic crisis narrative fashion, the storyline that got championed was that the government just happened to have a ready-made solution to the emerging crisis of the schools: that is, neoliberalization, with vouchers to support systems of school choice, charter schools to diversify the types of schools from which to choose, high-stakes testing to hold schools accountable and ensure students were learning what they needed, linking school funding and teacher pay to student test results, and so on.

The major legislation that was enacted in response to the education reform campaign that followed was No Child Left Behind, enacted in 2001 with bipartisan support. While only part of the education system's response to the crisis, this piece of national legislation reflected a highly neoliberal reading of how the nation was at risk and how policymakers should respond. First, it followed the idea that education was largely about creating employable workers with marketable skills rather than informed citizens who could effectively participate in a democracy. This was most noticeable in the law's system of "high-stakes" testing that emphasized math and reading skills at the expense of other forms of learning.[17] Second, the law put in motion reforms that relied on measuring school performance to create the basis for parents to choose from a menu of public and private schools (i.e., charter schools under contract with a local school district). This system of choice introduced the idea of a competitive market into local schools systems. These changes inevitably accelerated the instrumentalization and commodification of education as something that should be evaluated primarily in terms of how well it offered the opportunity for individual students to enhance their human capital via the development of marketable skills that would make them employable in the changing economy.[18]

With the crisis narrative in place, advocates for neoliberalizing education were ready to push through reforms. The story told was that public schools had failed and the logical solution was to turn it over to market actors. These market actors could come into local school districts and put in place market-based systems that allowed parents to act as consumers in choosing what schools were best for their individual children. In this way, parents could act to maximize each child's personal human capital by helping them learn what they needed to know so they could eventually acquire the skills needed to succeed in the changing economy.[19] Systems of competition would be initiated and schools would compete for students, and students and parents could evaluate schools based on how well the students at these schools tested.

NEOLIBERAL FAILURE: THE MIRAGE OF MARKETIZATION

As in other areas of public policy, bringing the private sector into public education has not really worked well.[20] For instance, voucher programs that subsidize students attending private schools have often led to creating tiers where more privileged students attend the better funded private schools that vouchers cannot pay for, leaving poorer students to attend inferior private schools.[21] Also charter schools have proven quite controversial. They do not evaluate better than public schools (often worse).[22] When they do better, it is for reasons having nothing to do with operating according to market principles. In some studies, their students can be shown to have improved scores compared with public schools, when the charter schools lengthen the time in school, per day and per academic year, work with students on more assignments at school rather than as part of homework, and take other actions associated with raising expectations for students. These are old ideas reaching back at least to *A Nation at Risk*, which energized the charter movement.[23] Yet public schools can get the same results with the same methods and there are studies from other countries indicating that a longer school year does not improve student performance.[24] In addition, it must not go unnoticed that charter schools have been sources of increased corruption in the education system, fudging performance numbers, paying exorbitant salaries to their executives, and using their resources to lobby governments to insulate them from oversight and control by local school districts.[25]

In the extreme, for-profit schools are finding ways to offer a stripped-down version of schools. They increasingly are partnering with other firms to provide more of their curriculum via the Internet while relying on volunteers from Teach for America to offer a program without the "frills" of music, arts, physical education, and sports. Rocketship, a for-profit provider from California, is spreading around the country with this "blended learning" model and attracting the interest of local government officials interested in cutting the cost of education regardless of the effects on student learning.[26]

Privatization has been equally vexing in higher education. For-profit colleges and universities have come under criticism, especially those promising a skills-based training for semiprofessional fields, such as medical technological specialists and other emerging fields. There have been charges of corruption among this group of schools as well. They often engage in deceptive advertising about providing a sure-fire path to employment when in reality their job placement rates for graduates are low.[27] These schools have also frequently been accused of loading students down with excessive amounts of education loans that they cannot pay off when they fail to get a job. It is very troubling that too little has been done to stop the proliferation of private, for-profit colleges and universities in various technical training fields where these schools basically have failed most of the students who are attracted to them.[28]

Yet if the past is any indication the failures of neoliberalism will lead to just more marketization. As the prevailing worldview, neoliberalism remains the baseline from which public policy reform is evaluated. A bipartisan consensus consolidates its hegemony in the area of education policy.[29] Private money from corporate and family foundations also has buttressed the commitment to marketizing the schools. Since 2000, the Walton Family Foundation alone has spent more than $1 billion on education reform, largely on Teach for America, voucher programs, and charter schools.[30] In other words, the concentration of wealth among the corporate elite has once again created opportunities for them to consolidate their position by using that wealth to affect politics and the public policymaking process.

Under these conditions, the emphasis on market-based approaches to education is likely to continue. As a result, the for-profit schools that have quickly become embedded in education at all levels continue to attract students and resist strict regulation, using their profits to effectively lobby Congress.[31] Much like the wealthy who have used their growing wealth to dominate the political process, charter schools have used the resources devoted to them to lobby effectively for their cause. Even as they fail to produce promised improvements in the public schools, they continue to garner political support from powerful politicians who often seek their campaign contributions.[32]

Part of the reason for the continued success of the for-profits is a key irony of neoliberalism. Neoliberal failure in fact may not be failure at all since much of the marketization of education in recent years seems designed to get people to comply with market forces rather than resist them.[33] If students fail or if a chosen school fails them, as market actors they must accept responsibility for their bad choices and work to improve their market participation in the future. This logic has spread from charter schools and for-profit colleges and universities to public schools and private nonprofit colleges and universities as they increasingly lean toward refashioning the curriculum to attract students with promises of opportunities to learn skills directly related to specific careers.[34] The bottom line is the commodification of education continues apace irrespective of effects on citizenship and democracy. As long as neoliberalism remains the prevailing ethic for evaluating education reform, the proposed responses to neoliberal failure are likely to be more neoliberalism that further accelerates the disciplining of market actors, students, parents, teachers, administrators, and program executives alike.

PERVERSE PERFORMANCE MEASUREMENT EFFECTS: TEACH
TO THE TEST AND TEACH TO THE RATE

Market logic now pervades all of education policymaking.[35] It foregrounds reliance on market actors, such as charter schools and for-profit colleges, to innovate and offer students more choice in obtaining a more commodifiable education that they can bank on for enhancing their human capital and becoming more successful market actors themselves. Schools engage in market competition in order to attract student customers; and students compete to get into the best schools. Performance standards are used to evaluate both schools and students, and increasingly teachers as well. Out of these changes emerge winners and losers as resources flow to the top performers at the expense of those who underperform. These market-based changes are occurring at all levels of education, producing the neoliberalization of education writ large.

Therefore, it is not difficult to see that performance measurement operates as a critical linchpin in the marketized education systems. In local school districts providing elementary and secondary education, performance measurement has become commonplace under the NCLB reforms.[36] Periodic mandatory testing of students in selected grades for particular subjects is required under the legislation and is implemented by local districts to the extent that states seek federal funding under the legislation. In higher education, the Obama administration has proposed tying federal aid to outcomes measures such as graduation rates.[37]

As discussed in chapter 5, performance measurement is well established in public management across a number of policy areas; however, this is in spite of sustained criticisms over the years. The response is to try to improve measurement rather than forgo it. Yet the insistence on improved measurement often overlooks some of the fundamental problems of insisting on a measurement system for evaluating policy implementation.[38] For this reason Beryl Radin calls performance measurement a "hydra-headed monster" that keeps returning irrespective of how many times its flaws are pointed out.[39]

If I have not made this clear, I should note that like most social scientists, I am personally not opposed to measuring social phenomena and using statistics to make social populations and problems more legible (in order for the state and its public policymakers to decide how to act in response).[40] Yet not only can people lie with statistics, as Mark Twain famously stated, those statistics can be used in ways that are more than just misleading. The key problem of performance measurement is the effect that such measures have on the way policies are implemented. Once a statistical benchmark is put in place and programs are held accountable for hitting a performance target, something profoundly dangerous happens to policy implementation. Depending on how critical the performance standard is, it can lead to a perverse form of administrative policy feedback, where the measurement tail comes to wag the program implementation dog.[41]

There is the risk of a means-ends inversion that comes from the instrumentalization of performance measurement. With a statistical benchmark hanging over program administrators, inevitably there is the concern that hitting the target must be given priority, even at the expense of other important programmatic considerations. If failure to hit the performance target means adverse actions will be taken against the program, including reductions in funding—or worse, termination of the program—then the performance management benchmarks not only inform decision making about how to implement the program but can become an exclusive obsession for administrators. To the extent that performance benchmarks become a preoccupation, they pose the risk that programming decisions will be made to hit the required targets irrespective of whether focusing on them might mean sacrificing other important, often less measureable dimensions of the program. Quantity can be emphasized at the expense of quality, and the program may then end up becoming an elaborate exercise in what public management theorists call "suboptimization," where the program objective is realized but in name only (see chapter 5).[42] Suboptimization produces an emphasis on "metrics over mission."[43]

High-stakes testing in the schools is probably the cardinal example of the perverse effects of performance measurement on policy implementation. For instance, in the case of education reforms that impose testing of students to evaluate school performance, a preoccupation with student scores in order to gain a positive evaluation might produce improvements in the scores even if students are not really improving in other dimensions of their education. An overemphasis on improving scores associated with basic skills related to enhancing human capital and employability might mean sacrificing other forms of education associated with helping students learn how to become thoughtful democratic citizens. Under No Child Left Behind, as enacted in 2001, states are required to conduct standardized tests annually on students in grades 3–8 in reading and math. These state-devised systems of high-stakes testing are designed to hold states and their schools accountable for the learning of their students. Failing schools can be defunded and closed. States have options under the law to link other concerns such as teacher pay to the student test scores.[44]

There are numerous reports of what is called the "teach to the test" effect, where instruction is warped to focus on students scoring better at the expense of overall learning. This means-ends inversion in which the test becomes the thing and learning is sacrificed for scoring better is probably the single most damning criticism of No Child Left Behind. It has helped energize opposition to the law to the point that states are pulling out of the program of testing in exchange for federal aid. As one statistical analysis comparing all states involved in testing under NCLB concluded:

> In light of the rapidly growing body of evidence of the deleterious unintended effects of high-stakes testing, and the fact that our study finds no convincing evidence that the pressure associated with high-stakes testing leads to increased achievement, there is no reason to continue the practice of high stakes testing. Thus, given (a) the unprofessional treatment of the educators who work in high-stakes testing situations, (b) the inevitable corruption of the indicators used in accountability systems where high-stakes testing is featured, (c) data from this and other studies that seriously question whether the intended effects of high-stakes testing actually occur, and (d) the acknowledged impossibility of reaching the achievement goals set by the NCLB act in a reasonable time frame, there is every reason to ask for a moratorium on testing policies that force us to rely on high-stakes testing.[45]

In the public management literature, the other major threat that comes from overemphasizing measurement in spite of its limitations is called "creaming."[46] Creaming, as also described in chapter 5, is where program administrators give priority to the clients who are likely to succeed without the program's help just so they can get credit for their success. These clients, who will contribute to the program meeting its performance target without being helped, are emphasized in program operations. It is like skimming the cream off the top of the milk and leaving the rest behind. It is not "teach to the test" but "teach to the rate."[47] There have been extensive efforts in creaming under

NCLB, much of it focused on gaming the system by way of limiting which students will be tested. The reports on reducing the pool of students to be tested under NCLB to include only the better students indicate some of the worst forms of creaming.[48] The NCLB's testing scheme ends up actually encouraging "schools to 'game the system' by excluding students from testing, and ultimately from school."[49]

Of course, neither creaming (as in teach to the rate) nor suboptimizing (as in teach to the test) need involve explicit corruption and can be conducted with the rules of any performance rating system such as the high-stakes testing of NCLB. Be that as it may, there have been major cheating scandals under No Child Left Behind.[50] Yet the bigger story is how the system can pervert education objectives without going outside the rules. Neoliberal systems of measurement are doing just that to public elementary and secondary education today. The pressure grows to extend this logic to deciding the allocation of federal funding to colleges and universities. While tracking graduation rates is important, tying funding to them as the Obama administration has proposed might just produce more neoliberal failure of the performance measurement kind. The hydra-headed, neoliberal monster of performance management has nine lives and like other zombies it can keep on keeping on, long after it should have been declared dead.

Neoliberal Education Manufactures Inequality

Education was once commonly considered the great equalizer. But no more. The failures of neoliberal education reform include growing inequities. A major debate among critics centers on neoliberalism's failure in reducing growing inequalities in recent decades. As mentioned earlier in this chapter, we need to consider the possibility that neoliberalism's failures could well be intentional rather than unintentional results of neoliberal policies and practices designed to redistribute resources toward the most aggressive market actors.[51] Given the role education plays in determining the economic prospects of so many, this debate undoubtedly has direct relevance for assessing education reform in the current era.

At one level, it is unremarkable that neoliberalism generates inequality. Neoliberalism is centrally about marketization; and markets have evolved to be about creating competitions with winners and losers. Under neoliberalism, each person has the primary responsibility to focus on how to enhance his or her own personal human capital in order to succeed as a market actor. Each person's job is to consider all choices according to the assumed market logic at that time. Yet as Andrew Dilts notes, this neoliberal orientation originally represented a break with the capitalism that preceded it. Adam Smith's form of capitalism emphasized mutually agreed-on exchanges between people who ideally were freely entering into those economic relationships.[52] For Michel Foucault, however, neoliberalism represents a fundamental shift in the orientation under capitalism, where *Homo oeconomicus* ceases to be "one of the two partners in the process of exchange" and becomes "an entrepreneur of himself."[53] Neoliberalization represents a shift in emphasis under capitalism whereby market actors are more preoccupied with enhancing their own human capital so they can win competitions. Therefore, when we emphasize that changes in education policy are producing neoliberal marketizing reforms, we are inevitably highlighting how those reforms are shifting education policy toward the introduction of market competitions where there are winners and losers and participants need to take responsibility for the choices they make. It is a system that responsibilizes bad choices that result in being unable to enhance one's human capital and be an effective entrepreneur of oneself.

So let the neoliberal student-consumer-buyer beware. If the charter school you choose fails to teach you what you need to know to get the career you are seeking, that is on you (or your parents, who may have made that bad choice for you). The same goes for your choice of college. If you took on massive amounts of debt to finance your education but cannot now get a decent job to pay off your student loans, then that is also on you as a failed market actor. Neoliberal logic is unimpressed with the record amounts of student debt, and campaigns for debt forgiveness have not gained traction politically (beyond limited gestures from sympathetic elected officials including President Obama). Yet it would seem that were it not for the hegemony of the neoliberal perspective the student debt crisis would receive more serious political discussion. Chris Maisano notes the troubling situation for those students with college loan debt:

In June 2010, total outstanding student loan debt became larger than total outstanding credit card debt for the first time in the country's history, and in the spring of 2012 this figure surpassed the astonishing figure of $1 trillion. This explosion in student loan indebtedness has been the logical result of the dramatic inflation in the cost of higher education (particularly public higher education) in recent decades. Economists estimate that the cost of tuition and fees has more than doubled since 2000, easily surpassing the rate of inflation in energy, housing, and even health care costs.

The driving force behind this explosion in higher education costs is the long-term disinvestment in public colleges and universities at the state level. While public higher education institutions have absorbed the majority of new undergraduate enrollments since 1990, the proportion of state spending on higher education has dramatically declined. According to a recent study by Demos, between 1990 and 2010, real funding per public full-time enrolled student declined by over 26%. This shortfall has not been filled by other sources of public funding, but rather by a marked increase of students' out-of-pocket costs. Over the same period, tuition and fees at four-year public colleges and universities rose by 112.5% while the price of public two-year colleges increased by 71%. Because household incomes have stagnated over the previous two decades, students and their families have been compelled to turn to student loans to cover these costs. According to the Department of Education, 45% of 1992–1993 graduates borrowed money from federal or private sources; today, at least two-thirds of graduates enter the workforce with educational debt.

Even though college-educated workers tend, on average, to earn higher incomes than their less-educated counterparts, young college-educated workers have not escaped the pressures of wage stagnation. In the last decade, the average annual earnings of workers ages 25 to 34 with Bachelors degrees fell by 15%. New graduates, meanwhile, saw their...average debt load increase by 24%. What makes this dramatic expansion of student loan indebtedness particularly troubling is the fact that unlike most other forms of personal debt, student loans cannot be discharged through the standard bankruptcy process. In the event of default on a private or federal student loan, borrowers face a range of invasive measures: wage garnishment, the interception of tax refunds or lottery winnings, and the withholding of future Social Security payments.[54]

Under these neoliberal conditions, it can be expected that education will begin to resemble a lottery that ends up creating what Suzanne Mettler has called "degrees of inequality."[55] In fact, we are seeing evidence that neoliberal marketizing reforms are leading to an education system that creates pathways to economic success for some while putting others who are seeking to advance educationally at a disadvantage. This is especially apparent in the postsecondary market, where many students attending for-profit colleges graduate (or not) with massive debt but no real job prospects, while students attending underfunded public colleges also are weighed down with student loans and face grim employment prospects. There is now growing evidence that seeking a college degree continues to be a safe financial investment but only for those students who attend the better, often exclusive private, nonprofit colleges and other elite universities.[56]

The public universities are increasingly confronting budget cuts as states fail to support them at prior levels. The antitax movement and the hollowing out of the welfare state have forced state universities to seek alternative sources of funding. Increases in tuition have led students to borrow more money but also work more while attending school, and the results indicate declining academic performance.[57] Neoliberalization results in more students learning less while shouldering more of the costs. The degrees of inequality continue to mount under neoliberalism's marketization of education.

Inequalities mount within the ranks of the professoriate as well. Increasingly the underfunded public colleges and universities turn to creating a casualized workforce of underpaid adjunct faculty to provide instruction for a growing majority of classes being taught at these institutions. Underpaid, most often without basic health or pension benefits, many of these adjuncts are graduate students or former graduate students with no real prospects of securing a permanent faculty appointment. They are increasingly seen as another contingent of microearners of the emerging "share economy."[58] As a result, a class division grows among the ranks of the faculty adding to the degrees of inequality wrought by the neoliberalization of higher education.

A recent report from Democrats in the U.S. House of Representatives in 2014 noted:

The post-secondary academic workforce has undergone a remarkable change over the last several decades. The tenure-track college professor with a stable salary, firmly grounded in the middle or upper-middle class, is becoming rare. Taking her place is the contingent faculty: nontenure-track teachers, such as part-time adjuncts or graduate instructors, with no job security from one semester to the next, working at a piece rate with few or no benefits across multiple workplaces, and far too often struggling to make ends meet. In 1970, adjuncts made up 20 percent of all higher education faculty. Today, they represent half.[59]

The change is even more drastic depending on how you count. More than 70 percent of all faculty are non–tenure track.[60] Yet a casualized professoriate of temporary instructors is evidently still not enough to balance the under-funded budgets of public colleges and universities. As a result, administrators are increasingly pushing use of the Internet to deliver instruction. Online instruction and other innovations are being developed, often relying on private corporate providers for content.[61] The result is yet another neoliberal market-based practice to introduce other forms of inequality among students in terms of how they take courses, and among instructors in terms of whether they are a featured lecturer or just an underpaid teaching assistant.

With the tumultuous changes to education today, it is difficult to predict whether cherished ideals of ensuring access to a decent education for all can be sustained. Also in doubt is whether education can continue to be a force that works to promote both equality and democracy. Instead, it may become an agent for generating greater inequality while ignoring its role in preparing the next generation to be effective democratic citizens.

The concern for democracy is not new but in the age of neoliberalism is at risk of being seen as an anachronistic extravagance. Nothing could be further from the truth. As far back as 1991, Carol Ziegler and Nancy Lederman discussed the implications of neoliberal education reforms such as vouchers in ways that resonate strongly today:

> Although First Amendment concerns have predominated in the debate over school choice, other important democratic ideals are at stake. Ironically, the commentators who have recognized this connection between good schooling and democratic controls have seen them as incompatible.
>
> John Chubb and Terry Moe's *Politics, Markets and America's Schools*, the seminal school choice study, postulates that a redesigned education system should vest authority directly in the schools, parents and students. Thus, the study argues, the school system should be disengaged from institutions of democratic control, such as federal and state government, to

the greatest extent possible. These advocates propose a free market system—with or without vouchers—in which schools are run autonomously, without governmental bureaucratic controls, as a way to improve schooling.

In fact, the schools that have been the successful models of "choice," like those in New York's East Harlem school district, have either seized or been granted some degree of autonomy in developing their own approaches to schooling. However, what supporters of the privatization of education ignore is that this autonomy is realized in public school systems like New York City's through a host of mechanisms which are *grounded* in law and policy, and are unavailable in the private schools. As such, this autonomy is built upon the underlying premise of our public schools, which is that all are included and that citizens should actively participate in decision-making. Those mechanisms empower parents, as well as teachers and students, in a way that does not, and cannot, exist in the private sector.

The rights of parents and students which are acknowledged and expected in our public schools are a direct extension of the Jeffersonian ideal of a nation enlightened though education. A voucher system that includes private schools inevitably involves a false choice between these accepted rights and "choice" in schooling. Thus, the challenge in education reform remains in the improvement of public education and not in its abandonment, and in strengthening the ties between schooling and democracy rather than in severing them.[62]

Education is essential for all of us individually and for society collectively. Without it, we cannot sustain democracy. That ideal is quintessentially American, or so it was before neoliberalism. We have marketized education, turning it into a commodity that individuals consume exclusively for the enhancement of their human capital. Yet even if that promise of enhanced human capital is increasingly not able to translate into decently paying jobs, the prevalence of neoliberal market logic in education has yet to peak and the negative consequences are at least as much political as economic.

THE NEXT NEOLIBERAL THING

SOCIAL IMPACT BONDS

Neoliberalism has moved from jargon to common parlance in a short time. It provides the dominant orientation for negotiating ordinary everyday existence writ large, in the market, civil society, the state, and their nexus. As a result, the economic logic that stands at the center of neoliberalism is assumed to stand for all logic. What is economically logical is logical per se. Neoliberalism is the default position for thinking about not just market participation but all behavior, public as well as private, inside government and out, for collective decision making as well as for individual choices. It has become the common sense of what passes for ordinary capitalism in the current era.[1]

Neoliberalism is a juggernaut. It is now basically an irresistible force not easily dislodged by simply showing it fails to achieve efficiency even as it exacerbates inequality.[2] It seems nothing can stop its increased application and dissemination across key social institutions and practices. The failures of neoliberalism beget nothing less than even more neoliberalism.[3] Showing that neoliberalism has made a problem like poverty worse, or that it has undermined government efforts to improve the lives of those disadvantaged by current policies, simply leads to new innovations in public policy that rely on even more intensified forms of marketization. Nothing better demonstrates this then social impact bonds as a new way of financing social welfare programs.

Social impact bonds are bonds that private investors buy to finance public services. They provide the incentive that the investors will make a profit if a service meets designated performance targets as determined by an independent evaluator. To paraphrase Jamie Peck and Nik Theodore, social impact bonds are a "fast-track global social policy" that spreads from one country to another, in this case as implemented first in England, then the United States, now Canada, Australia, New Zealand, and increasingly elsewhere.[4] They are more than just the latest example of neoliberalization of the welfare state, where state functions are marketized so as to run according to market logic. They do inject market logic into state operations and are a stark example of blurring the boundaries between the private and public spheres. Yet they go further. Social impact bonds are perhaps the paradigmatic example of welfare state neoliberalization because they explicitly financialize social welfare funding, putting it in the hands of private investors. These investors can reap substantial economic gains from their investments in state operations but only if the programs they fund are evaluated to be economically efficient in producing long-run savings that the government will get from a successful program. Social impact bonds represent nothing less than the financialization of the welfare state.

Social impact bonds are an excellent example of how neoliberalism replaces neoliberal failures with more intensified forms of neoliberalism. In particular, the bonds build on the failures of prior performance measurement schemes, upping the ante by proposing to pay private investors only if performance measurement benchmarks are met. Prior criticism of performance measurement systems focused in particular on their perverse effects, especially where meeting performance objectives actually had deleterious effects on addressing the fundamental underlying social problems being addressed (see chapters 5 and 6).[5] Such criticism might lead policymakers to move away from performance measurement schemes because of their less than optimal effects on public policy implementation via contract agencies in public-private partnerships. Yet Beryl Radin calls performance management a "hydra-headed monster," because, like the general outlook of neoliberalism itself, performance measurement schemes keep coming back into vogue every few years even though each time they do, people point out the fatal flaws underlying this way of enforcing accountability.[6] Instead of moving beyond flawed performance measurement schemes, these bonds intensify the emphasis on performance management by creating a situation where only programs that meet their performance measurement targets will attract funders as these investors will not receive a return on their investment if the program they back fails to meet its benchmarks. The result is essentially replacing performance measurement as it has previously been practiced with what we can call "high-stakes" performance measurement.

Social impact bonds were originally designed in the late 1980s to fund experimental, preventive programs to which governments could not commit dedicated funding from tax revenues. Yet they actually only started to get implemented in 2010 after governments found that they were broke. This is another way in which these bonds are an example of how neoliberalism's failures beget more neoliberalism. The neoliberal hollowing out of the welfare state made them popular. While they were originally a means to alternative funding for experimental programs, they are now an experiment for funding programs the government normally administers. Social impact bonds have become an increasingly popular method of social welfare financing if for no other reason than that neoliberal austerity has made governments desperate. The tax-cutting and deficit reduction strategies of neoliberal austerity have failed to get rid of the welfare state; instead, the welfare state must be funded by other means. In other words, the problems of neoliberalism beget not less but even more intensified forms of neoliberalism. As a result, social impact bonds are quickly becoming the paradigmatic practice of neoliberal financialization of social welfare programming, in which market actors in the form of private investors are given a determinative role in the decision-making process regarding state operations.

In this chapter, I examine the logic, operation, and implications of social impact bonds as one of the most dramatic examples of marketizing social welfare operations today. I begin the analysis explaining these bonds, then turn to placing them in the context of neoliberal trends related to getting corporate actors involved in funding public programs and working to achieve public outcomes: public-private partnerships, corporate social responsibility campaigns, and, last, what is being called "philanthrocapitalism." Next, I examine social impact bonds as an increasingly popular way of bringing these trends into convergence in a highly marketized way. This is followed by an analysis of how these bonds work in practice, a survey of the challenges confronting them, and finally critical assessment of the implications for democracy when capitalism gets so deeply involved in funding social welfare policy.

THE NEXT NEOLIBERAL THING: SOCIAL IMPACT BONDS

Social impact bonds might seem a recent innovation, but they were first talked about as early as 1988, when Ronnie Horesh, an economist from New Zealand, presented a paper before a meeting of the Australian Agricultural Economics Society that proposed what Horesh called "social policy bonds."[7] Subsequent variations sometimes referred to social benefit bonds and sometimes to social impact bonds. The key distinction between social policy bonds, on the one hand, and social impact or social benefit bonds, on the other, is that only social policy bonds (Horesh's original idea) would be tradable on a secondary market. If these types of bonds were to become tradable, they then would become no different than any other commodity that can be bought and sold in whatever markets there are buyers willing to purchase it. In fact, these types of bonds could then be bundled along with other financial investments or securities, further erasing the distinction between them and other financial commodities. Any social welfare programming financed in this fashion would be financialized to the point that it would seem almost inevitable that investors' interest in social welfare programs as profitable commodities would start to cast a long shadow over social welfare policymaking. In fact, as this chapter details, this is a distinct possibility even if these types of bonds never become tradable on secondary markets. So far, they are circulating among investors but they are not yet tradable on secondary markets. They are a source of funding for social welfare programs that investors can buy if not resell, and that in itself makes them worthy of critical scrutiny.

Regardless of whether we are talking about social policy, social benefit, or social impact bonds, it is important to note that none of these are technically bonds. Traditional bonds pay a guaranteed interest. These new bonds only promise a return on investment if the program being funded by the investors meets performance benchmarks. These benchmarks are determined by an independent, outside evaluator who is independent of both the agency providing the service and the investors putting up the funds. These bonds are designed to attract investors to preventive programs that, if successful, can reduce future costs to the government. The government agrees to share some of the projected savings for a program that is evaluated to be successfully preventing a problem from occurring or reoccurring, such as ex-felons returning to prison. Should the program being funded prove to be very successful, then the returns could conceivably exceed returns from long-term stock investments in publicly traded companies. Therefore social impact bonds may well prove to be attractive to private investors who can spot winning programs and are interested in taking a chance on fronting the funding for them. Additional investors might include philanthropists, charities, and private foundations that are less interested in profit and more interested in promoting public good. A third group of investors might be corporate financiers interested in improving their brand by having it associated with programs designed to solve public problems.

Horesh originally suggested that what he called social policy bonds would be ideal for experimental programs for which governments were reluctant to provide a dedicated stream of funding, even with initial evidence indicating that the intervention could prove to be an effective preventive program that would over time reduce government costs in addressing a major social problem. Hoersh mentioned long-term unemployment, homelessness, reincarceration, child welfare, and many other areas of concern in the social welfare arena. The idea was that investors might be interested in funding these experimental programs while governments could not.

The basic idea behind what Horesh called social policy bonds became the basis for the social impact (and social benefit) bonds that have emerged in recent years. It is important to consider that turning to private investors has implications beyond drawing on an alternative funding source. It is a profoundly neoliberal way of funding public programs that involves ceding public decision-making authority at least in part to financiers. These types of bonds make explicit the risks of neoliberal marketization of state functions. So it is therefore understandable that governments did not immediately jump to adopt this neoliberal innovation. In fact, it was not until governments became desperate for funding post the Great Recession that we saw a social impact bond program implemented. In 2010, the City of London initiated a social impact bond to fund a reentry program for ex-felons transitioning out of prison and back into the community. But since then, the idea of social impact bond programs has spread from London to New York, to selected states across the United States, and also to other countries, circumnavigating the globe to come back home to Australia and New Zealand, where the idea for these types of bonds started.

The fiscal condition of governments undoubtedly has helped make these new bonds seem to be an idea that is right for the times. Cash-strapped governments are likely to look favorably on this alternative source of funding. The Obama administration has recognized this opportunity and has embraced it, developing funding to support states and localities in developing the new type of bonds with its Pay for Success grants.[8] The grants are for building the infrastructure to create the bonds. President Obama has long been an advocate for what is called "evidence-based" policymaking. He very much wants to introduce accountability into funding of social welfare programs by insisting that the programs developed be grounded in empirical research that demonstrates their viability and that the programs once implemented correspondingly demonstrate that they produce positive outcomes.[9] Social impact bonds are consistent with this outlook in that they fund programs that are often developed out of successful pilot programs and investors only get repaid if the program achieves its performance benchmarks indicating that, as a preventive program, it has successfully worked to reduce future costs.

The Obama administration's Pay for Success initiative shows its commitment to social impact bonds. For 2014, the administration proposed $495 million in funding for Pay for Success. The White House announcement states:

> In the Fiscal Year 2014 Budget, President Obama proposed a nearly $500 million investment in Pay for Success, including the creation of a new $300 million Incentive Fund at the Treasury Department. The Fund is designed to empower cities, states and nonprofits to support more public-private partnerships that produce measurable results in their communities. In addition to the Incentive Fund, another $195 million is proposed to support Pay for Success programming in nine programs across three different Federal agencies: the Departments of Labor, Justice and Education.... The White House Pay for Success convening highlighted examples of innovative work underway at state and local levels across a wide array of sectors including workforce development, reducing recidivism, homelessness, aging, asthma management, disability and early childhood education. Currently, Pay for Success efforts are in some form of development in at least 14 states across the nation and that number continues to grow.[10]

In particular, California and Massachusetts have developed a strong interest in social impact bonds and are using Pay for Success funding to jump-start their programs. Massachusetts is using Pay for Success funding to develop a $27 million initiative to reduce recidivism among at-risk youth.

This funding is not in lieu of private investors. It is to help build the elaborate infrastructure required to implement social impact bonds. There is a lot of legwork required to bring the various partners together to get any one bond program up and running. In addition to recruiting investors, the government must enlist an agency (either public or private, new or existing) to oversee not just the financing but also the delivery of the service (which itself is often provided by a contract agency). Also, a critical feature in these new types of bond programs, as noted, is that investors are only paid if the service provided is evaluated favorably by an outside evaluator who is independent of both the investors and the contract agency providing the service. Social impact bonds therefore involve multiple partners who require extensive coordination. Much of the money the Obama administration is putting up for its Pay for Success initiative is to help cover the costs of initial payouts to investors and administering the bond programs.

Figure 7.1 specifies some of the key players in the typical social impact bond. First, the government agency responsible for the service being funded finds an intermediary that acts like a general contractor and oversees putting the pieces together. Then the intermediary contracts with a service provider (often a nonprofit) to provide the actual service being funded. Third, the intermediary also often works with an investment firm to recruit investors

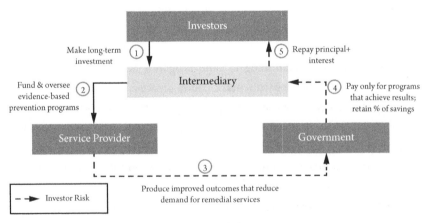

Figure 7.1 Social Impact Bond Basic Model.
(http://blog.centerforgiving.org/2013/08/26/understanding-the-social-impact-bond/).

on the basis of a prospectus that promises a schedule of payments should the program achieve designated outcome targets. The fourth missing piece of the puzzle (not shown in figure 7.1 but would appear on the right side at point number 4) is the outside evaluator who provides the independent assessment of whether the program has hit those benchmarks or met those targets, thereby creating the condition for authorizing payments to the investors. If the evaluator projects savings from a successful preventive program, then the government is expected to share some of that projected savings with the investors. This is the basic model for social impact bonds.

For instance, if a bond-funded program can reduce recidivism among those released from incarceration, the savings can be substantial. A commonly cited statistic in recent years is that on average, state governments in the United States spend considerably more a year to incarcerate somebody who has been convicted of a crime than to educate a student in the public schools (see figure 7.2).

These costs mount given the high levels of incarceration in the United States that have emerged over the last thirty to forty years (see figure 7.3). According to the U.S. Bureau of Justice Statistics, 2,266,800 adults were incarcerated in U.S. federal and state prisons and county jails at the end of 2011, just slightly less than 1 percent of the adult population.[11] Additionally, 4,814,200 adults in 2011 were on probation or on parole. In total, 6,977,700 adults were under correctional supervision (probation, parole, jail, or prison) in 2011, just under 3 percent of the adult population. In addition, there were 70,792 juveniles in juvenile detention in 2010.[12] The rise of mass incarceration in the United States has now reached the point where it produces a steady stream of prisoners being released back into the community. In 2008, for example, 735,454 people were released from state and federal prison. Many of those incarcerated, however, return for violations related to parole or probation. A study of 272,111 released inmates in 1994 found that two-thirds were rearrested, with about 55 percent returning to prison within three years.[13]

The federal government has responded with the passage of the Second Chance Act of 2008 to fund what are called reentry programs to work with those released so as to improve their chances of not recidivating.[14] These programs have not always evaluated well but there is some evidence they can reduce recidivism at the margin, usually around 5 percent.[15] If we can reduce the rate of recidivism further, it would reap substantial savings for state and local governments that could be used to improve funding for education and

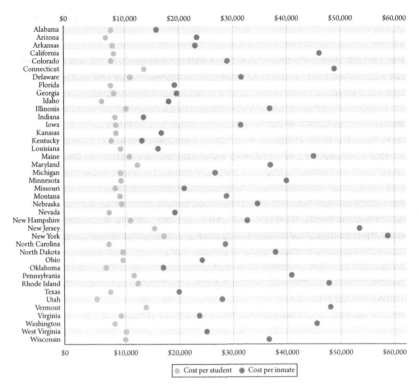

Figure 7.2 Cost of Students and Prisoners, by State.
Graphic: Tal Yellin/CNNMoney (http://www.money.cnn.com/infographic/
economy/education-vs-prison-costs/). Source: U.S. Census Data and Vera
Institute of Justice. Methodology: Education data was collected by the U.S. census
and covers public school children prekindergarten through twelfth grade. Prison
data from the Vera Institute was collected in each state using a department of
corrections survey. Corrections departments from forty states completed and
returned the survey, which asked respondents to provide prison expenditures paid
by the department of corrections, as well as prison costs paid by other agencies.
Tal Yellin/CNNMoney.

other service that would in turn help reduce what is spent on incarceration
in the future. Since Second Chance funding is limited and not all reentry
programs have proven worthy of backing, the idea of floating social impact
bonds to fund preferred programs has growing appeal. It is in fact now an
option for states under the law to use their federal grants to develop bond-
funded reentry programs. It is therefore not surprising that this area of huge
potential savings has proven to be where most of the energy around bonds
has been concentrated in this initial phase of rollout.

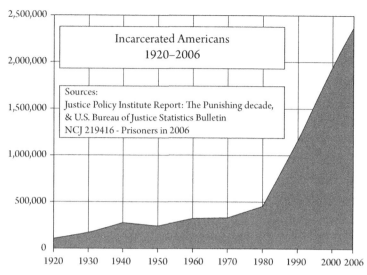

Figure 7.3   Incarcerated Americans, 1920–2006.

As noted earlier, the City of London was the first to initiate a bond-funded reentry program in 2010. In 2012, New York City initiated two bond-funded programs to work with juveniles coming out of detention.[16] Reentry programs like these are being developed in Massachusetts and other states. Some preventive programs under serious consideration for bond funding include services for at-risk youth or families at risk of losing custody of their children. Other preventive programs that could lead to long-run savings are being looked at as well.

It is too soon to know if social impact bond programs will produce outcomes that hit their performance management targets and people will conclude that they are a good thing for either governments or investors or both. A variety of questions remain to be answered. Will the programs attract enough investors? Even if they meet their targets will the projected savings actually ever materialize? Will the idea catch on and become more than experimental? Will this new type of bond evolve to become a major source of funding for social welfare programming? These are just a few of the "known unknowns" at this time.

The very idea of relying on private investors is sufficiently provocative that we must put social impact bonds under critical scrutiny, especially given the growing excitement around their potential to become a significant source of welfare state funding. As we have seen, already at this early stage there is great interest in the idea. Many people are excited about these bonds as an innovative source of funding that could provide needed resources for cash-starved governments. The structure of the bonds also holds out the prospect of increasing accountability by not paying for a service unless it proves it is successful in achieving agreed-upon objectives. For some people this is the ultimate neoliberal "win-win-win," where governments get needed funding, investors can make money, and programs come to operate according to the logic of "pay for success." A better funded, more accountable government that delivers services effectively arises as a result of allowing private investors to choose which programs in which they will invest. The government gets better as the investors get to make a profit. The whole thing seems irresistible.

The enthusiasm among private investors matches the interest of governments. For instance, Finance for Good, the Canadian intermediary promoting social impact bonds in their incubator stage, uses dramatic language to talk about them: "We are on the verge of a revolution in social service delivery. Our publically funded system does not have the resources to lead this revolution alone. Social impact bonds…allow private sector champions to make profitable investments to enhance our community and save our government money."[17] Can it be that these new bonds represent the dawning of a golden age of public-private partnerships in which private market actors and public state managers agree to finance public programs with private money in ways that redound to their mutual advantage? Or is all this hype glossing over both internal, technical problems with the mechanics of these bonds and external, substantive problems with the overall neoliberal project of marketizing the state?

RETHINKING SOCIAL IMPACT BONDS AS PUBLIC-PRIVATE PARTNERSHIPS

It is important to understand the context in which social impact bonds are emerging. They are part of the broader neoliberal movement to blur the boundaries between the state and the market in the name of bringing market actors into the state to improve its operations. They are just the latest example of what people are popularly referring to as public-private partnerships.[18] Public-private partnerships (or PPPs as they are often called) can range from privatization via contracting with private providers to offer public services to getting private firms or even private consortia (of multiple firms) to achieve public purposes, from administering public programs to forming consortia of private firms to agree voluntarily to enforce government-designated standards (as in regulations regarding private firm employment practices and other actions). The former (as in private firms delivering public services) are most common at the local level for the provision of basic services that can range from garbage collection to family planning. Increasingly, for-profit providers are relied on for even the incarceration of people convicted of felonies (though for-profit prisons still remain a minority of all prisons). The latter (as in private consortia) are increasingly common in the global economy, especially in creating voluntary programs to enforce agreed-on regulation of production in Third World countries.

Private actors taking steps to fulfill public purposes are also associated with another related development in the neoliberal world that goes by the name corporate social responsibility.[19] (These initiatives often go by the acronym CSRs.) There is overlap between the idea of public-private partnerships and organizations exhibiting corporate social responsibility; international voluntary trade enforcement networks or consortia are actually sometimes referred to as examples of corporate social responsibility or as examples of public-private partnerships. For some analysts, the concept of socially responsible corporations can be considered a type of public-private partnership. The reason why the idea of civic-minded corporations has become so popular is equally ambiguous. First, there is the lack of government in many settings in a globalizing economy. Private actors undertake what they think is the socially responsible thing that should be done but for which people cannot rely on government to enforce (especially in foreign countries where the U.S. government cannot impose its will as a regulator). First World corporations operating in the Third World might find themselves so motivated. They may also engage in these initiatives in order to protect their brand by avoiding being accused of exploiting workers and communities, people and environments.

Beyond public-private partnerships and corporate social responsibility, there is a related third development in the neoliberal blurring of the boundaries between the market and the state referred to as "philanthrocapitalism."[20] Philanthrocapitalism involves more than charity or private philanthropy. Instead, in philanthrocapitalism capitalists engage in philanthropic works but with an economic orientation that expects economic standards of efficiency and effectiveness to be met by those charitable efforts. Philanthrocapitalists do not just give away money for charitable purposes. They expect to see evidence that the money was well spent. Philanthrocapitalism includes the promotion of such ideas as the non-nonprofit, that is, a nonprofit that runs like a for-profit business.[21]

A significant dimension of philanthrocapitalism is found in the way it is changing how private foundations operate by insisting they fund only those public initiatives that can demonstrate positive economic outcomes. Philanthro-capitalist funding by private foundations looks for evidence of return on investment (or what is now commonly called ROI). A prime example is the Bill and Melinda Gates Foundation, which has focused on health and education policy, most controversially spending millions of dollars to promote the "Common Core" curriculum for public schools around the country.[22]

These three ideas, public-private partnerships, corporate social responsibility, and philanthrocapitalism, reflect neoliberalism's practice of blurring the boundary between the private and public sectors to get the latter to operate in market-compliant ways in the name of helping to promote market discipline in society overall. They blur the boundary between the public and the private either by marketizing public operations or publicly orienting private activities so that in either case they achieve public purposes based on market-based approaches. Social impact bonds fit this model perfectly. They reflect all three of these ideas. They involve public-private partnerships, use actors engaging in corporate social responsibility, and reflect efforts to practice philanthrocapitalism.

Given these definitions of public-private partnerships, corporate social responsibility, and philanthrocapitalism, social impact bonds could be seen as a manifestation of a very refreshing turn to beneficence within the neoliberal orientation. Yet the enthusiasm for these bonds should actually give us pause. The rush to adopt them comes at a very desperate time for the state, when governments are starved for cash and the antitax movement has deprived it of stable sources of funding. Desperation can lead people away from asking the difficult questions that need to be asked. In fact, the more we learn about these bonds, the more reasons there are to step back and think critically about this way of financing human services.

The history of public-private partnerships provides a factual track record that should raise concerns about this neoliberal financialization of human services. Bringing the private sector into government has most often led to achieving neither greater efficiencies nor improved effectiveness.[23] Activities of socially responsible corporations have often ended up being self-serving operations designed to legitimize a brand more than to actually advance the common good.[24] And philanthrocapitalism all too often involves wealthy elites imposing market discipline in order to achieve what they want done rather than what ordinary citizens would say we need.[25]

That checkered history should give us pause when it comes to social impact bonds. In particular it should make us wary that weaknesses in the operation of the bonds can potentially be exploited for private gain. At a minimum, it should raise some basic questions ranging from technical issues to substantive problems. For instance, bonds could:

1. encourage a preference for programs with clear, measureable objectives even if these are not focused on the most important social welfare issues that need to be addressed;
2. induce program administrators to aim at meeting measureable objectives but ignore other important social welfare policy goals;
3. discourage the more reliable taxpayer funding for social welfare programs; and
4. shift power from citizens, taxpayers, and voters to investors such that we need to worry about how capitalism comes to trump democracy.

The first two of these are technical issues internal to the operations of social impact bonds and the last two are probably the most significant substantive issues regarding the external implications of the turn to these bonds. I examine the first two technical issues in the next section before proceeding to the more substantive issues.

Social Impact Bonds Measurement Problems: Beyond Creaming and Suboptimizing

Performance measurement problems keep raising their hydra head in the age of neoliberalization.[26] As with high-stakes testing under No Child Left Behind and performance benchmarks in other human service programs (as discussed in chapters 5 and 6), social impact bonds offer really nothing new in this regard, other than doubling down on relying on performance measurement. This time performance measurement is being relied on for deciding whether the bond-funded experimental, preventive programs are successful enough that the government then needs to pay back investors with interest on the assumption that projected savings will eventually be realized.

The real problem here is not actually that programs will fail but that they will succeed, at least according to the performance measurement scheme. This is a problem that goes beyond suboptimizing and creaming to make a program seemingly hit its benchmark when in fact it has not. Instead, the larger problem of performance measurement in bonds is that hitting a performance benchmark, like reducing the recidivism rate for ex-felons or juveniles, does not necessarily mean the projected savings will actually ever materialize.

Doubling down on performance measurement only makes this irony more likely. With bonds, performance measures take on heightened significance. Everyone is invested in meeting the performance benchmark. Programs become all the more likely to be restructured to ensure that target is hit, perhaps at the expense of just about everything else worth doing in a program. Program changes are all the more likely to include giving less emphasis to other important, but perhaps less measureable, program objectives to the point at which even though the performance benchmark is met, the substantive effects of the program are diminished, reducing the likelihood that the projected savings will actually ever be realized. By the time that is discovered, however, the investors have been repaid and the government is left holding the bag. The measurement problems of bonds go well beyond the problems of creaming and suboptimizing that are widely discussed in the public management literature (see chapters 5 and 6).

CROWDING OUT CONVENTIONAL SOCIAL WELFARE FUNDING: WHAT WORKS VERSUS WHAT'S RIGHT

Preventing social and economic problems before they emerge has merit. Experimenting with different approaches does as well. Yet we need to ask why the bond-funded programs that are currently being rolled out focus only on preventive programs that address problems already manifest in the populations they serve. The whole approach seems to recoin the phrase "a day late and a dollar short." There is the risk in emphasizing these sorts of palliative programs that social impact bonds will be associated with attempts to forgo addressing the fundamental, political-economic, structural roots of poverty. These bonds could become yet another way that social welfare policy is about avoiding, covering up, mystifying, and denying what needs to be done to address persistent poverty as an enduring feature of the U.S. social order.

This in fact is a long-standing problem with social welfare policy in the United States and social impact bonds are just a new, neoliberal way to finance this type of indirection in an age of austerity and antitax sentiment. The whole idea that we need to conduct experiments on programs for the poor reflects several well-established practices in U.S. social welfare policy-making that with hindsight seem now nothing less than diversionary.[27] There are several dimensions to this misdirection.

First, the emphasis on experimentation reflects the shift away from grounding social welfare policies in rights and entitlements that citizens should get in order to ensure a decent standard of living. The trend for more than thirty years has been to give greater emphasis not to normative questions of what is right and who has what rights, but instead to empirical questions of what is factually correct and which programs work better. The "what works" agenda has replaced the "what's right" agenda. Second, this shift to the "what works" agenda reinforces the idea that the problems of poverty have mysterious causal pathways and experimental programs must be developed to figure out how to get at the causes and provide effective responses.

While it is undoubtedly true that the "what's right" and "what works" agendas are not inherently mutually exclusive, undue emphasis on experimentation can risk mystifying the issue of poverty, making it out to be a puzzle that can only be solved if we find the right programs that are proven to save money. We risk losing sight of the idea that poverty should be seen as a basic denial of rights, and that all humans should be protected as much as possible from this denial by their governments regardless of the costs (regardless whether existing programs are the most efficient or not).

Third, the fact that bond experiments have economic savings as their overriding benchmark for success is worrisome in its own right. The emphasis on saving money can potentially overshadow the commitment to doing good and actually helping people. Further, the prospect of savings appears only after poverty-related problems have been allowed to fester—something that is likely to happen once there is a shift away from doing "what's right" to focusing on "what works." Social impact bond experimentation therefore ineluctably constrains poverty reduction to only those efforts that are proven to save money by combatting problems they have been allowed to grow to the point that government must reluctantly consider requests that something be done to stop growing expenditures.

It is more than interesting that over the last few decades experimentation with addressing some people's needs continues to be accepted as legitimate without serious consideration of the deprivation and harm it poses for some of the needy who participate in these trials. We do not really experiment with various forms of providing Social Security to the elderly. We consider their right to collect those income transfers as having been earned and basically beyond the pale of political contestation. There has been a push over the years to privatize Social Security and let everyone invest their contributions themselves; however, tampering with Social Security in this way is consistently denigrated by popular majorities and the proposals from the marketers get dropped. Here is an instance where neoliberal marketization has confronted serious opposition on the grounds that Social Security benefits are an entitlement that has been earned and should not be taken away. Yet when it comes to the non-aged poor, the story is different. They are always already dismissed as the undeserving other who has not earned rights to benefits and whose poverty is the poor's own private responsibility. In this case, the government is authorized to experiment on possible solutions short of giving the poor entitlement rights to live a life outside poverty.

The implications for the politics of policymaking are perhaps the most worrisome. Well before bond funding of experimental programs became the next big neoliberal thing, Robin Rogers-Dillon insightfully noted, "It would be a bitter irony if the form and language of policy experimentation, promoted by academics and intellectuals to make policy choices more rational and transparent, created a back channel through which the American welfare state could be fundamentally altered with little public notice or debate."[28] In fact, one danger of social impact bonds, should they become increasingly popular, is that they will become a back channel for defunding mainline social welfare programs via taxation and mandatory contributions and lead to social welfare policy increasingly being funded by private investors. Rather than enhancing funding for social welfare initiatives, bonds could lead to crowding out public funding for basic social welfare programs, perhaps even eventually leading to the privatization of the sacred cow of Social Security.

Social impact bonds may discourage conventional funding for social welfare programming, if policymakers start to think that they should not fund programs unless they show enough promise to attract investor funding. This type of circular thinking can set in once bond funding starts to create its own form of path dependency with a negative policy feedback loop that discourages more traditional forms of funding on the grounds that that type of funding cannot be counted to deliver results like those promised by the bonds. Social impact bonds reinforce the idea that the state should not be funding social welfare policies, whether in the form of benefits or services, unless the policies have been tested and evaluated as successful in achieving specified objectives. This is a distinct possibility if "what works" thinking displaces an orientation to social welfare on the basis of "what's right," as in the basic right to live at a decent standard of living. From the shift to the "what works" agenda, it is a short step to the idea that all social welfare policies should be put under the experimental microscope and funded by private investors who decide which policies merit their backing. Once we get to that point, we have put the very idea of entitlement rights on the auction block and paved the way for investors to have a disproportionate say in what social welfare services and benefits will or will not be funded.

With Social Impact Bonds, Capitalism Trumps Democracy

Social impact bonds are not just an economic innovation; they have political consequences as well. They are a form of capitalism that has implications for democracy. Given their recent rollout, it may be too soon to evaluate the performance of bond-funded programs, and these bonds may never become so popular that we need concern ourselves with the threat they pose to ensuring there is appropriate funding for basic social welfare programs. Yet it is never too soon to examine the threats the very idea of social impact bonds pose for democracy. Such scrutiny is more than warranted because the way these bonds operate tells us a lot about the underlying logic of neoliberalism and the consequences that marketization poses for the welfare state going forward.

In other words, irrespective of whether bond-funded programs meet their performance targets, or perhaps especially if that is the case, we need to think about the political implications of this economic innovation. What happens to public policymaking once we start relying on private investors to decide which programs will be funded? The real back channel here might be that bonds, intentionally or not, become a public policymaking Trojan Horse for private investors. The more the state comes to rely on bonds for funding social welfare programs the greater the risk that that there will be a shift in power to private investors to decide what types of programs with which providers will be funded. Bonds pose the possibility that neoliberal marketization of the state ultimately leads to the private investor class getting to dominate the public policymaking process to an even greater extent than it already does.[29]

There is the distinct possibility that the neoliberal marketization of the state not only makes for questionable public policy but that it more critically makes for very troublesome politics. The neoliberal marketization of social welfare policy raises legitimate concerns that programs will get implemented in ways that overly insist on market logic to serve market purposes. Further, there are serious issues concerning the democratic implications of neoliberal marketization. We need to ask whether neoliberal marketizing initiatives like social impact bonds will lead to undermining our ability to promote democratic public policymaking, where citizens, taxpayers, and voters get to decide which social welfare policies will be funded and how. There is the distinct possibility that neoliberal marketizing efforts like bonds will make it less likely that the mass public via their elected representatives will be able to insist on social welfare policies that give people entitlement rights to live decently irrespective of whether the programs have been proven in experiments to be economically efficient and therefore can attract investor funding. These issues point to the ultimate form of privatization posed by neoliberal marketizing initiatives like social impact bonds. The real risk of neoliberal marketization is that we privatize public policymaking itself, not just the administration of the programs created by the public policymaking process. The public policymaking process is supposed to be open, transparent, and, most critically, democratic. Neoliberal marketization might well turn the process into a series of private decisions, made undemocratically by a select few private investors who negotiate with public officials about which programs they are willing to fund at what cost to the government.

While we might want to say that this dystopian nightmare of undemocratic decision making is already the reality in the age of neoliberal inequality, neoliberal marketizing practices like social impact bonds will enshrine that nightmare as our legitimate, legally authorized process for making public policy. Rule by economic elites will go from something that must be denied in public discourse to being something that can be publicly affirmed. That would undoubtedly have profound implications for democracy. Going forward we need to track the increasing popularity of social impact bonds not just in terms of their economic effects on funding public programs but also for their political effects on the ability of ordinary people to insist on a democratic public policymaking process.

Conclusion

Social impact bonds were originally conceived as a way to attract outside funding for promising experimental programs that could prevent social problems from worsening and as a result allow governments to reap long-term savings in reduced social welfare costs. Yet they have only now in an age of austerity started to be implemented as cash-starved governments beaten down by the antitax movement are forced to go hat in hand to private investors. It almost seems like extortion. First, you starve the beast; then you create a situation where the beast must beg for sustenance via the private investor market just to fund social welfare programs to attack problems that have been allowed to fester because we denied people basic entitlement rights in the first place. Neoliberal public policymaking has its own logic (which is not so logical).

Social impact bonds represent a dramatic instance of how neoliberal social welfare policy reform involves marketizing state operations. Market logic becomes the primary orientation in such programs and market actors come to play a significant role in social welfare policymaking and implementation. They legitimize experimenting with aid to the poor, making it ever more contingent on demonstrating economic efficiency in the form of saving the government money and economic efficacy in producing market-compliant actors. It is the latest way to discipline service providers and clients alike to adhere to market strictures above all else in the provision of human services.

There are technical challenges in implementing social impact bonds, including especially the reliance on questionable practices for determining whether programs have achieved negotiated performance targets. Yet the real challenges posed by these bonds occur not so much when the programs fail to meet their benchmarks and are deemed to have failed, but rather when they are deemed successful according to the performance standards in place. Gaming the system, via suboptimizing and creaming in particular, can result in programs being assessed as producing projected savings that will never materialize. But we might never know that until long after investors have been paid with money the state never gets to accrue. Social impact bonds could be therefore also characterized as a financing bait and switch. We loan you money that you have to repay only if the funded program achieves its performance objectives, even if meeting those objectives never actually produces the savings that are projected. Financializing social welfare policymaking has its own logic (which also is not so logical).

Social impact bonds are touted as manifestations of a new philanthro-capitalism, in which market actors practice corporate social responsibility by forming public-private partnerships with government to finance social welfare programs. Yet these bonds need to be examined with a critical eye; such examination remains in short supply as the excitement over these bonds as a neoliberal innovation has yet to abate. Once we take a critical eye toward bonds as a funding source for social welfare programs, we see they could well prove to be a back channel that undermines both social welfare entitlement rights and democratic decision making.

If social impact bonds become a prominent means to financing social welfare policies, we would need to monitor closely who gets to have the most influence over what social welfare policies are funded and to what effect. The potential political implications are possibly greater than the economic effects. As the next big neoliberal thing, social impact bonds point to how marketizing state operations poses threats to democratic decision making by accelerating the ongoing transfer of political power to the financial sector, thereby allowing it to dominate the public policymaking process. The next big neoliberal thing is here. It involves more than just marketizing state social welfare operations to get both program administrators and clients to be market compliant. It points to marketizing the public policymaking process itself, whereby capitalism trumps democracy. We must watch the rollout of social impact bonds with a critical eye for its political implications above all else.

GETTING BEYOND NEOLIBERALISM

THE ROAD TO RADICAL INCREMENTALISM

We live in dark times. A transformed economy has decoupled growth and wages, producing more riches for an elite few while many others confront a declining standard of living and a reduced quality of life. The resulting economic inequality has been translated into rapidly growing inequities in political influence that are being used to prevent public policy from addressing the malfunctioning economy and alleviating the hardships being imposed on ordinary Americans. Instead, we witness the continuing neoliberalization of social welfare policy, where a hollowed out and bankrupted welfare state must turn over decision-making power to private investors so as to raise what little financing it can from speculators, philanthropists, and corporate entrepreneurs. These private actors claim that their schemes for marketizing state operations are actually grounded in a commitment to social responsibility. The failures of neoliberalization and the turn to market-based public policies do not produce a return to a publicly funded welfare state but instead, the deficiencies of neoliberalized social welfare programming simply beget more neoliberalism. Neoliberalism has become a machine that moves of its own accord. It is the accepted logic of our time. It is a "zombie neoliberalism" that needs no legitimation other than that it offers new approaches to attack the problems its prior efforts ironically put in place.[1] We must marketize the state, and incentivize and sanction providers and clients alike. We must allow market logic to reign supreme. As a result, inexorably an ethic of private gain becomes the basis for public policymaking writ large. The return of ordinary capitalism post the Great Recession produces an inequitable economy where neoliberalism is the new normal.[2]

Today, there is growing concern about the inequities of neoliberal policies that manage poverty populations by disciplining them to be market compliant, but leave them bereft of economic opportunity. Yet efforts to move beyond neoliberalism must of necessity take into account the political constraints that neoliberalization had previously produced. We cannot simply wish neoliberalism away. It is firmly entrenched in the major institutions of society, social and political, as well as economic. In particular, there is a need to recognize that efforts to improve social welfare policy in the current period take place under the long shadow of decades of work to marketize state operations. Post–Great Recession, the return to a more ordinary capitalism occurs whereby neoliberalism is the new normal. Given the persistent preference for market-based approaches to public policymaking, there may be a need to recognize how deeply embedded the neoliberal philosophy has become in political-economic deliberations. We may need to work through rather than around neoliberal policies to address the inequities they create.

Protests like Occupy Wall Street and subsequent mobilizations such as Black Lives Matter on the issue of racialized policing are a critical ingredient of a more involved policy process. In discussing Black Lives Matter, Charles Blow has written: "[R]aising an issue to the point where it can no longer be ignored is the grist for the policy mill. Visibility and vocalization have value. In the same way that Occupy Wall Street forever elevated that concept of income inequality, the Black Lives Matter protesters have elevated the idea of inequity in policing as it relates to minority communities."[3] In other words, naming the problem has helped. Take the generic problem of neoliberalism itself. "Neoliberalism" is now increasingly a term that points to a recognizable problem—marketization of the state.

Yet more than naming is in order. We need strategy. The emerging struggle over neoliberalization today necessitates what I call "radical incrementalism," where we push for as much change as possible recognizing that elites will at best offer limited concessions that can nonetheless, we hope, be used to lay the groundwork for more ambitious transformations down the road. In the current period, this means recognizing that neoliberal social welfare policies are deeply path-dependent and, even in a time of crisis, cannot simply be replaced but must be more strategically countered. This also means recognizing that the most effective responses are likely to be grounded in everyday forms of resistance that work through rather than simply ignore neoliberalism as the ascendant practical rationality for getting things done in the public sector today.[4] Oppositional politics must of necessity, I would argue, take context into account when promoting social, economic, and political inclusion of marginalized groups.[5] In other words, a politics of radical incrementalism needs to be given serious consideration even if it is fraught with all kinds of pitfalls. The following analysis is designed to demonstrate the need to take radical incrementalism seriously, as the political orientation for our times.

Multilevel Mobilizing

A number of people on the left side of the political spectrum have sporadically voiced concern about the lack of sustained response to the new normal of neoliberalized inequality.[6] Their discontent joins that of the Right. Both Occupy and the Tea Party represent profound disappointment with the pervasive reality of a malfunctioning economy. We could say with confidence that there is as much melancholia on the Left as there is on the Right. While the Right bemoans the loss of the possibility of adhering to the ideal of the self-sufficient self, the Left longs for a return to a revitalized labor movement that can provide a center of gravity for a concerted takeover of the state to turn back the juggernaut of neoliberalism. The protests of Occupy are seen by many on the left as too episodic and disorganized to produce the political mobilization needed. Instead, we are told we must take a generation to build an organized Left that can compete for state power via elections and other means.

Yet the insistence that the Left exclusively focus on pulling back to organize on a grand scale for the long haul of structural change of the entire political-economic system relies too heavily on a false dichotomy that sets the Left up first for long-time irrelevance and ultimately permanent failure. The whole-cloth condemnation of the Left as lacking the willingness to do the difficult work of organizing along class lines overlooks the failures to do just that for several decades now. These failures are not the result of a lack of trying but of the increasing difficulties of doing so in a transformed economy. Today, the working class is a very diverse group of precarious workers, not just diverse racially and ethnically but divided by citizenship as well. It is more female than previously and more concentrated in human services and feminized work where caring relationships are emphasized, perhaps making labor less available to be organized for aggressive pushback against the forces producing its subordination.[7] Further, the precarity that is held in common across class lines compounds difficulties in organizing different types of workers in different classes. Casualization of work means different things for different types of workers and organizing in labor unions with an aim to form a popular labor party seems quite daunting. Casualized workers are dispersed as much as they are diversified, decreasingly on site together, especially as they work from home in the emerging "share economy."[8] To be sure, these micro-earners could join with the much more numerous conventional laborers to protest their conditions, just as fast-food workers have done with some frequency in recent years.[9] Yet we need to note that the state has increased its policing of protesters while at the same time making labor organizing that much more difficult.[10] And while public opinion of unions has rebounded from historic lows during the onset of the Great Recession, membership continues to decline. Today only about one in ten workers belongs to a union.[11]

Under these conditions, it seems now long past time to confront the reality that there is no going back to the halcyon days of union organizing. While it is commonplace to emphasize the importance of labor unions in working on behalf of improving the well-being of ordinary people, the lack of labor union militancy over time is itself a sign of how unlikely labor organizing is as a site for a sustained movement for political change today. Figure 8.1 shows the near total disappearance of strike activity by unions over the last thirty years. The most promising labor actions in recent years have been the wildcat strikes by ununionized fast-food workers, the sporadic efforts to unionize graduate students, and the initiation of attempts to give college athletes the right to form unions. Tammy Klein observes:

> So while the term 'labor movement' may still evoke midcentury images of blue-collar industrial organizing, today's version proceeds outside the confines of collective bargaining agreements. Put another way, labor now

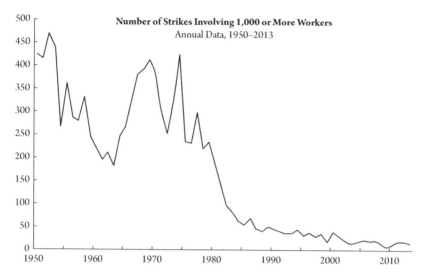

Figure 8.1 Number of Strikes Involving 1,000 or More Workers, 1950–2013. (http://lbo-news.com/2014/04/02/a-working-class-disarmed/).

faces a kind of post-legal environment. Recent court decisions have further weakened the National Labor Relations Act, which theoretically safeguards the right to organize, and Title VII [of the Civil Rights Act], which protects workers from discrimination.[12]

This transformed landscape suggests traditional labor organizing strategies must be revised radically. We must turn to a more coalitional politics that can bring diverse groups of people together, the status-anxious middle class, with the immigrant workers, documented and not, along with the unemployable and the unemployed, students joined with workers, and consumers with producers, all in the name of addressing the inequities of the transformed economy. An Occupy-like movement that celebrates how diverse "bodies in alliance" might be a better model than that touted by melancholic critics on the left who long to recreate the past successes of the labor movement.[13]

The failure to appreciate how the Occupy Left is already working post-Occupy on issues of debt, causualization, inequality, and related areas suggests a failure to appreciate the necessity of what I have been calling a "radical incrementalism" that operates, more rhizomatically than systematically, on multiple levels as a way to confront the reality of neoliberalism.[14] Multilevel radical incrementalism that synergistically integrates change efforts in protest movements, political party organizing, public policymaking, and program implementation enables us to work to make things better now in ways that lay the foundation for a better future.[15] Such synergistic activities involve working through neoliberalism rather than stubbornly denying it as the pervasive reality of our era. Yet sometimes we are too blinded by our past to appreciate what is needed in the present (to achieve a better future).

The Movement of Movements: The Occupy Left Versus the Organized Left

In the current era, there is much intellectual, if not political, credibility to be gained by refusing to practice the multilevel mobilizing of an Occupy Left and subsequent efforts like Black Lives Matter. There is a growing consensus that Occupy was a failure and its current extensions just fritter away energy that should be concentrated on building an organized Left that can push successfully for wholesale change.[16] Some on the left refuse to work with diverse groups on their different issues in real time. Instead, they insist on taking the long view that says such work is a distraction to the larger and critical cause of organizing for fundamental transformation of the existing political-economic system.

A major concern for this faction is maintaining the purity of the Left, striving to remain uncontaminated by the compromises of coalitional politics that are necessary when addressing the myriad of specific issues associated with the inequities of neoliberalism.[17] In this way, activism remains true to the tradition of radical politics as it was practiced during the age of revolution and especially the heyday of communist organizing. Sometimes this nostalgia for the history of radical politics can lead to blaming the victim, this time not so much blaming the poor for their own poverty but blaming the subordinated for their failure to organize effectively to enact fundamental change.[18]

Sometimes, the nostalgia for "one big union" to challenge the capitalist power structure is born of letting historical understanding crowd out the exigencies of the moment. In discussing the problem of combining scholarship and activism among leftist academics in the humanities, Bruce Robbins makes a point that has direct relevance to the academics of the organized Left as I am characterizing it. He asserts: "One trap the Left faces, at least to the extent that that Left is located in the academy, is an overemphasis on making a political program out of what it already does for a living."[19] Robbins is talking about bringing too much history into efforts to mobilize people who are focused on immediate concerns. Knowing about the history of the labor movement surely could help members of the precariat think about how to address their plight; from the perspective of ordinary citizens, they may not be all that open to hearing all that history when they are mostly concerned about landing a job once their unemployment has been cut off and they have had to declare bankruptcy. The bottom-up perspective encourages us to see things the way they do. And that might mean pushing to raise the minimum wage rather than holding out for the demise of capitalism or the adoption of a basic income.

Too much history can be matched with too much theory.[20] Too often today, the organized Left is joined by the theoretical Left. An overemphasis on theory produces what John Gunnell calls "epistemic privilege," that is, the idea that theory comes first and underwrites and authorizes the action that follows. Exercising epistemic privilege involves unquestioned acceptance of the cliché that without a sound theory there can never be effective political action.[21] Yet it is questionable to what extent we need to be able to theorize why things are the way they are to be able to do something about them. Theory is undoubtedly important for placing political action in context, deepening meaning, and clarifying the conditions of political possibility.[22] Yet an overemphasis on theory can be politically paralyzing. The preoccupation with theory can undermine the needed focus on strategy,[23] especially when theory is concerned with the big picture of understanding the current situation overall and over time, and strategy is more narrowly focused on what will connect with ordinary people's immediate concerns as they struggle to cope with the effects of a neoliberalizing economy.[24]

In other words, being an academic can get in the way of being an activist. A preoccupation with theory can distract us from working to achieve modest but worthwhile reforms that directly address people's immediate concerns. This is doubly unfortunate if those reforms actually work to lay the groundwork for larger, transformational change in the future. Epistemic privilege can lead us away from the radical incrementalism of making small, realistic changes now that can lay the groundwork for larger ones down the road.

In fact, the very idea of modest reform can be dismissed by those seeking more dramatic change because it poses the real possibility that it will defuse anger among the politically diverse precariat and thereby forestall the more dramatic systemic change that is needed to put the inequities of the new

normal of neoliberalism safely behind us. While largely limited to the ruminations of bloggers, it seems that many on the left have their own crisis
strategy that is premised on the idea that if things get bad enough, spreading
from the lower to the middle classes, mass mobilization against the existing
structure of power will finally gain traction and political transformation will
result. Yet this crisis strategy is indebted to the very same dichotomous thinking
that prevents some on the left from appreciating the value, and even the need,
to mobilize on multiple levels. It is a crisis strategy that trades off addressing
people's immediate needs in the short run for building up popular support
for more dramatic change in the long run. It pits a "politics of survival" against
a "politics of social change," seeing them as mutually exclusive.[25]

This bloggers' crisis strategy, however, seems at best an imagined strategy
that no one is really actively working to execute (especially since it would
impose growing hardship on the very people whom the Left wants to help).
Yet even those among the Occupy Left are vulnerable to this type of misplaced crisis thinking. Chris Hayes, in his otherwise thoughtful examination
of U.S. politics in the current age of hyperinequality, looks to a radicalized
middle class that has become frustrated with its ability to move ahead.[26] Hayes
writes:

> Crisis is not something to be longed for or embraced: as we've seen, war,
> financial crisis, natural disaster visit their most punitive blows upon the
> weakest, the poorest, the least powerful members of society. But political
> crises, moments when the keystone of authority of some major governing
> institution is whisked away like a Jenga block, can produce a tumbling cas-
> cade of new forms of politics. We've been looking at the tower for so long
> we forget it's made of blocks; we forget it can be put back together in a
> different way.[27]

Hayes sees the economic malaise spreading upward to the point that the privileged with resources can now be mobilized to redress the situation and push
for dramatic change. While the middle classes can indeed be a source of change,
especially today (see chapter 2), this type of top-down, elite-driven political
mobilization is vulnerable to being defused by concessions for those higher
up at the expense of those below them.

Yet a better crisis strategy actually was implemented. It was made famous
by Richard Cloward and Frances Fox Piven as the central means of mobilizing

support in the 1960s for reform of the welfare system and transition to a guaranteed income.[28] It was premised on a win-win that saw a politics of survival and a politics of social change as working synergistically. Piven and Cloward premised their strategy on their research, which estimated that about half of those eligible for welfare nationwide were not receiving it. If everyone who was eligible enrolled it would overload the system, create a crisis, and force elites to consider moving to a better system such as a guaranteed income (now called a basic income). The strategy worked in good part, with millions of people getting public assistance and Congress twice voting on a guaranteed income plan that was proposed by President Richard Nixon. While the plan was never adopted, many people got aid in the process. Signing up people for welfare helped address their immediate needs while growing membership in the cause for welfare rights intensified concern in the public that something had to be done to transform the broken system of aiding the poor. A politics of survival and a politics of social change were not pitted against each other; choosing one over the other was not required. Instead, the real crisis strategy was premised on the idea the two could work together synergistically.

This confusion about what is an effective crisis strategy is premised on overly dichotomous thinking that leads many on the left away from multi-level mobilizing. It also might explain why they are often better at resisting anything less than total transformation to a new society than in finding ways to support improvements that reduce people's suffering in the here and now. This resistance to reform also reflects nostalgic preoccupations with a lost past, when the revolution by the laboring classes was a real possibility. In contrast today the diverse people whose economic condition is made precarious by the changing economy are less available to be organized for mass mobilization on behalf of a fundamental transformation of the inequitable neoliberal political economy. As a result, many on the left are at risk of passing up on politics as it actually occurs today and instead contenting themselves with perfecting theoretical purity. Even left-leaning alternative political parties, such as the initially quite successful Working Families Party, get dismissed as not deserving of support as soon as the party makes questionable compromises as part of the effort to leverage power within the existing system.[29] In the hothouse environment born of frustration over the Left's inability to make a concerted and effective effort for transformational change, any misstep potentially becomes an excuse for continued inaction. Sometimes it seems the only political action the purists would support is a coup. They long for days when revolution was a real option. In this way, the Left continues to practice one of its more dominant forms of melancholia.

We may, however, come to look nostalgically on the academic Left, regardless of its disabling preoccupations. Today, that group is rapidly being replaced by academics fortunate enough to secure appointments but too insecure in them to dare to think of combining activism and scholarship.[30] This new generation is not even positioned to freely protest its own plight in the face of the ongoing corporatization of the academy, let alone start to work with ordinary Americans outside the academy who suffer the worst effects of the inequitable neoliberal economy. Confronting growing professional and institutional pressures from performance measurement schemes to publish in "high-impact" journals (i.e., highly cited, not highly influential politically), many academics now must publish constantly; however, their work is often assiduously theoretical and methodically arcane, as well as apolitical and disconnected from ongoing political struggle. Many of these younger academics are of the Left in their hearts and minds, but not on the printed page or in the streets.

Too often an insistence on organizing only for dramatic change can lead to immobilization on the grounds that proposed actions are less than entirely consistent with some blueprint about what is to be done to produce long-term structural change of society. Instead activism should be more humble, accepting that not all contingencies can be anticipated and social movement mobilization is not entirely predictable and cannot be planned out before it occurs.[31] In particular, the Left needs to stop making political action an either/or proposition and begin to think seriously about how political mobilization on multiple levels—protests, parties, policy, and program administration—can be made to work together to bring into being a better world for those suffering on the bottom of the socioeconomic ladder.

Radical movement politics in a variety of forms is what is needed today. Efforts focused on dramatic regime change still have their place, especially when there is a gnawing need to call out injustice and identify its structural sources embedded in the very foundations of the existing neoliberalized society. Yet what are we to do in the meantime? Is it possible to help alleviate suffering even while we work for more fundamental change? The ongoing resistance to anything less than wholesale societal change stems from the fact that it poses a falsely stark choice between radical movement politics and more conventional electoral and policy politics. This kind of thinking is overly dichotomous and fails to appreciate that mobilizing for change to redress the injustices of the neoliberalized economy does not always involve seeing the options as mutually exclusive.[32]

In fact, many activists today appreciate and participate in the diversity of movements involved in creating noteworthy changes in cultural practices, social relations, economics and politics.[33] Much of the energy of these movements comes from outside the academy where people are not weighed down with theoretical preoccupations. When big ideas, theory included, get to matter are when ordinary people confronting their difficulties in their everyday lives come to see the relevance of those ideas.[34] Today, there is a veritable movement of movements where change efforts take a diversity of forms, with some even working with, rather than against, the market system in ways that create more freedom and less oppression for ordinary people.[35] Just as we should not see protest politics and electoral politics as mutually exclusive, so should we learn to appreciate the value of a radical incrementalism that works to address people's problems in the here and now, while laying the groundwork for larger political transformation in the future. The protest politics of Occupy Wall Street has contributed to creating a context for the electoral successes of candidates such as Bill de Blasio, who became mayor of New York City with the support of the Working Families Party, which has strong ties to Occupy movement participants.[36] How de Blasio works with protest groups, including those that have become embroiled in the volatile issue of racialized policing, suggests real challenges but also hope for change.[37] Radical incrementalism suggests just this kind of synergy. It combines a politics of survival with a politics of social change to get significant improvements in state policy, following the successful model of welfare mobilization in the 1960s.[38]

THE ROAD TO RADICAL INCREMENTALISM

Radical incrementalism is not really an option: it is the prevailing reality of politics. It realistically recognizes the economic, social, and political constraints that limit mobilization on behalf of radical change. It also is based on an appreciation often shared by proponents for radical change that efforts at sustained political mobilization are not something that happen overnight. Instead, it works to help people in the short run within existing constraints but in ways that make more dramatic political transformation eventually more likely.

As much as people on the left hope for a radical swing away from neoliberal social welfare programming in the current era, the arc of history under U.S. capitalism suggests a more modest process of incrementalism. Incrementalism is defined in the public policy literature as a process of policymaking where a series of small remedial, corrective steps enable change in existing policy.[39] Yet the criticism of incrementalism is that it amounts to no more than tinkering with the existing system in ways that do nothing more than fine-tune the status quo. Perfecting neoliberalism means little more than making the ascendant disciplinary regime more effective in managing the poverty population and by extension everyone else who is made economically precarious by the transformed economy.[40] Incremental changes in neoliberal policies can result in nothing more than improving the system for embedding market logic more deeply into society and our daily lives.[41] It could amount to no more than perfecting the system for incentivizing market-consonant behavior in ways that end up leaving most people having to make do with the inadequate resources and opportunities afforded them in a changing economy.

Nonetheless, especially in an age of extreme political polarization that begets policy gridlock, incrementalism may be the prevailing reality more than ever. Under these conditions, it may be that ideas about more dramatic change need to be tempered with the reality of working for more limited changes that nonetheless do more than reinforce the existing system.[42] The issue then becomes how to practice a radical incrementalism.[43] By "radical incrementalism," I mean a process in which people push for change recognizing it will not necessarily be as large as they might like but also in which small changes can do more than fine-tune the existing system. Radical incrementalism is not about tweaking what is already in place to help perpetuate the status quo and the existing structure of power. It rejects changes that in all likelihood are going to lead to the continuation of the very problems that people are trying to address. Instead, the small changes of radical incrementalism lay the groundwork for further changes that over time can help build to a transformation of the existing structure of power, the source of the problems being attacked.[44] The key then is that when pushing for change as activists we must be able to distinguish radical incrementalism from the status-quo-reinforcing incrementalism most often offered by elites. This is often not easy but the goal is to try as much as possible to resist the co-optation elites will seek to gain by making minimal concessions. That is the focus we need today in an era of political gridlock born of polarization that stems in no small part from the wealthy using their wealth to block constructive responses to address the problems extreme inequality creates.

André Gorz highlighted the challenge in distinguishing between status quo incrementalism and radical incrementalism in his own terms when he distinguished what he called "non-reformist reform" from "reformist reform."[45] Gorz recognized that what distinguished progressive reform from status-quo-reinforcing reform was not easy to always identify, but nonreformist reforms are the progressive reforms that are essentially laying the groundwork to get beyond the inequities of capitalism by restructuring power relations. More recently David Harvey has called for appreciating the value of what he calls "revolutionary reforms" that provide the basis for challenging capitalist power over time.[46] Radical incrementalism similarly involves making small changes that lay the basis for restructuring embedded power relations that prevent more ambitious changes from happening.[47]

Radical incrementalism is focused on changing power relationships but it is not against the use of power, and it is focused on finding ways for government and the governance of populations to work to improve the lives of ordinary people. It does not simply resist oppressive state power, it seeks to bend it toward enhancing the conditions under which people live with, participate in, and benefit from state power. Radical incrementalism works to offer constructive answers to such questions as: what type of governance is appropriate for ordinary people today and how can we rework power relations to realize it?[48]

Radical incrementalism can be practiced on multiple levels and across different dimensions of the policy process. It can involve protest movements adroitly deciding to accept particular concessions elites offer to quell dissent.[49] It can also involve participating in electoral campaigns for candidates who resist capitulating to conventional politics as usual. It can involve pushing for changes in public policy that redistribute power and lay the foundation for broader changes in the future. Reallocating resources, such as to improve wages so that people can do more than just survive but also be better positioned to participate in the political process, is but one example.

Radical incrementalism can involve its own crisis strategy, just as it did with the welfare rights movement where improving access to benefits laid the groundwork for pushing for a guaranteed income. Radical incrementalism can exist within programs implementing public policies so as to implement them in ways that are more supportive of clients. Lisa Dodson's idea of a "moral underground" resonates with Carolyn and Martin Needleman's old idea of "guerrillas in the bureaucracy," where front-line workers bend the rules and develop workarounds so that clients are treated better.[50] Radical incrementalism need not be limited strictly to the state; it can involve working for change within civil society and even markets (often with supportive state action to enable those changes).[51] In this way, we can see how there are a variety of opportunities to practice radical incrementalism in ordinary everyday life with the result that conditions for improvements in people's well-being work together to lay the foundation to more fundamental social and economic transformation. The return of ordinary capitalism with neoliberalism as the new normal need not mean the end of politics; it means we need to start practicing radical incrementalism across multiple levels and different dimensions of the contemporary political scene.

That is not to say that the contemporary scene is an attractive one for progressive activists. Today, all kinds of deleterious political initiatives are afoot to marginalize the ability of ordinary people to address their increasing subordination. In fact, a lot of politics today is not just plain old-fashioned, status-quo-reinforcing incrementalism, but something much more insidious. Examples of status-quo-reinforcing incrementalism abound. Progress is stuck in enacting increases in minimum-wage laws. We could speed this up, while resisting the corresponding reductions in the earned income tax credit that result from the higher wages workers would get. Radical incrementalism is sensitive to these interactions in policy. When such marginal improvements in the minimum wage get enacted without accounting for the interaction with another policy like the earned income tax credit, policy change is basically treading water. Other thoughtful changes across the policy spectrum can lay the groundwork for a more empowered class of workers who can push for even greater changes.

Other marginal changes actually push backward. For instance, the ongoing push by the Right to roll back voting rights is a poignant reverse example of radical incrementalism, what we could call "retrograde incrementalism," that is, change that incrementally undoes progressive reforms in ways that reallocate power away from those pushing for change.[52] By requiring voter identification cards and restricting absentee, early, and extended hours voting, the Right has been able to make it more difficult for supporters of the

Democratic Party to show up at the polls, especially nonwhites, immigrants, students, and the elderly. Since President Barack Obama was reelected in 2012, at least eighteen states have imposed voting restrictions, bringing the total with such laws to over half of all states.[53] Should this wave of new restrictions continue to withstand legal challenges and tip elections to conservatives in the Republican Party, the chances for public policy to address the deleterious effects of the ongoing economic transformation decline. The 2014 elections are a sign of the challenges ahead. The election had the lowest turnout in seventy-two years as a disheartened electorate stayed home and gave the United States Senate back to the Republicans.[54]

WHY WE SHOULD CARE ABOUT THE AFFORDABLE CARE ACT

Public policies are where the issue of radical incrementalism is most intense. When deciding whether to support a policy proposal, the key issue is whether it will revise the existing structure of power or buttress existing power relationships and thereby prevent future changes that could lead to significant improvements in attacking the problem being addressed. A politically fraught example is the Affordable Care Act. Now here is a policy that provides a litmus test for radical incrementalism. It is as profoundly unpopular with the Left as with the Right. In spite of the hysteria it has provoked on the right as some kind of socialist government takeover of the U.S. health-care system, Obamacare (as it has come to be called) is actually very incremental and in many ways neoliberal. It builds off the existing systems of employer-based health insurance for workers and separate government health insurance for the elderly and the poor. In fact, the main complaints from the Left are that it is ill-conceived tinkering with the existing system of private health insurance and doomed to fail.

Yet Obamacare may end up being its own crisis strategy.[55] This is quite ironic since hatemongers like Glenn Beck and Rush Limbaugh for years argued that Obamacare was intentionally designed to wreck not just the U.S. health-care system but the entire government and our free enterprise system overall. Beck even invoked a paranoid and twisted version of what he called the "Cloward and Piven Strategy" as proof that Obama (allegedly as their acolyte) was out to bring down America.[56] None of this is in any way credible in spite of the Fox News website framing Beck's months-long tirade against Piven and Cloward as a "news report." A more sensible interpretation of Obamacare, however, is that over time as it comes to include more of the uninsured in the U.S. health-care system it will lay the groundwork for a transformation to a more equitable and efficient system. In fact, it is possible that all the attempts to block it reflect an implicit understanding that some of its innovations such as state-run online health insurance exchanges, where private health insurance companies compete to offer affordable health insurance to the uninsured, may over time begin a process of transforming our private health insurance system to become more accessible to and supportive of ordinary people who increasingly found private insurance unaffordable.

It is possible that the exchanges will spread to employers who will use them to offer employees more choice even as they garner savings that come from increased competition.[57] The requirements for participating in the exchanges also could make it increasingly difficult for private insurers to continue to participate and may even lead the private insurers that do survive to operate essentially like a public system. For this and other reasons, there is a glimmer of hope that Obamacare could be the basis for a fundamental transformation of health policy in the United States that would substantially benefit millions of Americans who have been denied access to needed care.

Yet Obamacare is not usually discussed this way. Given its implementation problems, talk is focused more on its survival than on whether it can transform the health insurance system. In fact, it could end up being little more than a neoliberal concession that seeks to co-opt health insurance advocates and get them to give up the quest for universal coverage under an equitable system enforced via public policy. Worse, the primary effect of insurances exchanges may be the marketization of a public good like health insurance. Health insurance will then get evaluated solely in highly neoliberal, individualistic terms to the neglect of how universal health coverage serves the interests of society overall. If exchanges lead to the ascendency of this kind of neoliberal logic, then the opportunity for Obamacare to ensure that we are providing health insurance for everyone to benefit society collectively will be lost. Any radical incrementalism implicit in Obamacare's implementation of health exchanges will have then been lost and it will become just another neoliberal policy informed by a highly individualistic market logic.[58] Then again, Obamacare's heavy reliance on big data to monitor outcomes for insured populations in the aggregate could lead to a disciplinary regime focused on lowering cost at the expense of individual freedoms.[59] In these ways, Obamacare may serve as a model to accelerate the neoliberalization of social insurance programs across the board.[60]

In the current period of neoliberalism the major challenge is to develop and implement meaningful reforms that do not further embed market logic throughout society. Just as neoliberals could not simply undo welfare state liberalism and had to resort to marketizing state operations as some kind of Plan B fallback position, so it is for those struggling to overcome the limitations of current neoliberal policies. We cannot simply wish them away but must first recognize the deep path dependencies of existing neoliberal social and economic policies. They are the new normal. We must find ways to move beyond them by taking them into account, refashioning them in socially equitable ways, and laying the groundwork for a more inclusive society. We need to find ways to practice a radical incrementalism within the prevailing context of neoliberalism.

Whether Obamacare proves to be the "camel's nose in tent" when it comes to health policy remains to be seen.[61] The rollout of the federal government's online private health insurance exchange for Obamacare demonstrates starkly the challenges under neoliberalism of trying to achieve progressive reform, such as making health insurance universally available.[62] The constraints of operating in such an environment require public policy to be fashioned in a way that is consonant with market principles rather than overriding them. Inevitably this adds additional layers of complexity to government programs already weighed down with the complexity that comes from our fragmented, decentralized, federal system of government and its multiple veto points that are frequently exploited by special interests. Steven Teles calls our system of government a "kludgeocracy."[63] Kludgeocracy promotes status-quo-reinforcing incrementalism. And neoliberalism actually leads to increased "kludginess" in public programs that are designed to work with markets rather than override them. Obamacare builds on top of existing systems for providing health insurance via employers to workers and via the government to the poor and the old. It involves states in expanding existing Medicaid programs to provide health insurance to the poor, it offers subsidies for people to buy private health insurance, it requires purchase of that insurance via online exchanges where people choose from competing plans. The complexity of a decentralized system is magnified by adding incrementally neoliberal reforms that offer market-consistent initiatives like the exchanges across fifty states rather than overriding the market with a single-payer, national health insurance system. The kludginess of the government health insurance system is intensified with its neoliberalization.

In fact there are reasons to think that Obamacare might not survive. It remains astoundingly unpopular, with Republicans in Congress staging vote after vote to repeal it and interest groups working day and night in state after state to undermine it. The U.S. Supreme Court even considered striking a stake in the heart Obamacare over what amounted to nothing more than a typo.[64] The difficulties of trying to shoehorn reform into the existing system of health care have proven to be formidable. In the end, Obamacare may just prove unworkable and be rolled back.[65]

The rollout of the federal exchange in late 2013 was nothing less than a debacle and as a result, it poses real dangers for building support for future policy improvements not just in health care but across social welfare policies. Mike Konczal has raised the important question of blame.[66] It remains unclear who will be blamed for the problems associated with Obamacare's intensified form of kludginess. Will it be liberalism or neoliberalism that will get blamed for the rollout debacle? And depending on how the blame is apportioned, will this mean that further advances in social welfare policy will be resisted or that the dominant tendency in the current era to champion marketized public policies (like the health insurance exchanges) will finally begin to lose sway? The answer, I suggest, will, however, only be learned incrementally as policy proposals get floated going forward.

For now, politics still takes place within this highly fraught, neoliberalized context. Market models remain ascendant across public policy arenas. Economic logic stands in for all logic: what is logical is what is economically efficient.[67] The emphasis across policy arenas is on using economic incentives and penalties to motivate desired behaviors.[68] Obamacare itself relies heavily on incentives and penalties to get people to buy health insurance and thereby achieve the public good of having a healthier national population that will be less of a financial burden for the whole society. The way to better public policies that help people combat the inequities of the transformed economy will involve at a minimum accounting for neoliberalism and its insistence on privileging market logic not just in personal decision making but public policy as well.

MICROMANAGING NEOLIBERALISM

As we see with Obamacare, the neoliberal mindset combines public policy and individual decision making such that the former is designed to improve the latter. The result is public policy structured to incentivize economically efficacious personal decisions that in theory will not just improve outcomes for the individual but also redound to the advantage of the whole society. The neoliberal turn to structuring public policy that promotes better individual decision making has spread to even progressively minded social scientists who are keen to understand the persistence of poverty and want to avoid inappropriately "blaming the victim." Many more conservative poverty scholars have for years emphasized that poor people often cause and perpetuate their own poverty, often across generations, because they make bad personal decisions. Yet liberal researchers have demonstrated a reverse causality: poverty causes bad decision making.[69] Their recommendations are to improve decision making by those living in poverty in spite of their circumstances.

The growing field that examines the neurobiology of poverty is a prominent case in point. Research in this area continues to accumulate with evidence that the "toxic stress" children confront from living in extremely adverse conditions can have long-term effects on cognitive development.[70] Solutions, however, often come in the form of helping the poor better manage their stress. Yet it would seem that more effort should be devoted to mitigating extremely adverse living conditions as a more systematic way to lower toxic stress and improve long-run cognitive development. While this is a long-term project itself, it could be approached by taking radically incremental steps that lay the foundation for improved living conditions, such as raising the minimum wage, making decently paying jobs more readily available, improving access to child care, and adding other social welfare benefits.

While there is strong empirical evidence for the negative effects of poverty on cognitive processing and by extension personal decision making, it is interesting how the neoliberal focus on personal decision making migrates from the right to the left, thereby displacing more structural approaches to reducing poverty. It is almost as if the hegemony of neoliberal thinking and its preoccupation with promoting more market-savvy decision making cannot be ignored and thus becomes the starting point for even progressive ruminations about poverty-reduction strategies. It shows the pervasiveness of neoliberalism such that it infiltrates progressive thinking for combating poverty. And neoliberalism is now not just wide but also deep. There are now even asset-building programs for the homeless, as if their homelessness is the result of their financial illiteracy and failure to save for future financial opportunities.[71] Under these conditions, it will take an extended effort to dig out of the neoliberal morass our political economy has produced.

It is undoubtedly true that aiding the poor to better cope with their circumstances need not reinscribe the victim blaming of the neoliberal paternalistic poverty management regime that seeks to discipline the poor to be more compliant with the economistic dictates of the current order. What the new biology of poverty scholarship seems to be saying but actually does not is that the real cure to poverty is preventing poverty in the first place. If children did not come into a world of fright that poor neighborhoods and family conditions pose, they would be far less likely to grow up to be such troubled adults. So it seems we should be working step-by-step to first reduce and eliminate poverty as the overwhelming stressor that powerfully works to reproduce itself across generations. Funding more nurses to reduce stress as opposed to raising wages and increasing jobs may help but also risks reinscribing that victim-blaming logic of neoliberalism.

The causal circuitry is actually even more complicated. Neoliberalism's disciplinary regime features a policing that is its own source of terror, as the killings of Michael Brown in Ferguson, Missouri, and Eric Garner in Staten Island, New York, have come to represent. Policing to discipline the poor to be compliant with the neoliberal order in spite of their being marginalized by it has resulted in growing illegitimacy of the state and its police power. As neoliberalism pushes relentlessly toward opening up new markets by marketizing the state and civil society, it creates the need to increase discipline on those who do not fit in, cannot participate, or will not benefit from such marketized systems. Heightened disciplinary responses to contain these marginalized populations just furthers the frustrations smoldering among the dispossessed that the neoliberal causes of their marginalization are not addressed.[72]

Now Time for Neoliberalism

Neoliberalism is the pervasive reality of the state today. It is the common sense of how to get things done. Whenever it fails for whatever reason, it is a good bet that the chosen responses will be to double down on neoliberalism and take it to another level. Privatized social welfare provision might lead to scandals of corruption and mismanagement as the profit motive trumps compassionate care for the disadvantaged clientele; however, the response that wins approval from state leaders is often to collaborate further with private actors, blurring the boundaries further between the market and the state, as with bringing financiers to invest in social welfare programs through social impact bonds. The cures to the inadequacies of neoliberalism are more neoliberalism. Neoliberalism is a juggernaut that goes on its own accord, with momentum enough to carry it long past anyone's expressed intentions.

What explains the persistence of neoliberalism? At one level, we can say it has very strong backing because it was originally the product of a conscious strategy of a politicized business class. In the 1970s this class started to seriously exercise its political muscle and deploy its massive resources to mobilize over its opposition to New Deal social policies that got amplified by the Great Society.[73] The primary objective of the business class was to roll back the welfare state, but given mass support for those policies, they had to resort to a Plan B of marketizing the state operations they could not eliminate. It could be that part of this conscious strategy was a desire to hollow out the welfare state so that the corporate sector could take it over and turn it into a source of profit, via privatization or even to the point of trading investments on social welfare funding via a secondary market. The goal was perhaps to financialize state operations so that they could be commodified and traded for profit. Yet less nefariously we could say that neoliberal marketization of the state is not so much a conscious design for those who practice it today since they may not even know of neoliberalism's origins in the deep recesses of the Mt. Pelerin Society and the thinking of people like Ludwig von Mises, Friedrich Hayek, and Milton Friedman.[74] Instead, it is now the "practical rationality" of how public policy choices are made.[75] It is the default position in the face of the hollowed-out welfare state in an age of manufactured austerity, where raising taxes is simply off the table. Now, all public initiatives must entertain enlisting private partners for developing, financing, and implementing programs. Or a third position also merits consideration, that regardless of its origins or how it has come to be the default position for public policymaking, it represents the outlook of many citizens, taxpayers, and voters who rightly or wrongly see government as discredited and refuse to pay for its operations unless it can demonstrate a return on investment.[76]

In any case, the default logic today is neoliberal: people should be empowered to choose how to make their own decisions as customers do in a free market. "Empowerment," "freedom," "choice" become the watchwords of the neoliberal order. Everything is unquestionably assumed in need of being evaluated under these terms, to the neglect of the power relations they mask and the inequities they thereby help perpetuate. We become at risk of succumbing to the "cunning of history" and reproducing the power relations that oppress us.[77] It is all deeply depoliticizing where being a change agent is reduced to producing "disruptive innovation" in service of corporate objectives.[78] Under these politically fraught conditions, the only social welfare policy initiatives likely to receive sufficient political support are the ones that evaluate well according to standards of economic logic.

Neoliberalism is both an economic project and a political project. It opens new markets by commodifying everything including state social provision. It also provides a way by which market logic and market actors insinuate themselves into the state's public policymaking process. Consciously or not, its marketization leads to dedemocratization in which capitalism gets to trump democracy in state decision making.[79]

Regardless of its origins, its location in conscious strategy or tacit understanding, or its manifestation as an artifact of an antigovernment age, neoliberalism is not likely to pass away anytime soon and we need to think about how to get beyond it rather than roll it back. This might mean moving beyond what Karl Polanyi called the "double movement" to counter the current neoliberalization of the state. The double movement countered market capriciousness with social protections but for the most part only if recipients were seen as acting consistently with prevailing social, cultural, and economic biases. Neoliberalism was in part a reaction to the paternalism of the double movement (even if it produced its own disciplinary regime that has a profound paternalism all its own).[80] We might need now what Nancy Fraser calls a "triple movement" that works through neoliberalism to lay the basis for empowering individuals to act more on their own terms rather than accept the social protections of the double movement that condition assistance with paternalist behavioral regulation.[81] For Michel Foucault and others, this means taking neoliberalism seriously as something that cannot be simply wished away but must be worked through.[82] But how we work through neoliberalism to this more empowering individualism is its own risky business that involves keeping open questions of strategy. As Piven and Cloward wisely once noted, we can no more offer a blueprint for social protest movements than we can plan for their spontaneous eruption.[83] We can, however, organize so that we can be prepared to make the most of them when they do occur. I would also argue that the most effective responses are going to be ones that resist the false choice of choosing one response over others. Instead, we must learn to work on multiple levels simultaneously, appreciating how they can produce synergy rather than undermine each other.

Getting beyond neoliberalism will take political mobilization on multiple levels inside and outside the conventional public policy system.[84] As neoliberalism's marketization increases profits and inequality, it inevitably undermines democracy while imposing greater discipline on dispossessed populations. Its own success economically becomes the basis for its crisis politically.[85] Protest movements such as Occupy Wall Street have helped highlight that the transformed economy is working for the wealthy (the 1 percent) at the expense of everyone else (the 99 percent). Protests against the policing of black neighborhoods can highlight the role of the disciplinary regime in helping to prop up a neoliberalized system that works increasingly for the privileged and leaves little for ordinary people. Yet once we account for neoliberalism's economic and political effects, we need to think seriously about what kinds of policy initiatives can start to lay the groundwork for moving beyond the obsession with instilling market logic everywhere and disciplining everyone who is left out.

The question of strategy might be posed as a choice of whether to resist the existing regime of power, work within it, or intensify its contradictions to accelerate transition to an alternative formation.[86] Yet the issue is better framed as not one at the expense of the other, but what is their relationship. There is the need to rethink how much emphasis should be given to pursuing a politics of resistance versus a politics that gives greater emphasis on affirmative actions. With Pierre Bourdieu we need to determine what is the proper mix for getting from social reproduction to social transformation.[87]

It is distinctly possible that sooner or later neoliberalism will run its course, after we recognize the limits of insisting on market logic in one policy arena after another. Simply applying Walter Benjamin's "emergency brake" on history by resisting neoliberalism on all fronts may eventually do the trick.[88] But that may take a long time. More constructive efforts will in all likelihood be needed, efforts requiring a shift from a politics of resistance to one that gives greater stress to the affirmative actions that can produce a radical incrementalism. Therefore, we might be better off thinking through how to refashion neoliberal policy regimes so that they do not put all the burden on the individual to figure out how to make perfect decisions with limited resources, whether it is in people deciding where their children go to school, where they decide to live, what health insurance to buy, what job to take, which child-care provider they will use when working, whether they dare to use their limited incomes to save for a better future. As the list suggests, the areas where social welfare policies in particular are being neoliberalized are numerous and growing. In turn, the list also implies at a minimum that there are multiple opportunities to reshape public policy in these areas so that we can practice a radical incrementalism that enables us to start to get beyond the failures of neoliberalism. Pushing for change policy by policy, program by program, we can begin to overcome the limitations of the new normal and begin anew to create supportive social policies, for workers, for parents, for children, for students, and so on.

Effective responses will of necessity leave room for working on multiple levels and resisting making false choices. In fact, even within affirmative efforts to work through neoliberalism, resistance has a role to play even within more constructive efforts that lay the groundwork for social transformation. We need the patient development of an alternative vision of the welfare state that allows us to live beyond the dehumanizing dimensions of the marketized state. That long-term perspective needs to be developed in ways that speak to the changing world going forward.[89] And while that is happening we can make incremental improvements in public policy that render that broader vision more credible to the mass public and more realizable in the long run. Even with the existing policy regime there are opportunities to do right by people in need by joining "guerrillas of the bureaucracy" who reside in the "moral underground" and work subversively to bend the implementation of existing policy toward the arc of justice, every day making a difference in the lives of ordinary people.[90] In other words, radical incrementalism can be, and in fact should be, conducted on a variety of levels, policy planning as well as policy implementation. We need guerrillas of the policy process as well as guerrillas of bureaucracy.

Getting to that better future beyond neoliberalism is contingent on working to ensure that there is a political process that is open to deliberating about the structure and role of the welfare state. To say that this latest iteration of ordinary capitalism presents difficult political challenges is an understatement. Today, what is most urgently needed is finding ways to constrain the undue influence of economic elites. The rapid concentration of wealth in their hands in the neoliberal era allows them to dominate the public policy-making process and convert our political system into what is best called an oligarchic plutocracy (rule by the richest few). As noted in chapter 1, Thomas Piketty has suggested that only a global wealth tax can prevent them from hoarding their disproportionate share of economic resources.[91] Yet as I mentioned in chapter 1, that idea at this point is perhaps too utopian given that there is not even a global government body available to impose the tax. Instead, others such as Dean Baker have noted that there are a variety of other domestic means at the disposal of national governments like the United States that can be taken to tax and rein in concentrated wealth. Pursuing these options in a way that evaluates them in terms of their ability to lay the groundwork to get beyond neoliberalism is the radically incremental way to proceed.[92]

Radical incrementalism is ultimately about politics; it resists economic determination. Concentrated wealth in itself cannot stop political change, especially if efforts are mobilized on multiple levels to work together. Participating in protests, elections, the policy process (including implementation), and other forms of activism can work together to help us get beyond the sad state of affairs that has made the welfare state a bankrupt, privatized, financialized, dehumanized basket case. The key is to get these different levels of effort to work together and not against each other. We must come to appreciate the need to operate on multiple levels and acknowledge that these efforts can work together rather than against each other. That requires more organizing to coordinate actions, as when welfare caseworkers protesting how they are being forced to treat clients gets coupled with incremental improvements in existing policy to support them, and both are connected to broader social movements of ordinary people to address the neoliberalization of the hollowed-out welfare state. A multipronged attack on the hydra-headed monster of neoliberalism is the way to fight the good fight today.

NOTES

CHAPTER 1

1. Joseph Stiglitz, *The Price of Inequality: How Today's Divided Society Endangers Our Future* (New York: W. W. Norton, 2012), pp. 1–37.

2. See Frances Fox Piven, "Welfare in a New Society: An End to Intentional Poverty and Degradation," in *Imagine: Living in a Socialist USA*, Frances Goldin, Debby Smith, and Michael Steve Smith, eds. (New York: Harper Perennial, 2014), pp. 125–34.

3. For some, today's politics is a sign of the failure of the Left to sustain itself as a meaningful force in the United States. See Adolph Reed, "Nothing Left: The Long, Slow Surrender of American Liberals," *Harper's*, March 2014, http://harpers.org/archive/2014/03/nothing-left-2/.

4. For instance, see Nancy Fraser, "Feminism, Capitalism and the Cunning of History," *New Left Review* 56 (March–April 2009): 97–117.

5. Paul Pierson, "Increasing Returns, Path Dependence, and the Study of Politics," *American Political Science Review* 94, 2 (2000): 251–67.

6. The persistence of not just economic depression but possibly economic collapse after the Great Recession continued to plague southern European countries like Greece, Spain, and Italy. See Liz Alderman, "Full Recovery Still Years Away for Many in Euro Zone," *New York Times*, May 16, 2013, http://www.nytimes.com/2014/05/16/business/international/full-recovery-still-years-away-for-many-in-euro-zone.html?ref=world&_r=0.

7. For an ethnographic account on how the transformed economy was changing the outlook of young people who were trying get a job or get off welfare, see Jennifer Silva, *Coming Up Short: Working Class Adulthood in an Age of Uncertainty* (New York: Oxford University Press, 2013).

8. Tayyab Mahmud, "Debt and Discipline," *American Quarterly* 64, 3 (2012): 469–94.

9. Wendy Brown, "Neo-Liberalism and the End of Liberal Democracy," *Theory and Event* 7 (2003), http://muse.jhu.edu/journals/theory_and_event/.

10. Andrew Dilts, *Punishment and Inclusion: Race, Membership, and the Limits of American Liberalism* (New York: Fordham University Press, 2014), chapter 2.

11. Philip Mirowski, *Never Let a Serious Crisis Go to Waste: How Neoliberalism Survived the Financial Meltdown* (London: Verso, 2013).

12. The phrase ordinary capitalism is open to multiple interpretations. One definition is that it is when the economy is functioning at a stable, efficient, and productive rate (even if it continues to generate winners and losers as capitalism always has). Another definition is that it is entirely normal to expect that ordinary capitalism changes with each swing back to a period of growth. The newest incarnation of ordinary capitalism seems to be an extreme version of the first definition with widening gaps between winners and losers (making it a good example of how it is entirely normal for ordinary capitalism to keep changing with each swing back to a period of growth).

13. Stiglitz, *The Price of Inequality*, chapter 1.

14. See Leo Pantich and Sam Gindin, *The Making of Global Capitalism: The Political Economic of American Empire* (New York: Verso, 2013); and David McNally, *Monsters of the Market: Zombies, Vampires and Global Capitalism* (Chicago: Haymarket Books, 2012).

15. See Joe Soss, Richard C. Fording, and Sanford F. Schram, *Disciplining the Poor: Neoliberal Paternalism and the Persistent Power of Race* (Chicago: University of Chicago Press, 2011), chapter 2.

16. George Lipsetz, "Separate and Unequal: Big Government Conservatism and the Racial State," in *State of White Supremacy: Racism, Governance, and the U.S.,* Moon-Kie Jung, Eduardo Bonilla-Silva, and João CostaVargas, eds. (Palo Alto, CA: Stanford University Press, 2011), pp. 110–29.

17. Sanford F. Schram, Joe Soss, and Richard C. Fording, "Neoliberal Paternalism: Race and the New Poverty Governance," in *State of White Supremacy: Racism, Governance, and the U.S.,* Moon-Kie Jung, Eduardo Bonilla-Silva, and João CostaVargas, eds. (Palo Alto, CA: Stanford University Press, 2011), pp. 130–57.

18. Löic Wacquant, *Punishing the Poor: The Neoliberal Government of Social Insecurity* (Durham, NC: Duke University Press, 2009).

19. See Ruth Wilson Gilmore, *Golden Gulag, Prisons, Surplus, Crisis, and Opposition in Globalizing California* (Berkeley: University of California Press, 2007).

20. The killing of Michael Brown by police officer Darren Wilson in Ferguson, Missouri, in the summer of 2014 led to an outpouring of not just protests but also extensive reporting on how race had been used in the St. Louis area, Missouri overall, and, in fact, the entire country for years as a convenient marker for demarcating marginal populations that could be treated in a more disciplinary fashion as a way of containing and refusing to address their poverty problems and related consequences. The protests grew larger the first week of December 2014 after a Staten Island, New York, grand jury refused to indict police officer Daniel Pantaleo for killing Eric Garner with a chokehold that seemingly violated police policy. See Tanzina Vega and John Eligon, "Deep Tensions Rise to Surface after Ferguson Shooting," *New York Times*, August 16, 2014, http://www.nytimes. com/2014/08/17/us/ferguson-mo-complex-racial-history-runs-deep-most-tensions-have-to-do-police-force.html?_r=0.

21. For the argument that ever-increasing inequality is now the inevitable result of how global capitalism is evolving, see Thomas Piketty, *Capital in the 21st Century*,

Arthur Goldhammer, trans. (Cambridge, MA: Belknap Press, 2014). On the "Great Compression," see Claudia Goldin and Robert A. Margo, "The Great Compression: The Wage Structure in the United States at Mid-Century" (National Bureau of Economic Research Working Paper No. 3817, 1991, Cambridge, MA), http://www.nber.org/papers/w3817.

22. Piketty, *Capital in the 21st Century*, chapter 15.

23. Piketty, *Capital in the 21st Century*, chapter 15.

24. Mark Stears has championed the idea that there should be more empirically informed political theory. See Mark Stears, "The Vocation of Political Theory: Principles, Empirical Inquiry and the Politics of Opportunity," *European Journal of Political Theory* 4, 4 (2005): 325–50. In this chapter and the others that follow, my analysis of the neoliberalization of the welfare state represents the obverse, i.e., theoretically informed empirical analysis.

25. See Bruce Ackerman, "Was Martin Luther King Wrong?" *Los Angeles Times*, April 28, 2014, http://www.latimes.com/opinion/op-ed/la-oe-ackerman-lbj-civil-rights-20140428-story.html#axzz30CjplggA. The quotation originates with abolitionist Theodore Parker. See Jamie Stiehm, "Oval Office Rug Gets History Wrong," *Washington Post*, September 4, 2010, http://www.washingtonpost.com/wp-dyn/content/article/2010/09/03/AR2010090305100.html.

26. Karl Marx's "The Eighteenth Brumaire of Louis Napoleon" appeared in a nonrecurring publication titled *Die Revolution* in 1852 and was republished with the title *The Eighteenth Brumaire of Louis Bonaparte* (as Marx had originally intended) in 1869. See the Progress edition (Moscow, 1937), translated by Saul K. Padover from the 1869 German edition.

27. Mircea Eliade, *The Myth of Eternal Return: Cosmos and History* (Princeton, NJ: Princeton University Press, 2005).

28. See John G. Gunnell, *Political Philosophy and Time: Plato and the Origins of Political Vision* (Chicago: University of Chicago Press, 1987 [1968]).

29. Carl Schmitt, "Three Possibilities for a Christian Conception of History," *Telos* 147 (2009 [1950]): 167–70, as quoted in Mitchell Dean, *The Signature of Power: Sovereignty, Governmentality and Biopolitics* (London: Sage, 2013), p. 142.

30. Dean, *The Signature of Power*, pp. 148–49.

31. We need to also consider the possibility that policy change occurring on one social issue or in one social field may not be matched by improvements on other fronts, making change uneven as well as cyclical. The uneven changes in the area of race relations is a case in point with an emerging black middle class growing alongside increasing marginalization of a demonized black inner-city poor.

32. On cyclical change in social welfare policy, see Frances Fox Piven and Richard A. Cloward, *Regulating the Poor: The Functions of Public Welfare* (New York: Vintage Books, 1971).

33. See Sanford F. Schram, *Praxis for the Poor: Piven and Cloward and the Future of Social Science in Social Welfare* (New York: New York University Press, 2002), pp. 93–95; Frances Fox Piven and Richard A. Cloward, *The New Class War: Reagan's Attack on the Welfare State and Its Consequences* (New York: Pantheon Books, 1982), pp. x–xi.

34. Piven and Cloward, *The New Class War*, pp. x–xi.

35. See Fred Block and Margaret R. Somers, *The Power of Market Fundamentalism: Karl Polanyi's Critique* (Cambridge, MA: Harvard University Press, 2014), p. 10. Nancy Fraser calls for a "triple movement" that would transcend the tensions between marketization and social protection with a shift toward emancipation. See Nancy Fraser, *Fortunes of Feminism: From State-Managed Capitalism to Neoliberal Crisis* (London: Verso, 2013), pp. 227–42.

36. Samuel Merrill III, Bernard Grofman, and Thomas L. Brunell, "Cycles in American National Electoral Politics, 1854–2006: Statistical Evidence and an Explanatory Model," *American Political Science Review* 102, 1 (2008): 1–17.

37. For the argument that all significant economic slumps are best understood by the unique conditions that gave rise to them, see Pantich and Gindin, *The Making of Global Capitalism*. For the argument that the Great Recession is best understood by long-term trends developing in the economy, see McNally, *Monsters of the Market*. My argument is that both long-term trends and unique conditions need to be taken into account in order to understand and respond to the Great Recession and its aftermath. In all three cases, there is a need to appreciate the role of the state in shaping the market. See Block and Somers, *The Power of Market Fundamentalism*, pp. 44–72.

38. Joseph Schumpeter, *Democracy, Socialism and Capitalism* (New York: Harper, 1942).

39. What is ordinary about ordinary capitalism includes the everyday experience of being exploited and oppressed by economic relationships. On the importance of the ordinariness of everyday lived experience in order to appreciate how the personal is political, see Kathleen Stewart, *Ordinary Affects* (Durham, NC: Duke University Press, 2007). On the importance of understanding structural changes from the bottom up in terms of the everyday experiences of the people most directly affected by them, see Nancy A. Naples, *Feminism and Method: Ethnography, Discourse Analysis, and Activist Research* (New York: Routledge, 2003), chapter 8; and Sanford F. Schram, *Words of Welfare: The Poverty of Social Science and the Social Science of Poverty* (Minneapolis: University of Minnesota Press, 1995), chapter 3. Naples proposes we conduct "everyday world policy analysis" (p. 143) as a way of understanding policy from the perspective of those on the bottom and I have proposed that we study policy from the "bottom up" in order to appreciate how those on the bottom are affected by those policies. On the importance of examining ideas in terms of ordinary experience, see Robyn Mansco, *The Highway of Despair: Critical Theory After Hegel* (New York: Columbia University Press, 2015), p. 156.

40. See Mahmud, "Debt and Discipline"; and Andrew Ross, *Creditocracy: And the Case for Debt Refusal* (New York: OR Books, 2014).

41. Colin Couch, "What Will Follow from the Demise of Privatised Keynesianism?" *Political Quarterly* 79, 4 (2008): 476–87; and Dean, *The Signature of Power*, pp. 218–19. Also see Maurizio Lazzarato, *The Making of the Indebted Man: An Essay on the Neoliberal Condition* (New York: Semiotexte, 2012).

42. Adam Bonica, Nolan McCarty, Keith T. Poole, and Howard Rosenthal, "Why Hasn't Democracy Slowed Rising Inequality?" *Journal of Economic Perspectives* 27, 3 (2013): 103–24.

43. Marx, "The Eighteenth Brumaire of Louis Napoleon," p. 1.

44. For an elegiac gesture toward a historical materialism that appreciates the need for even the most messianic among us to account for the force of history operating

in the present when seeking to make change, see Walter Benjamin, "Theses on the Concept of History," in *Illuminations: Essays and Reflections*, Hannah Arendt, ed. (New York: Schocken, 1969 [1955]), pp. 253–65.

45. Also from Marx, "The Eighteenth Brumaire of Louis Napoleon."

46. Avery F. Gordon, *Ghostly Matters: Haunting and the Sociological Imagination* (Minneapolis: University of Minnesota Press, 2008), p. 8.

47. See Jacques Derrida, *Specters of Marx: The State of the Debt, the Work of Mourning and the New International* (New York: Routledge, 2006).

48. This issue is addressed insightfully in a stunning portrait of the historian Martin Sklar, who developed the theory of "corporate liberalism." See John B. Judis, "Meet the Sarah Palin Enthusiast Who May Have Been the Best American Historian of His Generation," *New Republic*, June 17, 2014, http://www.newrepublic.com/article/118187/martin-j-sklar-and-search-usable-past/.

49. Fraser, "Feminism, Capitalism and the Cunning of History."

50. Walter Benjamin, *Selected Writings*, vol. 4, *1938–1940*, Walter Howard Eiland and Michael W. Jennings, eds. (Cambridge, MA: Harvard University Press, 2003), p. 402.

51. Benjamin Noys, *The Persistence of the Negative: A Critique of Contemporary Continental Theory* (Edinburgh: Edinburgh University Press, 2010).

52. See Dean, *The Signature of Power*, pp. 12–14.

53. See Nancy Fraser, "A Triple Movement? Parsing the Crisis after Polanyi," *New Left Review* 81 (May–June 2013): 119–32.

54. Piketty, *Capital in the 21st Century*, pp. 72–112.

55. U.S. House of Representatives, Committee on Ways and Means, "Welcome to the Obama Recovery—Four Years on Worst Recovery Ever Continues to Limp Along, Stranding Millions of Workers and Families," news release, Washington, DC, July 3, 2013, http://waysandmeans.house.gov/news/documentsingle.aspx?DocumentID=341434. Data from the U.S. Department of Labor, Bureau of Labor Statistics.

56. See Sheldon Danziger and Peter Gottschalk, *America Unequal*, Russell Sage Foundation Series (Cambridge, MA: Harvard University Press, 1997).

57. Emmanuel Saez, "Striking It Richer: The Evolution of Top Incomes in the United States (Updated with 2012 Preliminary Estimates)," Saez's website, September 3, 2013, http://elsa.berkeley.edu/~saez/saez-UStopincomes-2012.pdf.

58. See Robert D. Putnam, *Our Kids: The American Dream in Crisis* (New York: Simon and Shuster, 2015). Putnam offers a class analysis of the "opportunity gap" but ends up emphasizing that the primary response should be helping poor people access more "social capital," so they can help their children grow up with similar supports to those given to wealthier children. Yet increased social capital in a persistently unequal society does nothing to not create enough decently paying jobs and can leave those on the bottom still without opportunity. On how politics was critical in creating the "opportunity gap" and will be essential to successfully attacking it, see Jill Lepore, "Richer and Poorer," *New Yorker*, March 16, 2015, http://www.newyorker.com/magazine/2015/03/16/richer-and-poorer.

59. Piketty, *Capital in the 21st Century*, pp. 72–112.

60. Sheldon H. Danziger, "Fighting Poverty Revisited: What Did Researchers Know 40 Years Ago? What Do We Know Today?" *Focus* 25, 1 (2007): 3–11.

61. Colin Hay, "Globalisation, Welfare Retrenchment and the 'Logic of No Alternative': Why Second-Best Won't Do," *Journal of Social Policy* 27, 4 (1998): 525–32.

62. Stiglitz, *The Price of Inequality*, p. 4.

63. Michael B. Katz, "How America Abandoned Its 'Undeserving' Poor," *Salon*, December 21, 2013, http://www.salon.com/2013/12/21/how_america_abandoned_its_undeserving_poor/. Whether the transformed economy is one that inevitably leads to permanent decline in the economic fortunes of most Americans is surely subject to debate, but that argument is made forcefully by Stephen D. King, *When the Money Runs Out: The End of Western Affluence* (New Haven, CT: Yale University Press, 2013), and "When Wealth Disappears," *New York Times*, October 6, 2013, http://www.nytimes.com/2013/10/07/opinion/when-wealth-disappears.html?pagewanted=all.

64. Executive Pay Watch, "U.S. CEOs Paid 354 Times the Average Rank-and-File Worker—Largest Pay Gap in the World," http://www.aflcio.org/Press-Room/Press-Releases/U.S.-CEOs-Paid-354-Times-the-Average-Rank-and-File-Worker-Largest-Pay-Gap-in-the-World.

65. Paul Krugman, "Piketty Day Notes," *New York Times*, April 16, 2014, http://krugman.blogs.nytimes.com/2014/04/16/piketty-day-notes/.

66. Block and Somers, *The Power of Market Fundamentalism*, pp. 44–72; and Fred Block, "Varieties of What? Should We Still Be Using the Concept of Capitalism?" *Political Power and Social Theory* 23 (2012): 269–91.

67. Wolfgang Streeck, "On Fred Block, Varieties of What? Should We Still Be Using the Concept of Capitalism?" *Political Power and Social Theory* 23 (2012): 311–21.

68. Thomas Piketty, Emmanuel Saez, and Stefanie Stantcheva, "Optimal Taxation of Top Incomes: A Tale of Three Elasticities," *American Economic Journal: Economic Policy* 6, 1 (2014): 230–271.

69. Ross, *Creditocracy*; and Mahmud, "Debt and Discipline."

70. John Shinal, "Finance Set to Surpass Tech as Most-Profitable U.S. Industry," *USA Today*, July 14, 2013, http://www.usatoday.com/story/tech/columnist/shinal/2013/07/14/finance-and-tech-industry-outlook/2509349/.

71. Stiglitz, *The Price of Inequality*, chapter 5.

72. See Bonica et al., "Why Hasn't Democracy Slowed Rising Inequality?" and Peter K. Enns, Nathan J. Kelly, Jana Morgan, Thomas Volscho, and Christopher Witko, "Conditional Status Quo Bias and Top Income Shares: How U.S. Political Institutions Have Benefited the Rich," *Journal of Politics* 76, 2 (2014): 289–303.

73. Thomas E. Mann and Norman J. Ornstein, *It's Even Worse Than It Looks: How the American Constitutional System Collided with the New Politics of Extremism* (New York: Basic Books, 2013).

74. Martin Gilens, *Affluence and Influence: Economic Inequality and Political Power in America* (Princeton, NJ: Princeton University Press, 2012), pp. 1–11.

75. Martin Gilens and Benjamin I. Page, "Testing Theories of American Politics: Elites, Interest Groups, and Average Citizens," *Perspectives on Politics* 12, 4 (2014): 564–81, http://www.princeton.edu/~mgilens/Gilens%20homepage%20materials/Gilens%20and%20Page/Gilens%20and%20Page%202014-Testing%20Theories%203-7-14.pdf.

76. Pierson, "Increasing Returns, Path Dependence, and the Study of Politics."

77. Pierson, "Increasing Returns, Path Dependence, and the Study of Politics;" and Joe Soss and Sanford F. Schram, "The Promise of a Public Transformed: Welfare Reform as Policy Feedback," *American Political Science Review* 101, 1 (2007): 111–27.

78. See B. Guy Peters, Jon Pierre, and Desmond S. King, "The Politics of Path Dependency: Political Conflict in Historical Institutionalism," *Journal of Politics* 67, 4 (2005): 1275–1300.

79. Jacob Hacker, "Privatizing Risk without Privatizing the Welfare State: The Hidden Politics of Social Policy Retrenchment in the United States," *American Political Science Review* 98, 2 (2004): 243–60. Also see Jacob S. Hacker and Paul Pierson, "After the 'Master Theory': Downs, Schattschneider, and the Rebirth of Policy-Focused Analysis," *Perspectives on Politics*, 12, 3 (2014): 643–62.

80. For evidence of a growing gap in life expectancy between the rich and poor, see Steven Hargreaves, "How Inequality Hurts America," *CNN Money*, September 25, 2013, http://money.cnn.com/2013/09/25/news/economy/income-inequality/index.html. For declines in life expectancy among the poor, see Sabrina Tavernise, "Life Spans Shrink for Least-Educated Whites in the U.S.," *New York Times*, September 20, 2012, http://www.nytimes.com/2012/09/21/us/life-expectancy-for-less-educated-whites-in-us-is-shrinking.html?pagewanted=all&_moc.semityn.www.

81. Kathleen Geier, "Shocker Stat of the Day: Life Expectancy Decreases by 4 Years among Poor White People in the U.S.," *Washington Monthly*, September 22, 2012, http://www.washingtonmonthly.com/political-animal-a/2012_09/shocker_stat_of_the_day_life_e040058.php.

82. David Harvey, *A Brief History of Neoliberalism* (New York: Oxford University Press, 2007), p. 118.

83. On the issue of whether neoliberalism is race neutral, see Lester Spence, "Race and the Neoliberal City" (paper presented at the Sawyer Seminar on Capitalism in the 21st Century, Arrighi Center for Global Studies, March 28, 2014). Also see Stuart Hall, *The Hard Road to Renewal: Thatcherism and the Crisis of the Left* (London: Verso 1988).

84. Sandy Fitzgerald, "Nation's Prisons Becoming Modern-Day Asylums for Mentally Ill," *Newsmax*, September 26, 2013, http://www.newsmax.com/US/prison-mental-health-inmantes/2013/09/26/id/527895.

85. For a history of the cyclical shifts in the warehousing of the mentally ill in the United States, see Andrew Scull, *Decarceration: Community Treatment and the Deviant—a Radical View* (Upper Saddle River, NJ: Prentice Hall, 1977). Also see Timothy Williams, "Jails Have Become Warehouses for the Poor, Ill and Addicted, a Report Says," *New York Times*, February 11, 2015, http://www.nytimes.com/2015/02/11/us/jails-have-become-warehouses-for-the-poor-ill-and-addicted-a-report-says.html?smid=fb-share.

86. Ruth Wilson Gilmore, "Forgotten Places and the Seeds of Grassroots Planning," in *Engaging Contradictions: Theory, Politics, and Methods of Activist Scholarship*, Charles R. Hale, ed. (Berkeley: University of California Press, 2008), pp. 31–61.

87. See Jacob Hacker, *The Great Risk Shift: The Assault on American Jobs, Families, Health Care, and Retirement—and How You Can Fight Back* (New York: Oxford University Press, 2006).

88. See Jacob Hacker and Paul Pierson, "What Krugman and Stiglitz Can Tell Us." *New York Review of Books*, September 27, 2012, http://www.nybooks.com/articles/archives/2012/sep/27/what-krugman-stiglitz-can-tell-us/.

89. See Jared Bernstein, "The Impact of Inequality on Growth," Center for American Progress, accessed December 14, 2013, http://www.americanprogress.org/wp-content/uploads/2013/12/BerensteinInequality.pdf.

90. Michael Edesess, "The Great Debate on Inequality: Stiglitz versus Krugman," *Advisor Perspectives*, June 25, 2013, http://www.advisorperspectives.com/newsletters13/The_Great_Debate_on_Inequality.php.

91. See Paul Krugman, "Why We Are in a New Gilded Age," *New York Review of Books*, May 8, 2014, http://www.nybooks.com/articles/archives/2014/may/08/thomas-piketty-new-gilded-age/.

92. Enns et al., "Conditional Status Quo."

93. Lane Kenworthy, *Progress for the Poor* (New York: Oxford University Press, 2011).

94. Edward McClelland, "RIP, the Middle Class: 1946–2013," *Alternet*, September 20, 2013, http://www.alternet.org/rip-middle-class-1946-2013.

95. See Bonica et al., "Why Hasn't Democracy Slowed Rising Inequality?"

96. Soss, Fording, and Schram, *Disciplining the Poor*, chapter 2.

97. Brown, "Neo-Liberalism and the End of Liberal Democracy," and "American Nightmare: Neoliberalism, Neoconservatism, and De-Democratization." *Political Theory* 34, 6 (2006): 690–714.

98. Nicholas J. Kiersey, "Everyday Neoliberalism and the Subjectivity of Crisis: Post-Political Control in an Era of Financial Turmoil," *Journal of Critical Globalisation Studies* 4 (2011): 23–44.

99. Lucy Heady, "Social Return on Investment Position Paper," *New Philanthropy Capital*, April 2010, http://www.thinknpc.org/publications/social-return-on-investment-position-paper/.

100. Sanford F. Schram, *Welfare Discipline: Discourse, Governance and Globalization* (Philadelphia: Temple University Press, 2006), chapter 5.

101. See Jodi Dean, *Democracy and Other Neoliberal Fantasies: Communicative Capitalism and Left Politics* (Durham, NC: Duke University Press, 2009), pp. 19–48.

102. Now even retirees are being reconstructed in the neoliberal imaginary as proto-workers who must produce or find other ways to reduce their reliance on state-funded pensions. See Diana Coole, "Reconstructing the Elderly: A Critical Analysis of Pensions and Population Policies in an Era of Demographic Aging," *Contemporary Political Theory* 11 (2012): 41–67.

103. Jodi Dean, "Paul Ryan Has a 20-Year Plan to Destroy the Government: Where's Ours?" *I Cite*, August 15, 2012, http://jdeanicite.typepad.com/i_cite/2012/08/paul-ryan-has-a-20-year-plan-to-destroy-the-government-wheres-ours.html.

104. See Sanford F. Schram and Basha Silverman, "The End of Social Work: Neoliberalizing Social Policy Implementation," *Critical Policy Studies* 6, 2 (2012): 128–45, and chapter 5 here.

105. See Soss, Fording, and Schram, *Disciplining the Poor*, pp. 2–3.

106. Soss and Schram, "The Promise of a Public Transformed," pp. 124–27.

107. Diane Ravitch, *Reign of Error: The Hoax of the Privatization Movement and the Danger to America's Public Schools* (New York: Knopf, 2013).

108. See Todd Gitlin, *Occupy Nation: The Roots, the Spirit, and the Promise of Occupy Wall Street* (New York: IT Books, 2012).

109. Bob Master, "The Zeitgeist Tracked Down Bill de Blasio: How the Rise of Occupy and Decline of the Neoliberal Narrative Helped Shape the 'de Blasio Moment,'" *The Nation*, December 26, 2013, http://www.thenation.com/article/177720/zeitgeist-tracked-down-bill-de-blasio#.

110. Matt Taibbi, "The Police in America Are Becoming Illegitimate," *Rolling Stone*, December 5, 2014, http://www.rollingstone.com/politics/news/the-police-in-america-are-becoming-illegitimate-20141205.

111. See Denise Chen, "Goldman to Invest in City Jail Program, Profiting if Recidivism Falls Sharply," *New York Times*, August 2, 2012. See chapter 7 here.

112. Jamie Peck and Nik Theodore, "Recombinant Workfare, across the Americas: Transnationalizing 'Fast' Social Policy," *Geoforum* 41, 2 (2010): 195–208.

113. Kelly Walsh and John Roman, "Social Impact Bonds: Testimony before the Committee of the Whole Council of the District of Columbia," Urban Institute, June 6, 2013, http://www.urban.org/publications/904589.html.

114. One troubling development in the de Blasio administration is his appointment of a social impact bond maven to be deputy mayor for housing and economic development. See Michael Belinsky, "Bill de Blasio Appoints Social Impact Bond Financier as Deputy Mayor for Housing and Economic Development," December 24, 2013. http://mikebelinsky.wordpress.com/2013/12/24/bill-de-blasio-appoints-social-impact-bond-financier-as-deputy-mayor-for-housing-and-economic-development/.

115. Paul Heideman, "Bulletproof Neoliberalism," *Jacobin* 14 (June 2014), https://www.jacobinmag.com/2014/06/bulletproof-neoliberalism/. On neoliberalism as embedded in everyday life, see Mirowski, *Never Let a Serious Crisis Go to Waste*.

CHAPTER 2

1. See Robert Reich, "Robert Reich on What's Really Destroying the American Middle Class," *Alternet*, September 29, 2014, http://www.alternet.org/economy/robert-reich-whats-really-destroying-american-middle-class; Pew Research Center, *Most Say Government Policies since the Recession Have Done Little to Help Middle Class, Poor: 'Partial' Recovery Seen in Jobs, Household Incomes*, March 2015, http://www.people-press.org/files/2015/03/03-04-15-Economy-release.pdf.

2. Andrew Ross, *Creditocracy: And the Case for Debt Refusal* (New York: OR Books, 2014).

3. For a discussion of the political implications of these economic developments, see Jacob Hacker, *The Great Risk Shift: The Assault on American Jobs, Families, Health Care, and Retirement—and How You Can Fight Back* (New York: Oxford University Press, 2006).

4. Barbara Ehrenreich, *Fear of Falling: The Inner Life of the Middle Class* (New York: Pantheon, 1989). I can think of no better depiction of this class-status anxiety than René Magritte's painting *Golconda* (see the cover of this book).

5. The turn to melancholia to capture society's mood post–Great Recession spans literature, film, and the arts more generally. An overly allegorical and eschatological

rendition can be seen in the Lars von Trier 2011 film *Melancholia* (Zentropia, Denmark), which can be loosely interpreted as suggesting the end of the capitalist way of life as the equivalent to the end of the world (especially for some particularly isolated, privileged people).

6. Sigmund Freud, "Mourning and Melancholia," in *The Standard Edition of the Complete Psychological Works of Sigmund Freud*, vol. 14, *(1914–1916): On the History of the Psycho-Analytic Movement, Papers on Metapsychology and Other Works*, James Stachey, ed., (New York: Vintage Books, 2001 [1917]), pp. 237–58.

7. Ilit Ferber, "Melancholy Philosophy: Freud and Benjamin," *E-rea: Revue Électronique d'Études Sur Le Monde Anglophone—Discourses of Melancholy* 4, 1 (2006), paragraph 1: http://erea.revues.org/413.

8. See Ferber, "Melancholy Philosophy," and "Leibniz's Monad: A Study in Melancholy and Harmony," in *Philosophy's Moods: The Affective Grounds of Thinking*, Hagi Kenaan and Ilit Ferber, eds. (Dordrecht: Springer Press, 2011), pp. 53–68.

9. Ilit Ferber, *Philosophy and Melancholy: Benjamin's Early Reflections on Theater and Language* (Stanford, CA: Stanford University Press, 2013).

10. Giorgio Agamben, *Stanzas: Word and Phantasm in Western Culture* (Minneapolis: University of Minnesota Press, 1993). Von Trier's film *Melancholia* suggests a deep anxiety about an impending doom for people who in spite of their wealth were never satisfied that they had come to possess the safety and comfort they had desired.

11. See Elisabeth Anker, "Heroic Identifications: Or, 'You Can Love Me Too—I Am So Like the State,'" *Theory & Event* 15, 1 (2012), https://muse.jhu.edu/login?auth=0&type=summary&url=/journals/theory_and_event/v015/15.1.anker.html.

12. On the self-hatred that comes with the splitting of the melancholic self, Ferber relies on Walter Benjamin to distinguish pathological melancholia from melancholy as a generic human condition, which she says has a much longer history and "is a mood that allows one privileged access to truth and meaning." See Ferber, "Leibniz's Monad," p. 61.

13. Edward McClelland, "RIP, the Middle Class: 1946–2013," *Alternet*, September 20, 2013, http://www.salon.com/2013/09/20/rip_the_middle_class_1946_2013/.

14. Robert Reich, "Where Is the Angry Middle Class Revolution?" *Salon*, January 27, 2014, http://www.salon.com/2014/01/27/robert_reich_3_reason_why_we_havent_had_a_progressive_revolution_yet_partner/; and Francis Fukuyama, "The Middle Class Revolution," *Wall Street Journal*, June 28, 2013, http://m.us.wsj.com/articles/SB10001424127887323873904578571472700348086?mobile=y.

15. For analysis of survey data demonstrating the effects of economic shocks on personal worries and both on policy attitudes, see Jacob S. Hacker, Philipp Rehm, and Mark Schlesinger, "The Insecure American: Economic Experiences, Financial Worries, and Policy Attitudes," *Perspectives on Politics* 11, 1 (2013): 23–49.

16. See Joseph E. Stiglitz, "A Tax System Stacked against the 99 Percent," *New York Times*, April 15, 2013, http://opinionator.blogs.nytimes.com/2013/04/14/a-tax-system-stacked-against-the-99-percent/?ref=opinion. Also see Robert J. Samuelson, "The Twilight of Entitlement," *Washington Post*, April 28, 2013,

http://www.washingtonpost.com/opinions/robert-samuelson-the-end-of-entitlement/2013/04/28/90356b1a-ae90-11e2-8bf6-e70cb6ae066e_story.html.

17. On the role of demonization of others in the name of vouchsafing one's precarious political identity, see Michael Rogin, *Ronald Reagan, the Movie: And Other Episodes in Political Demonology* (Berkeley: University of California Press: 1988).

18. Guy Standing, *The Precariat: The New and Dangerous Class* (New York: Bloomsbury, 2011).

19. For an insightful analysis of how changes in fiction in recent years reflect a melancholic turn, see David Marcus, "Post-Hysterics: Zadie Smith and the Fiction of Austerity," *Dissent* (Spring 2013), http://www.dissentmagazine.org/article/post-hysterics-zadie-smith-and-the-fiction-of-austerity. Marcus writes about Zadie Smith's fiction: "but in our present moment, we need fiction that is dedicated to exposing the ways in which we can no longer realize ourselves—the ways in which we are just not that free. Smith's *NW*—a novel that captures the taxing human and social costs of austerity—might help lead the way. If nothing else, its pointed sense of direction reminds us just how lost we now are."

20. Natasha Singer, "In the Sharing Economy, Workers Find Both Freedom and Uncertainty," *New York Times*, August 16, 2014, http://www.nytimes.com/2014/08/17/technology/in-the-sharing-economy-workers-find-both-freedom-and-uncertainty.html.

21. Tayyab Mahmud, "Debt and Discipline," *American Quarterly* 64, 3 (2012): 469–94.

22. On neoliberal governmentality, I rely on but also part from Mitchell Dean and Kaspar Villadsen, *State Phobia and Civil Society: The Legacy of Michel Foucault* (Palo Alto, CA: Stanford University Press, forthcoming). See Andrew Dilts, "From 'Entrepreneur of the Self' to 'Care of the Self': Neo-liberal Governmentality and Foucault's Ethics," *Foucault Studies* 12 (October 2011):130–46. The quintessential strategy of neoliberal governmentality is "assets building," whereby each person is expected to save, accumulate capital, and build assets for long-term financial well-being. See Michael Sherraden, ed., *Inclusion in the American Dream: Assets, Poverty, and Public Policy* (New York: Oxford University Press, 2005). For a poignant example of promoting the kind of "subjectivation" (activating a particular type of subjectivity) associated with neoliberal governmentality, see Bree Kessler, "Home Run: How Neoliberalism Took Over Home-Makeover Shows," *Bitch* 57 (Winter 2012): 38–41.

23. See Jodi Dean, *The Communist Horizon (Pocket Communism)* (London: Verso, 2012), p. 173, where she states: "in contrast with desire, drive isn't a quest for a fantastic lost object; it's the force loss exerts on the field of desire. Drives don't circulate around a space that was once occupied by an ideal, impossible object. Rather, drive is the sublimation of desire as it turns back in on itself."

24. See Christopher S. Parker and Matt Baretto, *Change They Can't Believe In: The Tea Party and Reactionary Politics in America* (Princeton, NJ: Princeton University Press, 2013); and Kate Zernike and Megan Thee-Brenan, "Poll Finds Tea Party Backers Wealthier and More Educated," *New York Times*, April 14, 2010, http://www.nytimes.com/2010/04/15/us/politics/15poll.html?src=me&ref=general.

25. On the performative dimensions of anger as manifested in the Tea Party and paradigmatically represented in Rick Santelli's CNN tirade, see Holloway Sparks, "Mamma Grizzlies and the Guardians of the Republic: The Democratic and Intersectional Politics of Anger in the Tea Party Movement," *New Political Science*, August 30, 2014, http://www.tandfonline.com/doi/abs/10.1080/07393148.20 14.945252#.VAX4rPldWPs.

26. See on Flickr, http://www.flickr.com/photos/susanad813/3447487250/.

27. Opposition to immigration reform is high among members of the Tea Party in no small part due to anxiety about how immigration reform would tip the demographic and, by extension, electoral balance against them. See Alexander Bolton and Russell Berman, "Immigration Reform Battle Centers on Conservative Tea Party Bloc," *The Hill*, January 26, 2014, http://thehill.com/homenews/house/ 196427-the-gop-lawmakers-who-may-decide-fate-of-immigration-reform.

28. Kristen A. Lee, "Louisiana Gov. Bobby Jindal Tells GOP 'Stop Being the Stupid Party,'" *New York Daily News,* January 25, 2013, http://www.nydailynews.com/ news/politics/gov-bobby-jindal-gop-stop-stupid-party-article-1.1247645.

29. Zernike and Thee-Brenan, "Poll Finds Tea Party Backers Wealthier and More Educated."

30. Suzanne Mettler, *The Submerged State: How Invisible Government Policies Undermine American Democracy* (Chicago: University of Chicago Press, 2011), p. 2.

31. See Sanford F. Schram, *After Welfare: The Culture of Postindustrial Social Policy* (New York: University Press, 2002), pp. 149–84. Also see chapter 5 here.

32. Stiglitz, "A Tax System Stacked against the 99 Percent."

33. The relationship of private debt to public debt is not just a U.S. problem, as the sovereign debt crisis in Europe has shown. Even the usually fiscally prudent Netherlands increasingly cannot meet its European Union debt limits. Fiscal prudence with social protections as a backstop has resulted in both becoming relics of the past in the face of a massive housing bubble bursting. See Christoph Schult and Anne Seith, "The Netherlands Falls Prey to Economic Crisis," *Speigel Online International,* April 2, 2013, http://www.spiegel.de/international/europe/economic-crisis-hits-the-netherlands-a-891919.html.

34. William E. Connolly, *Christianity and Capitalism, American Style* (Durham, NC: Duke University Press, 2008), pp. 39–68.

35. Fred Block and Margaret R. Somers, *The Power of Market Fundamentalism: Karl Polanyi's Critique* (Cambridge, MA: Harvard University Press, 2014).

36. Block and Somers, *The Power of Market Fundamentalism*, p. 4.

37. Quoted in Block and Somers, *The Power of Market Fundamentalism*, pp. 30–31.

38. C. Wright Mills, *White Collar: The American Middle Classes*, 50th anniversary ed. (New York: Oxford University Press, 2002), pp. 10–11.

39. Grover Norquist, founder and president of Americans for Tax Reform, pushed his Tax Protection Pledge, which was signed by 95 percent of Republicans in Congress before 2012 and is a forerunner of the Tea Party antitax stance. He famously once said: "I'm not in favor of abolishing the government. I just want to shrink it down to the size where we can drown it in the bathtub" (http://www .sourcewatch.org/index.php?title=Grover_Norquist). Norquist's attempt to bankrupt the government by starving it of needed tax revenue that then could help the

middle class cover its debts represents the quintessential example of someone who enacts the drive of middle-class melancholia long after the desire to realize the idealized self-sufficient self has gone away from an increasingly anxious and precarious middle class. See Theda Skocpol and Vanessa Williamson, *The Tea Party and the Remaking of the Republican Conservatism* (New York: Oxford University Press, 2011), p. 172.

40. Sonia Smith, "Drug Tests for Welfare Recipients," *Texas Monthly*, March 27, 2013, http://www.texasmonthly.com/story/drug-tests-welfare-recipients; and Joe Soss, "Penalties Will Hurt Students, Families," *Knoxville News-Sentinel*, April 4, 2013, http://www.knoxnews.com/news/2013/apr/04/joe-soss-penalties-will-hurt-students-families/.
41. See Josh Feldman, "Fox News IDs, Reports New Details on Stenographer Who Went on Bizarre Rant on House Floor," *Mediaite*, October 17, 2013, http://www.mediaite.com/tv/fox-news-ids-reports-new-details-on-stenographer-who-went-on-bizarre-rant-on-house-floor/.
42. Parker and Baretto, *Change They Can't Believe In*, p. 3.
43. Paul Krugman, "The Austerity Agenda," *New York Times*, May 12, 2013, http://www.nytimes.com/2012/06/01/opinion/krugman-the-austerity-agenda.html?_r=0
44. See Ian Haney Lopez, "Is Paul Ryan Racist?" *Politico Magazine*, March 14, 2014, http://www.politico.com/magazine/story/2014/03/is-paul-ryan-racist-104687_Page2.html#.U01ZPlc_RSB.
45. See Ian Haney Lopez, *Dog Whistle Politics: How Coded Racial Appeals Have Reinvented Racism and Wrecked the Middle Class* (New York: Oxford University Press, 2014).
46. See Wendy Brown, "Resisting Left Melancholy," *Boundary* 2, 26 (1999): 19–27. For a recent Hollywood film on left melancholia and the guilt over giving up the struggle for revolutionary transformation of the United States, see Robert Redford's *The Company You Keep* (Voltage Pictures, Los Angeles, 2012). See Kelly Candaele, "The Foam on a Sea of Rage: The Weather Underground, 'The Company You Keep,' and What to Read Instead," *Los Angeles Review of Books*, April 21, 2013, http://lareviewofbooks.org/article.php?id=1599.
47. Elisabeth Anker, "Left Melodrama," *Contemporary Political Theory* 11, 2 (2012): 133. For Anker, melodrama is a useful idiom for articulating the melancholic pre-occupations of the Manichean struggle between the rivaling classes of haves and have-nots.
48. Walter Benjamin, *Selected Writings*, vol. 4, *1938–1940*, ed. Howard Eiland and Michael W. Jennings (Cambridge, Ma: Harvard University Press, 2003), p. 402.
49. Benjamin Noys, *The Persistence of the Negative: A Critique of Contemporary Continental Theory* (Edinburgh: Edinburgh University Press, 2010).
50. Ruth Milkman, Stephanie Luce, and Penny Lewis, *Changing the Subject: A Bottom-Up Account of Occupy Wall Street* (New York: Murphy Institute, City University of New York, 2013), http://sps.cuny.edu/filestore/1/5/7/1_a05051d2117901d/1571_92f562221b8041e.pdf. This report provides empirical evidence the authors use to indicate the middle-class representation in both the Tea Party and Occupy: "[T]he Tea Party is dominated by older whites, including many retired

people (who are thus also 'biographically available,' at the other end of life), and focuses much of its energy on influencing candidates for elected office, with enormous funding from right-wing advocacy groups. As we have seen, Occupy has a much younger profile, its supporters are more highly educated (although many Tea Party members did attend college, contrary to popular belief)."

51. The focus on the 1 percent emerged prior to Occupy in the research Thomas Piketty conducted with Emanuel Saez and others. See Timothy Shenk, "Thomas Piketty and Millennial Marxists on the Scourge of Inequality," *The Nation*, April 14, 2014, http://www.thenation.com/article/179337/thomas-piketty-and-millennial-marxists-scourge-inequality.

52. Dean, *Communist Horizon*, p. 237.

53. Dean, *Communist Horizon*, p. 236.

54. Brown, "Resisting Left Melancholy."

55. See Michael Kazin, "Anarchism Now: Occupy Wall Street Revives an Ideology," *New Republic*, November 7, 2011, www.tnr.com/article/politics/97114/anarchy-occupy-wall-street-throwback. Kazin's concern is that Occupy reflects an excessive willingness to just let people express themselves rather than organizing around an explicit agenda for change. This critique resonates with Dean's even if it comes from a different political position. See Dean, *The Communist Horizon*, pp. 236–37.

56. See Brown, "Resisting Left Melancholy."

57. David Laitin, "Political Remedies to Economic Inequality," in *Occupy the Future*, David Grusky, Doug McAdam, Rob Reich, and Debra Satz, eds. (Boston: Boston Review Books, 2013), p. 152.

58. Gloria Browne-Marshall, "'Occupy Wall Street' Is No Civil Rights Movement," *InsightNews.com*, December 14, 2011, http://insightnews.com/news/8270-occupy-wall-street-is-no-civil-rights-movement.

59. Ta-Nehisi Coates, "Whither the Occupy Wall Street Movement?" *The Root*, February 4, 2012, http://www.theroot.com/buzz/whither-occupy-wall-street-movement.

60. Jacques Derrida, *Specters of Marx: The State of the Debt, The Work of Mourning and the New International* (New York: Routledge, 2006), p. 1.

61. Anker, "Heroic Identifications," http://muse.jhu.edu.proxy.wexler.hunter.cuny .edu/journals/theory_and_event/v015/15.1.anker.html#f29-text.

62. Frances Fox Piven, "Occupy! And Make Them Do It," *The Nation*, April 2, 2012, http://www.thenation.com/article/166821/occupy-and-make-them-do-it.

63. On the "work of mourning" regarding debt as in paying homage to what has been lost, see Derrida, *Specters of Marx*, pp. 61–95. Also see Jacques Derrida, *Given Time: I. Counterfeit Money* (Chicago: University of Chicago Press, 1994).

64. Anker, "Heroic Identifications," http://muse.jhu.edu.proxy.wexler.hunter.cuny .edu/journals/theory_and_event/v015/15.1.anker.html#f29-text.

65. Mahmud, "Debt and Discipline." Also see Ross, *Creditocracy*.

66. See Andrew Dilts, *Punishment and Inclusion: Race, Membership, and the Limits of American Liberalism* (New York: Fordham University Press, 2014), chapter 2, regarding neoliberal governmentality as centered on promoting the entrepreneurial self who leverages his or her human capital to become personally responsible or risks being subject to the state's disciplinary regime.

67. On Foucault's focus on oppression as opposed to Freud's emphasis on repression, see Michel Foucault, *The History of Sexuality*, vol. 1, *An Introduction*, 5th ed. (New York: Vintage, 1990), pp. 15–16.

68. The preoccupation with debt post–Great Recession was immortalized by Jimmy Fallon with Brian Williams and company on *Late Night*, in "Slow Jam the News: The Debt Ceiling," December 3, 2014, http://www.latenightwithjimmyfallon.com/video/slow-jam-the-news-debt-ceiling/n32088/.

69. Andrew Ross, "Creditocracy or Democracy?" *Aljazeera America*, May 10, 2014, http://america.aljazeera.com/opinions/2014/5/credit-card-debtclassoccupy-creditocracy.html.

70. Mahmud, "Debt and Discipline," pp. 487–88. Also see Joseph E. Stiglitz, "Student Debt and the Crushing of the American Dream," *New York Times*, May 12, 2013, http://opinionator.blogs.nytimes.com/2013/05/12/student-debt-and-the-crushing-of-the-american-dream/?smid=fb-share.

71. Occupy's diversity parallels the diversity of the Tea Party, with both having a significant group coming from the middle class, in the case of Occupy that being younger professionals and students who are concerned about how the transformed economy is denying them careers at that stratum. See Slavoj Žižek, *The Year of Dreaming Dangerously* (London: Verso, 2012), p. 12.

72. Rolling Jubilee, "A Bailout of the People by the People," http://rollingjubilee.org/.The antiglobalization movement of the prior decade focused on debt forgiveness for Third World countries struggling to conform to repayment plans imposed by the International Monetary Fund. David Graeber envisioned this effort as analogous to a "biblical jubilee," as in a sabbatical year where the land is not tilled. See David Graeber, *Debt: The First 5,000 Years* (Brooklyn, New York: Melville House, 2011), p. 2, http://libcom.org/files/__Debt__The_First_5_000_Years.pdf.

73. Rolling Jubilee, "A Bailout of the People by the People." Also see Astra Taylor, "A Strike against Student Debt," *New York Times*, February 27, 2015, http://www.nytimes.com/2015/02/28/opinion/a-strike-against-student-debt.html?_r=0.

74. The shift from Occupy protests to the Rolling Jubilee parallels a New Orleans jazz funeral march, first solemn on the way to the burial ground but then jubilant in song on the way back in the name of carrying on. See Joseph Roach, *Cities of the Dead: Circum-Atlantic Performance* (New York: Columbia University Press, 1996), pp. 61–63.

75. On the Right's insistence that government debt is immoral, see Paul Krugman, "Immorality, Debt, and Fiscal Policy," *New York Times*, March 31, 2013.

76. While Jacques Derrida played with Freud's mourning-melancholy distinction, Tammy Clewell notes: "Derrida also argues for an understanding [of] mourning as an affirmative incorporation of the lost other, emphasizing that we internalize lost loves at the same time the lost other cannot be fully assimilated in the mourner's psyche. While recognizing that otherness in the self may give rise to forms of melancholy depression, Derrida also argues that the mourning subject 'welcomes' its own bereaved decentering as the very condition of 'hospitality, love or friendship.'" See Tammy Clewell, "Mourning beyond Melancholia: Freud's Psychoanalysis of Loss," *Journal of the American Psychoanalytic Association*, 52, 1 (2004): 43–67, 63.

77. See Sarah Palin, *America by Heart: Reflections on Family, Faith and Flag* (New York: Harper, 2010), p. 85.
78. "In Florida, Palin Criticizes Occupy Protesters, Says They Want Bailout," *HT Politics*, November 4, 2011, http://politics.heraldtribune.com/2011/11/04/in-florida-palin-criticizes-occupy-protesters-says-they-want-bailout/. Palin's comments anticipated presidential candidate Mitt Romney's infamous 2012 private comment to wealthy campaign donors that the "47 percent" of Americans who did not pay any taxes were voting for President Barack Obama out of a sense of entitlement as victims that the government should take care of them. See Geoffrey Dunn, "'If You Know What I Mean': The Crony Capitalism of Sarah Palin," *Huffington Post*, June 15, 2012, http://www.huffingtonpost.com/geoffrey-dunn/if-you-know-what-i-mean-t_b_1601185.html; and Alfredo Quintana, "I am the 99 Percent and the 47 Percent—and anything but the Romney-Percent," *Huffington Post*, September 18, 2012, http://www.huffingtonpost.com/alfredo-quintana/i-am-the-99-percent-and-t_b_1893916.html.
79. Ferber, "Melancholy Philosophy."
80. Slavoj Žižek, "Only a Radicalised Left Can Save Europe," *New Statesman*, June 25, 2014, http://www.newstatesman.com/politics/2014/06/slavoj-i-ek-only-radicalised-left-can-save-europe.

CHAPTER 3

1. Frances Fox Piven, "Movements Making Noise," *The Nation*, February 18, 2013, http://www.thenation.com/article/172542/movements-making-noise.
2. David Harvey, *Seventeen Contradictions and the End of Capitalism* (New York: Oxford University Press, 2014), p. 91.
3. Frances Fox Piven and Richard A. Cloward, *Regulating the Poor: The Functions of Public Welfare* (New York: Vintage Books, 1971), p. 338.
4. See Judith Butler, "Bodies in Alliance and the Politics of the Street," *#Occupy Los Angeles Reader*, issues 1–3 November 2011, http://suebellyank.com/wp-content/uploads/2011/11/ola-reader-full.pdf.
5. See Maarten Simons and Jan Masschelein, "Governmental, Political and Pedagogic Subjectivation: Foucault with Rancière," *Education Philosophy and Theory* 42 (August 2010): 588–605.
6. See Andrew Dilts, "From 'Entrepreneur of the Self' to 'Care of the Self': Neoliberal Governmentality and Foucault's Ethics," *Foucault Studies* 12 (October 2011): 130–46.
7. On "the people" as manifested in Occupy, see Jodi Dean, *The Communist Horizon* (New York: Verso, 2012), p. 232, e-book. Another notion of the people that highlights its internal diversity is "the multitude." See Michael Hardt and Antonio Negri, *Empire* (Cambridge, MA: Harvard University Press, 2000). On the process by which the multitude becomes a people, see Dilip Gaonkar, "After the Fictions: Notes towards a Phenomenology of the Multitude," *e-flux* 10, 58 (2014), http://www.e-flux.com/journal/after-the-fictions-notes-towards-a-phenomenology-of-the-multitude/.

8. Judith Butler, *Precarious Life: The Powers of Mourning and Violence* (London: Verso, 2006).

9. See Butler, "Bodies in Alliance and the Politics of the Street."

10. On how the appeal to a universally shared human vulnerability constitutes a depoliticizing "mortalist humanism" that prizes ethics over politics, see Bonnie Honig, "Antigone's Two Laws: Greek Tragedy and the Politics of Humanism," *New Literary History* 41, 1 (2010): 1–33; doi:10.1353/nlh.0.0140. Also see Glenn David Mackin, *The Politics of Social Welfare in America* (New York: Cambridge University Press, 2013), pp. 130–34.

11. See Frances Fox Piven and Richard C. Cloward, *Poor People's Movements: How They Succeed, Why They Fail* (New York: Vintage, 1977).

12. Guy Standing, *The Precariat: The New and Dangerous Class* (New York: Bloomsbury USA, 2011). The upper tier of the precariat could be seen as a new "New Class." The "New Class" was a popular neoconservative conceit in the 1980s to suggest that professionals were a new propertyless ruling class who had much more liberal political interests given that their income and wealth was not tied to owning private property but rather derived from their standing in the occupational structure as important experts. It seems the class system has come full circle and Standing stands this idea on its head with his precariat, which includes many professionals dislodged from upper-middle-class status with the economic transformation under way. On the New Class, see B. Bruce-Briggs, *The New Class?* (New Brunswick, NJ: Transaction, 1979).

13. On performativity as centered in the transgressive act of reusing a discursive practice outside its originating context, see Judith Butler, *Excitable Speech: A Politics of the Performative* (New York: Routledge, 1997).

14. On the lumpiness of the "homeless" categorization, see Mark J. Stern, "The Emergence of the Homeless as a Public Problem," *Social Service Review* 58 (1984): 291–301.

15. Andrew Robinson, "In Theory Precariatans of All Countries, Unite!" *Ceasefire*, March 18, 2011.

16. Michael J. Shapiro, introduction, *Language and Politics*, Michael J. Shapiro, ed. (New York: New York University Press, 1994), p. 5.

17. On shared vulnerability as the basis for citizenship, see Martha Fineman, *The Autonomy Myth: A Theory of Dependency* (New York: New Press, 2004).

18. See "There Is Diversity at Occupy Wall Street," October 20, 2011: http://www.theroot.com/multimedia/video-diversity-occupy-wall-street. Also see Errin Haines, "Occupy Protesters Eye Diversity as Movement Grows," *Huffington Post*, October 17, 2011; and Melanie Eversley, "Occupy Wall Street Shows Diversity in Age, Politics," *USA Today*, November 1, 2011.

19. Butler, "Bodies in Alliance and the Politics of the Street."

20. The relation of bodies in alliance to the space of appearance is analogous to music, where the spaces between the individual notes make the melody audible and comprehendible, where the silences between the sounds are constitutive of the song itself. See John Cage, *Silence: Lectures and Writings* (Middletown, CT: Wesleyan University Press, 1961).

21. Butler, "Bodies in Alliance and the Politics of the Street."

22. See Janell Watson, "Butler's Biopolitics: Precarious Community," *Theory and Event* 15, 2 (2012), http://muse.jhu.edu/login?auth=0&type=summary&url=/journals/theory_and_event/v015/15.2.watson.html.

23. On coalitional politics that emphasizes a shared marginal status in relation to power among diverse identity groups, see Cathy Cohen, "Punks, Bulldaggers, and Welfare Queens: The Radical Potential of Queer Politics?" *GQL: A Journal of Lesbian and Gay Studies* 3 (May 1997): 437–65.

24. John Muse, "Preoccupations: Looking at Pictures with Judith Butler," (paper presented at Bryn Mawr College, November 9, 2011). Michel Foucault calls the text/image imbrication a "calligram." See Michel Foucault, *This Is Not a Pipe*, James Harkness, trans. (Berkeley: University of California Press, 1983 [1969]). The calligram highlights in particular how texts and images imply each other in the act of supplementation, where the audience interprets the text to imagine an image and vice versa. Also see W. J. T. Mitchell, *Picture Theory: Essays on Verbal and Visual Representation* (Chicago: University of Chicago Press, 1993).

25. "We Are the 99 Percent," Tumblr, http://wearethe99percent.tumblr.com/.

26. Alfredo Quintana, "I Am the 99 Percent and the 47 Percent—and Anything But the Romney-Percent," *Huffington Post*, September 18, 2012, http://www.huffingtonpost.com/alfredo-quintana/i-am-the-99-percent-and- t_b_1893916.html.

27. Gary Langer, "A Draw on the Economy, a Win on Empathy—and the Face of a Changing Nation," *ABC News*, November 7, 2012, http://abcnews.go.com/blogs/politics/2012/11/a-draw-on-the-economy-a-win-on-empathy-and-the-face-of-a-changing-nation/.

28. Jennifer Silva, *Coming Up Short: Working Class Adulthood in an Age of Uncertainty* (New York: Oxford University Press, 2013), p. 18. The "mood economy" Silva describes as prevailing among the economically disenfranchised working-class young people she interviewed is profoundly melancholic in its focus on individualized detachment from collective efforts to address ongoing economic marginalization. The "We Are the 99 Percent" Tumblr website provides a way of articulating an individual to the collective, i.e., how the individual's plight can be articulated with the common condition. On melancholy as a fundamental mood for articulating the individual's relationship to the world, see Ilit Ferber, "Leibniz's Monad: A Study in Melancholy and Harmony," in *Philosophy's Moods: The Affective Grounds of Thinking*, Hagi Kenaan and Ilit Ferber, eds. (Dordrecht: Springer Press, 2011), p. 61.

29. See Joseph Stiglitz, *The Price of Inequality: How Today's Divided Society Endangers Our Future* (New York: W. W. Norton, 2012).

30. See Jodi Dean, "Enclosing the Subject," *Political Theory* (2014), doi:10.1177/0090591714560377.

31. See Sanford F. Schram, "The Artful Study of Not Being Governed: Better Political Science for a Better World," *Common Knowledge* 18, 2 (2012): 528–37.

32. Karl Marx, "The Eighteenth Brumaire of Louis Napoleon," p. 1. This quotation is taken from the Progress edition (Moscow, 1937), translated by Saul K. Padover from the 1869 German edition.

33. On how contemporary feminism may be unreflectively realizing the goals of neoliberalism that overvalorize individual choice via market participation, see Nancy

Fraser, "Feminism, Capitalism and the Cunning of History," *New Left Review* 56 (March–April 2009): 97–117.

34. Slavoj Žižek, "The True Blasphemy," *I Cite*, http://jdeanicite.typepad.com/i_cite/zizek/.

35. The "We Are the 99 Percent" Tumblr page and the bagged Telefonica strikers represent individuals as anonymous members of a collective action in ways that imply their collective strength in resisting their oppression. The political significance of depicting the individual as an anonymous part of the collective, however, can take a fascist turn, as in Leni Riefenstahl's depictions of the massive Nazi rallies of Nuremberg on behalf of Adolph Hitler in her film *Triumph of the Will*. (Berlin, *Reichspropagandaleitung der NSDAP*, 1935). Magritte's *Golconda* represents a more sardonic statement on "massification" of the status-anxious middle class (see the cover to this book). The political significance of visual representations such as these is perhaps best analyzed in Walter Benjamin, "The Work of Art in the Age of Mechanical Reproduction," in *Illuminations: Essay and Reflections*, Hannah Arendt, ed. (New York: Schocken, 1969), pp. 217–52.

36. Carl Schmitt, *Constitutional Theory* (Durham, NC: Duke University Press, 2008), p. 274, quoted in Mitchell Dean, *The Signature of Power: Sovereignty, Governmentality and Biopolitics* (Los Angeles: Sage, 2013), p. 205.

37. On the one hand, Schmitt's preoccupation with the political as ineliminably public and collective unfortunately is perhaps the greatest example of how such thinking can tip when overemphasized toward the insistence that only "the people" are legitimate and can even form the natural basis for something like National Socialism. On the other hand, the Internet as the neoliberal privatization of political action poses a challenge that the "We Are the 99 Percent" Tumblr page must, and in my mind, evidently does, meet by virtue of its making explicit the various ways that individual narratives are part of the collective understanding of who have been pushed into the precariat and how. The poles between the individual and the collective, it seems, must be traversed in order to keep political agency alive (and healthy).

38. Edward Andrew, "Class in Itself and Class against Capital: Karl Marx and His Classifiers," *Canadian Journal of Political Science/Revue Canadienne de Science Politique* 16, 3 (1983): 577–84.

39. See Karl Marx, *Das Kapital* (Seattle: CreateSpace, 2012), p. 2, where he asserts: people are "the personification of economic categories, the bearers [Träger] of particular class-relations and interests."

40. See Alain Badiou, *Pocket Pantheon: Figures in Postwar Philosophy* (New York: Verso, 2009), p. 31, where Badiou attributes to Jean Paul Sartre the idea that "[c]ollective action is the pure moment of revolt. Everything else is an expression of man's inevitable inhumanity, which is passivity." Badiou himself, however, suggests that more than protest, the dispossessed need a party to channel their agency toward meaningful change.

41. For the argument that stressing precarity as a universally shared condition depoliticizes differences, see Honig, "Antigone's Two Laws." On how marginalization of some implies the inevitability of a politics of recuperation, see Bernard Williams's use of the "moral remainder." Bernard Williams, "Ethical Consistency," in *Problems of the Self* (Cambridge: Cambridge University Press, 1973), pp. 166–86.

42. Dean, *The Communist Horizon*, pp. 229–30.

43. Karen Zivi, "Rights and the Politics of Performativity," in *Judith Butler's Precarious Politics: Critical Encounters*, Terrell Carver and Samuel Chambers, eds. (New York: Routledge, 2008), pp. 157–70. Also see Butler, *Excitable Speech*.

44. See Dilts, "From 'Entrepreneur of the Self' to 'Care of the Self.'"

45. On the *Leviathan* frontispiece, see Ernst Kantorowicz, *The King's Two Bodies: A Study in Mediaeval Political Theology* (Princeton, NJ: Princeton University Press, 1957).

46. See Sanford F. Schram, "Now Time for Neoliberalism: Resisting Plan B from Below," in *Critical Issues for Social Work Practice*, Michael Lavalette and Iain Ferguson, eds. (London: Palgrave Macmillan, 2013). Also see Wendy Brown, "Neo-liberalism and the End of Liberal Democracy," *Theory and Event* 7, 1 (2003), http://muse.jhu.edu/login?uri=/journals/theory_and_event/v007/7.1brown.html.

47. Jacob Hacker, *The Great Risk Shift: The Assault on American Jobs, Families, Health Care, and Retirement—and How You Can Fight Back* (New York: Oxford University Press, 2006).

48. See Naomi Klein, *The Shock Doctrine: The Rise of Disaster Capitalism* (New York: Picador, 2008).

49. Dennis Saleebey, "The Strengths Perspective in Social Work Practice: Extensions and Cautions," *Social Work* 41, 3 (1996): 296–305.

50. Robinson, "In Theory Precariatans of All Countries, Unite!"

51. Franco Barchiesi, "Precarity as Capture: A Conceptual Reconstruction and Critique of the Worker-Slave Analogy," *UniNomade*, October 10, 2012, http://www.uninomade.org/precarity-as-capture/.

52. "Precarity" is what Michael Shapiro calls an "action framework" constitutive of political action itself and not just a reflection of it. See Shapiro, introduction, p. 5.

53. See Michael Kazin, "Anarchism Now: Occupy Wall Street Revives an Ideology," *New Republic*, November 7, 2011, www.tnr.com/article/politics/97114/anarchy-occupy-wall-street-throwback.

54. Dean, *The Communist Horizon*, pp. 238–48.

55. Lois Ruskai Melina, "Being the Change: Protest as Performative Discourse in the Occupy Portland Encampment," *Global Discourse*, 2014, doi:10.1080/23269995.2014.903719.

56. See Adolph Reed, "Nothing Left: The Long, Slow Surrender of American Liberals," *Harper's*, March 2014, http://harpers.org/archive/2014/03/nothing-left-2/.

57. For a good review of the scholarship on the relationship of protest politics to conventional politics, see Doug McAdam and Sidney Tarrow, "Ballots and Barricades: On the Reciprocal Relationship between Social Movements and Elections," *Perspectives on Politics* 8, 2 (2010): 529–42. Not all scholarship has always appreciated the role of protest politics. One noteworthy example is the debate about the role of protest movements in influencing the New Deal. See Jacob S. Hacker and Paul Pierson, "Business Power and Social Policy: Employers and the Formation of the American Welfare State," *Politics and Society* 30, 2 (2002): 277–325.

58. The relationship of protest politics and more conventional politics for the civil rights movement is discussed in Katherine Tate, *From Protest to Politics: The New Black Voters in American Elections* (Cambridge, MA: Harvard University Press, 1998).

59. For just one important example, see Dara Z. Strolovitch, "Do Interest Groups Represent the Disadvantaged? Advocacy at the Intersections of Race, Class, and Gender," *Journal of Politics* 68, 4 (2006): 893–908.

60. See Piven and Cloward, *Poor People's Movements*; and Frances Fox Piven and Richard Cloward, *Why Americans Don't Vote* (New York: Pantheon Books, 1989).

61. See Sanford F. Schram, *Praxis for the Poor: Piven and Cloward and the Future of Social Science in Social Welfare* (New York: New York University Press, 2002), chapter 3.

62. See Schram, *Praxis for the Poor*, chapter 3. Piven's talk to the Occupy Wall Street encampment in Zuccotti Park on October 3, 2011, spoke to the role of the protest in distinction from the efforts of parties to win elections: Frances Fox Piven, "We Desperately Need a Popular Uprising in the U.S.," Youtube, http://www.youtube.com/watch?v=gBbnnqlX9Jw.

63. Frances Fox Piven, "Occupy! And Make Them Do It," *The Nation*, April 2, 2012, http://www.thenation.com/article/166821/occupy-and-make-them-do-it.

64. On protest politics as something that is not done at a distance from the state, see Alain Badiou as cited in Mackin, *The Politics of Social Welfare in America*, p. 203.

65. See Schram, *Praxis for the Poor*, chapter 3.

66. Frances Fox Piven, "Occupy's Protest Is Not Over: It Has Barely Begun," *Guardian*, September 17, 2012.

67. See Jeffrey C. Alexander, "The Arc of Civil Liberation: Obama-Tahrir-Occupy," *Philosophy and Social Criticism* 39, 4–5 (2013): 341–47.

CHAPTER 4

1. See Micaela di Leonardo, *Exotics at Home: Anthropologies, Others, and American Modernity* (Chicago: University of Chicago Press, 1998), p. 1.

2. Stephen J. Ball, *Education Policy and Social Class: The Selected Works of Stephen J. Ball* (New York: Routledge, 2007), p. 48. Also see Eduardo Bonilla-Silva, *Racism without Racists: Color-Blind Racism and the Persistence of Racial Inequality in the United States* (Lanham, MD: Rowman and Littlefield, 2003).

3. See Martin Gilens, *Why Americans Hate Welfare: Race, Media, and the Politics of Antipoverty Policy* (Chicago: University of Chicago Press, 2000).

4. Sanford F. Schram, *Words of Welfare: The Poverty of Social Science and the Social Science of Poverty* (Minneapolis: University of Minnesota Press, 1995).

5. See J. M. Balkin, *Cultural Software: A Theory of Ideology* (New Haven, CT: Yale University Press, 2003).

6. Jeffrey Alexander, *The Performance of Politics: Obama's Victory and the Democratic Struggle for Power* (New York: Oxford University Press, 2010), 81.

7. Barbara J. Nelson, "The Origins of the Two-Channel Welfare State: Workmen's Compensation and Mothers' Aid," in *Women, the State, and Welfare*, Linda Gordon, ed. (Madison: University of Wisconsin Press, 1990), 123–51.

8. Joe Soss and Sanford F. Schram, "A Public Transformed? Welfare Reform as Policy Feedback," *American Political Science Review* 101, 1 (2007): 111–27.

9. Soss and Schram, "A Public Transformed?"

10. See Kathryn Edin and Laura Lein, *Making Ends Meet: How Single Mothers Survive Welfare and Low-Wage Work* (New York: Russell Sage Foundation, 1998).

11. Even Michael Harrington, in *The Other America,* ended up reinscribing the deep semiotic structure of deservingness by suggesting the poor had a different culture than the middle class. See Barbara Ehrenreich, "Rediscovering American Poverty: How We Cured 'The Culture of Poverty,' Not Poverty Itself," *TomDispatch.com,* March 15, 2012, http://www.tomdispatch.com/post/175516/tomgram%3A_barbara_ehrenreich%2C_american_poverty%2C_50_years_later/.

12. Martha Feldman, Kaj Sköldberg, Ruth Nicole Brown, and Debra Horner, "Making Sense of Stories: A Rhetorical Approach to Narrative Analysis," *Journal of Public Administration Research and Theory* 14, 2 (2004): 147–70.

13. "The Literary Apprentice," http://www.cod.edu/people/faculty/fitchf/readlit/theory.htm.

14. See Slavoj Žižek, *Enjoy Your Symptom: Jacques Lacan in Hollywood and Out* (New York: Routledge, 2001).

15. Michael Klein, "Narrative and Discourse in Kubrick's Modern Tragedy," in *The English Novel and the Movies,* Michael Klein and Gillian Parker, eds. (New York: Frederick Ungar, 1981), pp. 95–107, 95, 107.

16. Deborah Stone, *Policy Paradox and Political Reason* (New York: W. W. Norton, 2010).

17. Sanford F. Schram, "Postmodern Policy Analysis: Identity and Difference in Social Policy," *Policy Sciences* 26, 2 (1993): 249–70.

18. Frank Fischer, *Democracy and Expertise: Reorienting Policy Inquiry* (New York: Oxford University Press, 2009), p. 206.

19. See Michael B. Katz, *The Undeserving Poor: America's Enduring Confrontation with Poverty,* 2nd ed. (New York: Oxford University Press, 2013).

20. Charles Murray is presented as the most significant contemporary proponent of the perversity thesis in Fred Block and Margaret Somers, *The Power of Market Fundamentalism: Karl Polanyi's Critique* (Cambridge, MA: Harvard University Press, 2014), chapter 7.

21. See Margaret Somers and Fred Block, "From Poverty to Perversity: Ideas, Markets, and Institutions over 200 Years of Welfare Debate," *American Sociological Review* 70 (2005): 260–87.

22. Matthew A. Crenson, *Building the Invisible Orphanage: A Prehistory of the American Welfare System* (Cambridge, MA: Harvard University Press, 2001).

23. Deborah E. Ward, *The White Welfare State: The Racialization of U.S. Welfare Policy* (Ann Arbor: University of Michigan Press, 2005).

24. Frances Fox Piven and Richard A. Cloward, *Regulating the Poor: The Functions of Public Welfare* (New York: Pantheon Books, 1971).

25. Joe Soss, Richard C. Fording, and Sanford F. Schram, *Disciplining the Poor: Neoliberal Paternalism and the Persistent Power of Race* (Chicago: University of Chicago Press, 2011).

26. Sanford F. Schram and Joe Soss, "Success Stories: Welfare Reform, Policy Discourse, and the Politics of Research," *The Annals of the American Academy of Political and Social Science* 577 (2001): 49–65.

27. See Thomas Lemke, "The Birth of Bio-Politics: Michel Foucault's Lecture at the Collège de France on Neo-Liberal Governmentality," *Economy and Society* 30, 2 (2001): 190–207.

28. See Patrick Kaylor, "Wraparound: Medicalization and Governmentality" (Ph.d. dissertation, Graduate School of Social Work and Social Research, Bryn Mawr College, 2008).

29. Schram, *Words of Welfare*, pp. 3–19.

30. In many ways, neoliberal governmentality ends up undermining the individualization that comes when human services work to empower clients to practice self-determination. See Anna Yeatman, Gary Wayne Dowsett, and Diane Gursansky, *Individualization and the Delivery of Welfare Services: Contestation and Complexity* (London: Palgrave Macmillan, 2009).

31. Sanford F. Schram, *After Welfare: The Culture of Postindustrial Social Policy* (New York: New York University Press, 2000), pp. 62–63.

32. Sanford F. Schram, *Welfare Discipline: Discourse, Governance, and Globalization* (Philadelphia: Temple University Press, 2006), pp. 136–39.

33. See Linda Houser, Sanford F. Schram, Joe Soss, and Richard C. Fording, "Babies as Barriers: Welfare Policy Discourse in an Era of Neoliberalism," *The Rutledge Handbook of Poverty in the United States*, Stephen Nathan Haymes, Maria Vidal de Haymes, and Rueben Miller, eds. (New York: Routledge, 2015), pp. 143–60.

34. Soss, Fording, and Schram, *Disciplining the Poor*, chapters 9–10.

35. Sheldon H. Danziger, Richard Frank, and Ellen Meara, "Mental Illness, Work and Income Support Programs," *American Journal of Psychiatry* 166, 4 (2009): 398–404.

36. Pew Research Center, "Independents Take Center Stage in Obama Era," 2009, http://www.people-press.org/2009/05/21/independents-take-center-stage-in-obama-era/.

37. Gilens, *Why Americans Hate Welfare*.

38. See Murray Edelman, *Political Language: Words That Succeed and Polities* (Lanham, MD: Academic Press, 1974).

39. Peter Conrad, *The Medicalization of Society: On the Transformation of Human Conditions into Treatable Disorders* (Baltimore: Johns Hopkins University Press, 2007).

40. Alison Mitchell, "Gingrich's Views on Slayings Draw Fire," *New York Times*, November 23, 1995, http://www.nytimes.com/1995/11/23/us/gingrich-s-views-on-slayings-draw-fire.html.

41. Lemke, "The Birth of Bio-Politics," p. 203.

42. Anna Korteweg, "Welfare Reform and the Subject of the Working Mother: Get a Job, a Better Job, Then a Career," *Theory and Society* 32, 4 (2003): 445–80, 468.

43. See Theda Skocpol and Vanessa Williamson, *The Tea Party and the Remaking of Republican Conservatism* (New York: Oxford University Press, 2011).

44. Adam Liptak, "In Court, Sharp Questions on Health Law's Mandate," *New York Times*, March 28, 2012, http://www.nytimes.com/slideshow/2012/03/27/us/20120328_SCOTUS.html?ref=us.

45. On the framing of issues by political elites to first agitate the mass public and then re-create their acquiescence to policies that elites wanted to enact in the first place, see Murray Edelman, *Politics as Symbolic Action: Mass Arousal and Quiescence* (Chicago: Markham, 1971).

CHAPTER 5

1. Iain Ferguson and Michael Lavalette, "Globalization and Social Justice: Toward a Social Work of Resistance," *International Social Work* 49, 3 (2006): 309–18.

2. Catherine McDonald and Gregory Marston, *Analysing Social Policy: A Governmental Approach* (London: Algar, 2006); Michael Fabricant and Steve Burghardt, *The Welfare State Crisis and the Transformation of Social Service Work* (Armonk, NY: M. E. Sharpe, 1992); David Stoesz, *Poverty of Imagination: Bootstrap Capitalism, Sequel to Welfare Reform* (Madison: University of Wisconsin Press, 2000); Jane Aronson and Kristin Smith, "Managing Restructured Social Services: Expanding the Social?" *British Journal of Social Work* 40 (2010): 530–47; John Wallace and Bob Pease, "Neoliberalism and Australian Social Work: Accommodation or Resistance?" *Journal of Social Work* 11 (2011): 132–42; Dennis R. Young et al., *Financing Nonprofits: Putting Theory into Practice* (Lanham, MD: AltaMira Press, 2006).

3. Joe Soss, Richard C. Fording, and Sanford F. Schram, "The Organization of Discipline: From Performance; Management to Perversity and Punishment," *Journal of Public Administration Research and Theory* 21 (2011): i202–i232.

4. Wendy Brown, "Neo-Liberalism and the End of Liberal Democracy," *Theory and Event* 7 (2003), http://muse.jhu.edu/journals/theory_and_event/.

5. Michael Lipsky, *Street-level Bureaucracy: Dilemmas of the Individual in Public Service* (New York: Russell Sage Foundation, 2010 [1983]).

6. Joe Soss, Richard C. Fording, and Sanford F. Schram, *Disciplining the Poor: Neoliberal Paternalism and the Persistent Power of Race* (Chicago: University of Chicago Press, 2011).

7. Soss, Fording, and Schram, "The Organization of Discipline."

8. Michael Katz, *Improving Poor People: The Welfare State, the "Underclass," and Urban Schools as History* (Princeton, NJ: Princeton University Press, 1997).

9. Richard A. Cloward and Frances Fox Piven, "Notes toward a Radical Social Work," in *Radical Social Work*, Roy Bailey and Mike Brake, eds. (New York: Pantheon, 1975), pp. vii–xlviii.

10. Linda Gordon, *Pitied but Not Entitled: Single Mothers and the History of Welfare, 1890–1935* (New York: Free Press, 1994).

11. Scott Allard, *Out of Reach: Place, Poverty, and the New American Welfare State* (New Haven, CT: Yale University Press, 2009).

12. Brown, "Neo-Liberalism and the End of Liberal Democracy."

13. Soss, Fording, and Schram, *Disciplining the Poor*, chapter 2.

14. Sanford F. Schram and Joe Soss, "Success Stories: Welfare Reform, Policy Discourse, and the Politics of Research," *Annals of the American Academy of Political and Social Science* 577 (2001): 49–65.

15. Lawrence Mead, ed., *The New Paternalism: Supervisory Approaches to Poverty* (Washington, DC: Brookings Institution Press, 1997).

16. Jon Carroll, "Mr. Newt Explains It All for You," *San Francisco Chronicle*, November 27, 1995, p. B8.

17. Sanford F. Schram, *Welfare Discipline: Discourse, Governance and Globalization* (Philadelphia: Temple University Press, 2006), chapter 7.

18. Celeste Watkins-Hayes, *The New Welfare Bureaucrats: Entanglements of Race, Class, and Policy Reform* (Chicago: University of Chicago Press, 2009), p. 14; and Frank Ridzi, *Selling Welfare Reform: Work-first and the New Common Sense of Employment* (New York: New York University Press, 2009), p. 137.
19. Catherine J. Turco, "Cultural Foundations of Tokenism: Evidence from the Leveraged Buyout Industry," *American Sociological Review* 75, 6 (2010): 894–913.
20. Kenneth J. Meier, "Representative Bureaucracy: An Empirical Analysis," *American Political Science Review* 69 (1975): 526–42.
21. Michael Brintnall, "Preparing the Public Service for Working in the Multiethnic Democracies: An Assessment and Ideas for Action," *Journal of Public Affairs Education* 14, 1 (2008): 39–50.
22. Frank J. Omowale Satterwhite, and Shiree Teng, *Culturally Based Capacity Building: An Approach to Working in Communities of Color for Social Change* (Los Angeles: California Endowment and CompassPoint Nonprofit Services, 2007), p. 2.
23. Tony Carrizales, "Exploring Cultural Competency within the Public Affairs Curriculum," *Journal of Public Affairs Education* 16, 4 (2010): 593–606.
24. Ridzi, *Selling Welfare Reform*; and Watkins-Hayes, *The New Welfare Bureaucrats*.
25. Cathy Cohen, *The Boundaries of Blackness: AIDS and the Breakdown of Black Politics* (Chicago: University of Chicago Press, 1999).
26. Schram and Soss, "Success Stories."
27. Alcoholics Anonymous, *Twelve Steps and Twelve Traditions* (New York: Alcoholics Anonymous, 1953).
28. Donald P. Moynihan, *The Dynamics of Performance Management: Constructing Information and Reform* (Washington, DC: Georgetown University Press, 2008), p. 9.
29. Beryl A. Radin, *Challenging the Performance Movement: Accountability, Complexity, and Democratic Values* (Washington, DC: Georgetown University Press, 2006).
30. Stephen H. Bell and Larry L. Orr, "Screening (and Creaming?) Applicants to Job Training Programs: The AFDC Homemaker–Home Health Aide Demonstrations," *Labour Economics* 9, 2 (2002): 279–301.
31. Soss, Fording, and Schram, *Disciplining the Poor*, p. 213.
32. Radin, *Challenging the Performance Movement*.
33. Irene Lurie, *At the Frontlines of the Welfare System: A Perspective on the Decline in Welfare Caseloads* (Albany: State University of New York Press, 2006).
34. Lawrence Mead, *Government Matters: Welfare Reform in Wisconsin* (Princeton, NJ: Princeton University Press, 2004), p. 158.
35. Soss, Fording, and Schram, *Disciplining the Poor*, pp. 223–26.
36. Simon Guilfoyle, "On Target?—Public Sector Performance Management: Recurrent Themes, Consequences and Questions," *Policing* 6, 3 (2012): 250–60.
37. Richard C. Fording, Sanford F. Schram, and Joe Soss, "Do Welfare Sanctions Help or Hurt the Poor? Estimating the Causal Effect of Sanctioning on Client Earnings," *Social Service Review* 87, 4 (2013): 641–76.
38. Mary Ellen Klas, "Federal Labor Officials to Investigate Questionable Contracts at Florida Workforce Boards," *St. Petersburg Times*, July 15, 2011.
39. National Institute on Drug Abuse, *Principles of Drug Addiction Treatment* (Bethesda, MD: National Institute on Drug Abuse, 1999).

40. Institute of Medicine, *Improving the Quality of Health Care for Mental and Substance-Use Conditions*, Committee on Crossing the Quality Chasm: Adaptation to Mental Health and Addictive Disorders (Washington, DC: Institute of Medicine of the National Academies on Health Care Services and National Academies Press, 2006), www.nap.edu.

41. Thomas A. McLellan, Jack Kemp, Adam Brooks, and Deni Carisea, "Improving Public Addiction Treatment through Performance Contracting: The Delaware Experiment," *Health Policy* 87, 3 (2008): 296–308.

42. Stephen T. Higgins and Nancy M. Petry, "Contingency Management: Incentives for Sobriety," *Alcohol Research and Health* 23, 2 (1999): 122–29.

43. Anita Marton, John Daigle, and Grace de la Gueronniere, *Identifying State Purchasing Levers for Promoting the Use of Evidence-Based Practice in Substance Abuse Treatment*, resource paper, Center for Health Care Strategies, (Princeton, NJ: Robert Wood Johnson Foundation's Medicaid Managed Care Program, 2005), http://www.chcs.org/media/PurchasingLeversFinal.pdf.

44. Marton, Daigle, and de la Gueronniere, *Identifying State Purchasing Levers.*

45. Join Together *Rewarding Results: Improving the Quality of Treatment for People Alcohol and Drug Problems* (Boston: Boston University School of Public Health, 2003), p. ii, http://www.washingtoncircle.org/pdfs/JTO_Report.pdf.

46. McLellan et al., "Improving Public Addiction Treatment through Performance Contracting," p. 297.

47. As quoted in Maureen Stewart, *Use of Performance-Based Contracts in Outpatient Alcohol and Drug Abuse Treatment* (Phd dissertation, Brandeis University, Heller School of Public Policy, 2009), p. 148.

48. McLellan et al., "Improving Public Addiction Treatment through Performance Contracting."

49. McLellan et al., "Improving Public Addiction Treatment through Performance Contracting," pp. 302–4.

50. Teresa Gowan and Sarah Whetstone,"Making the Criminal Addict: Subjectivity and Social Control in a Strong-Arm Rehab," *Punishment and Society* 14, 1 (2012): 69–93.

51. Alcoholics Anonymous, *Twelve Steps and Twelve Traditions.*

52. National Institute on Drug Abuse, *A Manual to Reduce the Risk of HIV and Other Blood-Borne Infections in Drug Users*, NIH Publication 00-4812 (Washington, DC: National Institute on Drug Abuse, U.S. Department of Health and Human Services, National Institutes of Health, 2000).

53. Dánica M. Diaz, "Comparing the Effectiveness of Behavioral Contracts that Use Function Based Reinforcers versus Highly Preferred Items for Attention Maintained Behaviors" (MAthesis, University of South Florida, Department of Child and Family Studies,), http://scholarcommons.usf.edu/etd/1614.

54. Toba Schwaber Kerson et al., *Social Work in Health Settings: Practice in Context* (New York: Routledge, 2010).

55. Gowan and Whetstone,"Making the Criminal Addict."

56. Aronson and Smith, "Managing Restructured Social Services."

57. Lisa Dodson, *The Moral Underground: How Ordinary Americans Subvert an Unfair Economy* (New York: New Press, 2011).

58. See Kathleen Stewart, *Ordinary Affects* (Durham, NC: Duke University Press, 2007). On "radical incrementalism," see chapter 8.

CHAPTER 6

1. Jesse Hessler Rhodes, "Progressive Policy Making in a Conservative Age? Civil Rights and the Politics of Federal Education Standards, Testing, and Accountability," *Perspectives on Politics* 9, 3 (2011): 519–44.
2. Diane Ravitch, *Reign of Error: The Hoax of the Privatization Movement and the Danger to America's Public Schools* (New York: Knopf, 2012).
3. Henry Giroux, "Neoliberalism, Corporate Culture, and the Promise of Higher Education: The University as a Democratic Public Sphere," *Harvard Educational Review* 72, 4 (2002): 425–63. Also see Suzanne Mettler, *Degrees of Inequality: How the Politics of Higher Education Sabotaged the American Dream* (New York: Basic Books, 2014).
4. Pierre Bourdieu, "Rethinking the State: On the Genesis and Structure of the Bureaucratic Field," *Sociological Theory* 12, 1 (1994): 1–19.
5. Löic Wacquant, *Punishing the Poor: The Neoliberal Government of Social Insecurity* (Durham, NC: Duke University Press, 2009).
6. Joe Soss, Richard C. Fording, and Sanford F. Schram, *Disciplining the Poor: Neoliberal Paternalism and the Persistent Power of Race* (Chicago: University of Chicago Press, 2011).
7. See Soss, Fording, and Schram, *Disciplining the Poor*, pp. 6–9.
8. Deborah Stone, *Policy Paradox: The Art of Political Decision Making* (New York: W. W. Norton, 2012); and Murray Edelman, *Political Language: Words/That Succeed and Polities* (Lanham, MD: Academic Press, 1974). See chapter 4 for how their theorizing the role of crisis narratives in public policy deliberation can be applied to welfare reform.
9. *A Nation at Risk: The Imperative for Educational Reform* (Washington, DC: U.S. Department of Education, National Commission on Excellence in Education, 1983), http://www2.ed.gov/pubs/NatAtRisk/intro.html.
10. *A Nation at Risk*, introduction, http://www2.ed.gov/pubs/NatAtRisk/intro.html.
11. See Henry Giroux, *Neoliberalism's War on Higher Education* (Chicago: Haymarket Books, 2014).
12. Garnet Kindervater and Joe Soss, "Governing through Crisis: How States Produce the Present in the Future Tense" (paper presented at the Annual Meeting of the Western Political Science Association, Seattle, WA, April 19, 2014).
13. *A Nation at Risk*, risk section, http://www2.ed.gov/pubs/NatAtRisk/risk.html.
14. *A Nation at Risk*, recommendations, http://www2.ed.gov/pubs/NatAtRisk/recomm.html.
15. Kindervater and Soss, "Governing through Crisis," pp. 28–29.
16. See Sanford F. Schram, *Words of Welfare: The Poverty of Social Science and the Social Science of Poverty* (Minneapolis: University of Minnesota Press, 1995), pp. 20–21.
17. David Hursh, *High-Stakes Testing and the Decline of Teaching and Learning: The Real Crisis in Education* (Lanham, MD: Rowman & Littlefield, 2008).

18. Henry A. Giroux, "Can Democratic Education Survive in a Neoliberal Society?" *Truthout*, October 16, 2012, http://truth-out.org/opinion/item/12126-can-democratic-education-survive-in-a-neoliberal-society.

19. The neoliberal preoccupation with risk is demonstrated in lotteries for admission to exclusive charter schools that in some communities provide basically the only chance for a child to escape poverty. This situation is poignantly depicted in the Davis Guggenheim film *Waiting for Superman* (Santa Monica, CA, Electric Kinney Films, 2010).

20. In particular, see Ravitch, *Reign of Error*; and Giroux, *Neoliberalism's War on Higher Education*. Also see Gordon Lafer, *Do Poor Kids Deserve Lower-Quality Education than Rich Kids? Evaluating School Privatization Proposals in Milwaukee, Wisconsin*, Briefing Paper #375 (Washington, DC: Economic Policy Institute, 2014).

21. Barbara Miner, "Vouchers: Special Ed Students Need Not Apply," *Rethinking Our Schools* (Winter 2003), http://www.rethinkingschools.org/special_reports/voucher_report/v_vouc182.shtml.

22. *National Charter School Study, 2013* (Stanford, CA: Center for Research on Education Outcomes, Stanford University, 2013), http://credo.stanford.edu/documents/NCSS%202013%20Final%20Draft.pdf.

23. Amy Crawford, "Should the School Year Be Longer? A Large-Scale Study Throws Cold Water on a Popular Idea," *Boston Globe*, June 2, 2013, http://www.bostonglobe.com/ideas/2013/06/01/should-school-year-longer/yHLI249RX-COfVVHWe1g9pO/story.html.

24. Crawford, "Should the School Year Be Longer?"

25. Ravitch, *Reign of Error*, pp. 156–79.

26. Lafer, *Do Poor Kids Deserve Lower-Quality Education than Rich Kids?*, pp. 3–5.

27. See Mettler, *Degrees of Inequality*, pp. 87–109.

28. Mettler, *Degrees of Inequality*, pp. 37–38.

29. See Jesse Rhodes, *An Education in Politics: The Origins and Evolution of No Child Left Behind* (Ithaca, NY: Cornell University Press, 2012).

30. Motoko Rich, "A Walmart Fortune Spreading Charter Schools," *New York Times*, April 26, 2013, http://www.nytimes.com/2014/04/26/us/a-walmart-fortune-spreading-charter-schools.html?hpw&rref=us&_r=0.

31. Mettler, *Inequalities of Degrees*, p. 15.

32. Andrea Gabor, "Charter School Refugees," *New York Times*, April 4, 2013, http://www.nytimes.com/2014/04/05/opinion/charter-school-refugees.html?_r=0.

33. David Harvey, *A Brief History of Neoliberalism* (New York: Oxford University Press, 2007).

34. Wesley Shumar, *College for Sale: A Critique of the Commodification of Higher Education* (New York: Routledge, 1997).

35. Michael Apple, *Educating the "Right" Way: Markets, Standards, God, and Inequality* (New York: Routledge, 2006).

36. See Rhodes, *An Education in Politics*, pp. 185–86.

37. Tamar Lewin, "Obama's Plan Aims to Lower Cost of College," *New York Times*, August 22, 2013, http://www.nytimes.com/2013/08/22/education/obamas-plan-aims-to-lower-cost-of-college.html?_r=0.

38. See Donald P. Moynihan, *The Dynamics of Performance Management: Constructing Information and Reform* (Washington, DC: Georgetown University Press, 2008); and Beryl A. Radin, *Challenging the Performance Movement: Accountability, Complexity, and Democratic Values* (Washington, DC: Georgetown University Press, 2006).

39. Beryl A. Radin, "The Government and Performance Review Act (GPRA): Hydra-Headed Monster or Flexible Management Tool?" *Public Administration Review* 58, 4 (1988): 307–17.

40. At its etymological root, the word "statistics" implies numbers for the state. See Mary Poovey, "Figures of Arithmetic, Figures of Speech: The Discourse of *Statistics* in the 1830s," *Critical Inquiry* 19, 2 (1993): 256–76.

41. On administrative policy feedback, see Joe Soss and Donald P. Moynihan, "Feedback and the Politics of Administration," *Public Administration Review*, April 16, 2014, doi: 10.1111/puar.12200.

42. On suboptimization and No Child Left Behind, see Mark Graban, "Texas Snow Days Expose the Gaming of Standardized Tests," *Learn Blog*, February 12, 2011, http://www.leanblog.org/2011/02/texas-snow-days-expose-the-gaming-of-standardized-tests/.

43. See Mario Morino, *Leap of Reason: Managing Outcomes in an Age of Scarcity* (Washington, DC: Venture Philanthrophy Partners, 2011), p. 7.

44. Jeffrey P. Braden and Jennifer L. Schroeder, "High-Stakes Testing and No Child Left Behind: Information and Strategies for Educators," *National Association of School Psychologists* (2004), http://www.nasponline.org/communications/spawareness/highstakes.pdf.

45. Sharon L. Nichols, Gene V. Glass, and David C. Berliner, *High-Stakes Testing and Student Achievement: Problems for the No Child Left Behind Act* (Tempe, AZ: Education Policy Studies Laboratory, Arizona State University, 2005), p. 109, http://epsl.asu.edu/epru/documents/EPSL-0509-105-EPRU.pdf.

46. See James J. Heckman, Carolyn J. Heinrich, and Jeffrey Smith, "The Performance of Performance Standards," *Journal of Human Resources* 37, 4 (2002): 778–811; and Robert Klitgaard and Paul Light, eds., *High Performance Government: Structure, Leadership, Incentives* (Santa Monica, CA: Rand, 2005), p. 6.

47. Randal Reback, "Teaching to the Rating: School Accountability and the Distribution of Student Achievement," *Journal of Public Economics* 92 (2008): 1394–1415.

48. Diane Elliot Kearn, "Zombie Ideas in Education: High-Stakes Testing and Graduation Policies," *New England Reading Association Journal* 49, 1 (2013): 96–103. For instance, see "Louisiana Believes—SPED Students Should Be Reclassified before Test Time to Optimize Test Scores," *Crazy Crawfish Blog*, February 6, 2013, http://crazycrawfish.wordpress.com/2013/02/06/louisiana-believes-sped-students-should-be-reclassified-before-test-time-to-optimize-test-scores/.

49. Julian V. Heilig and Linda L. Darling-Hammond, "Accountability Texas-Style: The Progress and Learning of Urban Minority Students in a High-Stakes Testing Context," *Educational Evaluation and Policy Analysis* 30, 2 (2008): 75. The NCLB legislation includes test accommodations for students with disability, which can lead to gaming the system in the opposite direction of including students with

disabilities but testing them in ways that allow them to score higher than previously. See Thomas S. Dee and Brian Jacob, "The Impact of No Child Left Behind on Student Achievement," *Journal of Policy Analysis and Management* 30, 3 (2011): 418–46.

50. Valerie Strauss, "Atlanta Test Cheating: The Tip of the Iceberg?" *Washington Post*, April 1, 2013, http://www.washingtonpost.com/blogs/answer-sheet/wp/2013/04/01/atlanta-test-cheating-tip-of-the-iceberg/.

51. See Harvey, *A Brief History of Neoliberalism*, p. 98.

52. Andrew Dilts, "From 'Entrepreneur of the Self' to 'Care of the Self': Neo-liberal Governmentality and Foucault's Ethics," *Foucault Studies* 12 (October 2011): 130–46. Also see Andreas Kalyvas and Ira Katznelson, "Rhetoric of the Market: Adam Smith on Recognition, Speech and Exchange," *Review of Politics* 63, 3 (2001): 549–80.

53. Michel Foucault, *The Birth of Biopolitics: Lectures at the Collège de France, 1978–79*, Translated by Graham Burchell, trans. (New York: Palgrave Macmillan, 2008), p. 226.

54. Chris Maisano, "The Soul of Student Debt," *Jacobin* 9 (2012), https://www.jacobinmag.com/2012/12/the-soul-of-student-debt/.

55. Mettler, *Degrees of Inequality*.

56. Mettler, *Degrees of Inequality*, pp. 30–39.

57. Richard Arum and Josipa Roska, *Academically Adrift: Limited Learning on College Campuses* (Chicago: University of Chicago Press, 2010).

58. Steven Strauss, "'Welcome' to the Sharing Economy—Also Known as the Collapse of the American Dream," *Huffington Post*, December 29, 2013, http://www.huffingtonpost.com/steven-strauss/welcome-to-the-sharing-economy_b_4516707.html.

59. U.S. House of Representatives, Committee on Education and the Workforce, Democratic staff, *The Just-in-Time Professor: A Staff Report Summarizing eForum Responses on the Working Conditions of Contingent Faculty in Higher Education*, January 2014), http://democrats.edworkforce.house.gov/sites/democrats.edworkforce.house.gov/files/documents/1.24.14-AdjunctEforumReport.pdf.

60. Adrianna Kezar, "Changing Faculty Workload Models," *TIAA-CREF Institute*, November 2013, https://www.tiaa-crefinstitute.org/public/pdf/changing-faculty-workforce-models.pdf.

61. "Major Players in the MOOC Universe," *Chronicle of Higher Education*, April 22, 2014, http://chronicle.com/article/Major-Players-in-the-MOOC/138817/?cid=wc.

62. Carol L. Ziegler and Nancy M. Lederman, "School Vouchers: Are Urban Students Surrendering Rights for Choice?" *Fordham Urban Law Journal* 19, 3 (1991): 813–31.

CHAPTER 7

1. Relying on Kathleen Stewart, we can say that neoliberalism exudes its own form of agency, operating on us as much as we operate on it, producing effects in relationship between people, things, and spaces. It is something that must be contended

with rather than simply dismissed. We must work through rather than ignore its power, by engaging its "ordinary affects" in everyday life. See Kathleen Stewart, *Ordinary Affects* (Durham, NC: Duke University Press, 2007).

2. See Philip Mirowski, *Never Let a Serious Crisis Go to Waste: How Neoliberalism Survived the Financial Meltdown* (London: Verso, 2013).

3. Jamie Peck, "Zombie Neoliberalism and the Ambidexterous State," *Theoretical Criminology* 14, 1 (2010): 104–10; and Mitchell Dean, *The Signature of Power: Sovereignty, Governmentality and Biopolitics* (Los Angeles: Sage, 2013), p. 220.

4. On the growing popularity of social impact bonds, see Kristina Costa, "Social Impact Bonds: Investing for Success," Center for American Progress, March 3, 2014, https://www.americanprogress.org/issues/open-government/report/2014/03/03/85099/investing-for-success/. On fast-track global social policy, see Jamie Peck and Nik Theodore, "Recombinant Workfare, across the Americas: Transnationalizing 'Fast' Social Policy," *Geoforum* 41, 2 (2010): 195–208. Also see Jay F. Hein, "Ideas as Exports: The National and International Welfare Reform Efforts of the Past Decade Got Their Start in Madison, Wisconsin," *American Outlook*, Summer 2002, http://www.sagamoreinstitute.org/ao/index/article/id/1877. Hein talks about what he calls "global domestic policy," i.e., social policies that get disseminated around the world.

5. See Donald Moynihan, *The Dynamics of Performance Management: Constructing Information and Reform* (Washington, DC: Georgetown University Press, 2008), pp. 3–5.

6. Beryl A. Radin, "The Government and Performance Review Act (GPRA): Hydra-Headed Monster or Flexible Management Tool?" *Public Administration Review* 58, 4 (1988): 307–17.

7. Horesh would come to insist on the distinction between social policy bonds and social impact bonds because the former are tradable on a secondary market whereas the latter are not. See Ronnie Horesh, "Social Policy Bonds" (paper presented at New Zealand Branch of the Australian Agricultural Economics Society, Discussion Paper No. 121, Blenheim, July 1988), http://socialgoals.com/SPBsBlenheim.pdf.

8. Steven VanRoekel and Jonathan Greenblatt, "Pay for Success—an Innovative Approach to Improve Results and Save Money," July 10, 2013, Office of Management and Budget, Washington, DC, http://www.whitehouse.gov/blog/2013/07/10/paying-success-innovative-approach-improve-results-and-save-money.

9. Ron Haskins, Christina Paxson, and Jeanne Brooks-Gunn, *Social Science Rising: A Tale of Evidence Shaping Public Policy*, policy brief (Princeton, NJ: Future of Children, Princeton-Brookings, 2009), http://futureofchildren.org/futureof-children/publications/docs/19_02_PolicyBrief.pdf.

10. VanRoekel and Greenblatt, "Pay for Success."

11. *Correctional Population in the United States* (Washington, DC: Department of Justice, Bureau of Justice Statistics, 2011).

12. National Center for Juvenile Justice, "Easy Access to the Census of Juveniles in Residential Placement: 1997–2011," http://www.ojjdp.gov/ojstatbb/ezacjrp/, accessed March 5, 2015.

13. David J. Lavin and Patrick A. Langan, *Recidivism of Prisoners Released in 1994*, Special Report NCJ 193427 (Washington, DC: U.S. Department of Justice, Office of Justice Programs, Bureau of Justice Statistics, 2002).

14. Council of State Governments, Justice Center, "Second Chance Act," http://csgjusticecenter.org/nrrc/projects/second-chance-act/, accessed March 5, 2015.

15. David B. Mullhausen, "The Second Chance Act: More Evaluations of Effectiveness Needed," *Heritage Foundation*, July 27, 2010, http://www.heritage.org/research/testimony/second-chance-act-how-effective-are-prisoner-reentry-programs.

16. Brian Peteritas, "New York City Tests Social Impact Bonds," *Governing*, August 23, 2012, http://www.governing.com/news/local/gov-new-york-city-tests-social-impact-bonds.html.

17. See Finance for Good, http://financeforgood.ca/social-impact-bonds-and-their-role-in-canada/.

18. Chris Skelcher, "Public-Private Partnerships and Hybridity," *Oxford Handbook of Public Administration* (New York: Oxford University Press, 2005), pp. 347–70.

19. Jeb Brugman and C. K. Prahalad, "Co-creating Business's New Social Compact," *Harvard Business Review* (February 2007): 80–91.

20. Christine Letts, William Ryan, and Allen Grossman, "Virtuous Capital: What Foundations Can Learn from Venture Capitalists," *Harvard Business Review* (March–April 1997): 36–44.

21. Steve Rothschild and Bill George, *The Non Nonprofit: For-Profit Thinking for Nonprofit Success* (San Francisco: Josey-Bass, 2012).

22. Matthew Bishop and Michael Green, *Philanthrocapitalism: How the Rich Can Save the World* (London: Bloomsbury Press, 2008); and Linsey McGoey, "Philanthrocapitalism and Its Critics," *Poetics* 40 (2): 185–99.

23. Matthew Flinders, "The Politics of Public-Private Partnerships," *British Journal of Politicsand International Relations* 7 (2005): 215–39.

24. Gerard Hanlon, "Rethinking Corporate Social Responsibility and the Role of the Firm—on the Denial of Politics," in *The Oxford Handbook of Corporate Social Responsibility*, Andrew Crane et al., eds. (New York: Oxford University Press, 2008), pp. 156–72.

25. Michael Edwards, *Just Another Emperor? The Myths and Realities of Philanthrocapitalism* (New York: Demos/Young Foundation, 2008), pp. 11–92.

26. Radin, "The Government and Performance Review Act."

27. See Sanford F. Schram, *Words of Welfare: The Poverty of Social Science and the Social Science of Poverty* (Minneapolis: University of Minnesota, 1995), pp. 8–15. Also see Julie A. Nice, "Forty Years of Welfare Policy Experimentation: No Acres, No Mule, No Politics, No Rights," *Northwestern Journal of Law and Social Policy* 4, 1 (2009): 1–13, http://scholarlycommons.law.northwestern.edu/njlsp/vol4/iss1/1.

28. Robin H. Rogers-Dillon, *The Welfare Experiments: Politics and Policy Evaluation* (Palo Alto, CA: Stanford University Press, 2004), p. 180.

29. See Martin Gilens and Benjamin I. Page, "Testing Theories of American Politics: Elites, Interest Groups, and Average Citizens," *Perspectives on Politics* 12, 4 (2014): 564–81, http://www.princeton.edu/~mgilens/Gilens%20homepage%20materials/Gilens%20and%20Page/Gilens%20and%20Page%202014-Testing%20Theories%203-7-14.pdf.

CHAPTER 8

1. Jamie Peck, "Zombie Neoliberalism and the Ambidexterous State," *Theoretical Criminology* 14, 1 (2010): 104–10; and Mitchell Dean, *The Signature of Power: Sovereignty, Governmentality and Biopolitics* (Los Angeles: Sage, 2013), p. 220.

2. This concluding chapter returns to the themes that informed the first chapter of this book, this time pursuing in depth the question of what is to be done to effectively respond to neoliberalism as the new normal and the challenges it poses for ordinary people going forward.

3. Charles Blow, "Beyond Black Lives Matter," *New York Times*, February 9, 2015, http://www.nytimes.com/2015/02/09/opinion/charles-blow-beyond-black-lives-matter.html?&hp&action=click&pgtype=Homepage&module=c-column-top-span-region&region=c-column-top-span-region&WT.nav=c-column-top-span-region&_r=0.

4. This resistance takes place on multiple levels. On the micro level, see Kathleen Stewart, *Ordinary Affects* (Durham, NC: Duke University Press, 2007); and James C. Scott, *The Art of Not Being Governed* (New Haven, CT: Yale University Press, 2012). For the macro, see Frances Fox Piven and Richard A. Cloward, *Poor People's Movements: How They Succeed, Why They Fail* (New York: Pantheon, 1977).

5. In this sense, effective oppositional politics must of necessity come to grips with the agency and power of neoliberalism as it operates in relationships between people, places, and things. Its contextual power to shape what is politically possible is perhaps best understood by how it operates as the practical rationality for getting things done in the public sector today. As a result, as I said, neoliberalism needs to be worked through, rather than around, and that difficult work perhaps is best done, as Kathleen Stewart reminds us, via ordinary everyday experience where we actually grapple with neoliberalism's palpably negative effects for growing numbers of people. See Stewart, *Ordinary Affects*, pp. 2–9.

6. Adolph Reed, "Nothing Left: The Long, Slow Surrender of American Liberals," *Harper's*, March 2014, http://harpers.org/archive/2014/03/nothing-left-2/.

7. On the issue of the lack of aggressive action by the working classes in response to their deteriorating economic plight, see David Graeber, "Caring Too Much: That's the Curse of the Working Classes," *The Guardian*, March 26 , 2014, http://www.theguardian.com/commentisfree/2014/mar/26/caring-curse-working-class-austerity-solidarity-scourge.

8. Natasha Singer, "In the Sharing Economy, Workers Find Both Freedom and Uncertainty," *New York Times*, August 16, 2014, http://www.nytimes.com/2014/08/17/technology/in-the-sharing-economy-workers-find-both-freedom-and-uncertainty.html.

9. Steven Greenhouse, "Hundreds of Fast-Food Workers Striking for Higher Wages Are Arrested," *New York Times*, September 4, 2014, http://www.nytimes.com/2014/09/05/business/economy/fast-food-workers-seeking-higher-wages-are-arrested-during-sit-ins.html?_r=0.

10. See Erik Haffner, "Punishing Protest, Policing Dissent: What Is the Justice System For?" *Common Dreams*, February 12, 2012, http://www.commondreams.org/view/2012/02/12-6; and Michael D. Yates, *Why Unions Matter* (New York: Monthly Review Press, 2009).

11. See Bruce Drake, "Opinion of Unions Is Up, Membership Down," *Fact Tank*, September 2, 2013, http://www.pewresearch.org/fact-tank/2013/09/02/opinion-of-unions-is-up-membership-down/: "In August 2011, a time when there were fears of a new economic downturn and widespread dissatisfaction with national conditions, favorable ratings for labor unions among the public hit an all-time low of 41%." By 2013, ratings had rebounded to 51 percent but they were still below the levels of support of prior decades. Union membership has continued to decline, with only 11.3 percent of the workforce in unions by 2013. Also see Sam Grindlin, "Underestimating Capital, Overestimating Labour: A Response to Andrew Kliman," *New Left Project*, March 17, 2014, http://www.newleftproject.org/index.php/site/article_comments/underestimating_capital_overestimating_labour_a_response_to_andrew_kliman.

12. E. Tammy Kim, "The Year in Labor: Fast-food Workers Lead a New Working Class," *Aljazeera America*, December 20, 2013, http://america.aljazeera.com/articles/2013/12/20/the-year-in-laborfastfoodworkersandanewworkingclass.html.

13. Judith Butler, "Bodies in Alliance and the Politics of the Street," #Occupy Los Angeles Reader, issue 1–3 (November 2011), http://suebellyank.com/wp-content/uploads/2011/11/ola-reader-full.pdf.

14. See Peter Funke, "Rhizomatic Resistance: Social Movement Politics from Porto Alegre to Tunis and Frankfurt" (paper presented at the Annual Meeting of the American Political Science Association, Washington, DC, August 29, 2014).

15. On the need for experiments that can produce synergies across different levels of activism in thought as well as action, see William E. Connolly, *The Fragility of Things: Self-Organizing Processes, Neoliberal Fantasies and Democratic Activism* (Durham, NC: Duke University Press, 2013), postlude. Julian Zelizer underscores the importance of what I am calling "multilevel mobilizing" when pointing out that even a strong president like Lyndon Baines Johnson could not be effective in passing civil rights reform without it. He writes: "the interconnected world of grass roots activists, interest groups, intellectuals, and non-profit organizations gave liberalism its muscle." See Julian Zelizer, "The Power of Lyndon Johnson Is a Myth," *Washington Post*, January 11, 2015, http://www.washingtonpost.com/blogs/monkey-cage/wp/2015/01/11/the-power-of-lyndon-johnson-is-a-myth/. Also see Julian Zelizer, *The Fierce Urgency of Now: Lyndon Johnson, Congress, and the Battle for the Great Society* (New York: Penguin Press, 2015).

16. See Reed, "Nothing Left"; and Jodi Dean, *The Communist Horizon (Pocket Communism)* (London: Verso, 2012), pp. 207–15. In addition, see John Ehrenberg's informed contrast between what I am calling the "organized Left" and the Occupy Left, in "Occupying Occupy: What Went Wrong?" (paper presented at the Annual Meeting of the American Political Science Association, August 29, 2014, Washington, DC).

17. The issue of the need to resist getting involved in minor political battles that can fritter away the needed energy for the bigger struggle to transform the system is more of an issue for Reed in "Nothing Left" and Dean in *The Communist Horizon* than Ehrenberg in "Occupying Occupy." Yet it is a common refrain in response to the alleged failures of Occupy.

18. A case in point is criticism of the protestors in Ferguson, Missouri, in response to the killing of Michael Brown in the summer of 2014 and the alleged failures of low-income African Americans there over time to organize to challenge the white power structure. See Charles Cobb, "Black People Had the Power to Fix the Problems in Ferguson before the Brown Shooting; They Failed," *Washington Post*, September 18, 2014, http://www.washingtonpost.com/posteverything/wp/2014/09/18/black-people-had-the-power-to-fix-the-problems-in-ferguson-before-the-brown-shooting-they-failed/.

19. Bruce Robbins, "How Much History Does the American Left Need?" *Tikkun*, April 8, 2014, http://www.tikkun.org/nextgen/how-much-history-does-the-american-left-need.

20. See Jacques Rancière, *The Philosopher and His Poor* (Durham, NC: Duke University Press, 2004).

21. John G. Gunnell, *Orders of Discourse: Philosophy, Social Science, and Politics* (Lanham, MD: Rowman & Littlefield, 1998), p. 196.

22. On the importance of theory for sustaining the Occupy Wall Street protest beyond its event horizon to realize its potential as a new type of revolutionary movement, see Thomas Nail, "Deleuze, Occupy, and the Actuality of Revolution," *Theory and Event* 16, 1 (2003), http://muse.jhu.edu/login?auth=0&type=summary&url=/journals/theory_and_event/v016/16.1.nail.html.

23. See Marc Stears, "The Vocation of Political Theory: Principles, Empirical Inquiry and the Politics of Opportunity," *European Journal of Political Theory* 4, 4 (2005): 325–50, 344–45.

24. Jodi Dean's discussion of her participation in the antifracking group We Are Seneca Lake simultaneously supports activism not overly encumbered with theoretical concepts like the anthropocene (the age of human-made climate warming) while dismissing less disruptive forms of activism on the grounds they will reinforce the hegemony of what she calls "communicative capitalism" (as a regime that enlists people in unreflectively reproducing their own subordination). See Jodi Dean, "Living the Lake," *I Cite*, January 3, 2015, http://jdeanicite.typepad.com/, and comments in the subsequent Facebook discussion: https://www.facebook.com/jodi.dean3?fref=ts. Radical incrementalism is a concept designed to promote incremental changes that not only avoid the social reproduction of the existing hegemony but also lay the groundwork for future transformational changes. Dean alludes to articulating affinities across different forms of activism and associated knowledges (each of which is not encumbered with too much abstract theorizing) in "Learning, Liveliness, and Expanding the World," *I Cite*, January 5, 2015, http://jdeanicite.typepad.com/i_cite/2015/01/learning-liveliness-and-expanding-the-world.html.

25. For a discussion of the "politics of survival" versus a "politics of social change," see Joe Soss, *Unwanted Claims: The Politics of Participation in the U.S. Welfare System* (Ann Arbor: University of Michigan Press, 2000), pp. 87–89.

26. Christopher Hayes, *Twilight of the Elites: America after Meritocracy* (New York: Crown, 2013), chapter 7.

27. Hayes, *Twilight of the Elites*, p. 237.

28. Richard A. Cloward and Frances Fox Piven, "A Strategy to End Poverty," *The Nation*, May 2, 1966, pp. 510–517. Also see Sanford F. Schram, *Praxis for the Poor:*

Piven and Cloward and the Future of Social Science in Social Welfare (New York: New York University Press, 2002), chapter 3. Piven and Cloward's "crisis strategy" is often put forward as a form of resistance; however, it shares more than the goal of a basic income guarantee with neo-Marxist accelerationism in looking to speed up the current regime in working to its logical transformation to something better. Thanks to Jason Adams for making this connection.

29. Ari Paul, "The Rise and Fall of the Working Families Party," *Jacobin*, November 15, 2013, https://www.jacobinmag.com/2013/11/the-rise-and-fall-of-the-working-families-party/.

30. See Sanford F. Schram, "The Future of Higher Education and American Democracy: An Introduction," *New Political Science*, 36, 4 (2014): 425–37.

31. See Sanford F. Schram, "The Praxis of *Poor People's Movements*: Strategy and Theory in Dissensus Politics," *Perspectives on Politics* 1, 4 (2003): 715–20.

32. Doug Henwood, "The Top of the World: An Ambitious Study Documents the Long-Term Reign of the 1 Percent," *Bookforum*, April–May 2014, http://www.bookforum.com/inprint/021_01/12987. In this review, Henwood responds to Thomas Piketty's analysis that concludes that capitalism has returned to its normal pattern of increasing inequality with economic growth. Henwood concludes that the only reasonable response is one that combines a protest politics of aggressive resistance coupled with efforts to improve "rational democratic deliberation." Neither one nor the other on its own, however, is likely to provide effective responses.

33. Romand Coles, *Beyond Gated Politics: Reflections for the Possibility of Democracy* (Minneapolis: University of Minnesota Press, 2005).

34. See Stears, "The Vocation of Political Theory." A promising development is that more published theory in recent years engages contemporary political issues and uses empirical evidence about those issues. For instance, see Elizabeth Ben-Ishai, *Fostering Autonomy, a Theory of Citizenship, the State, and Social Service Delivery* (University Park: Pennsylvania State University Press, 2012).

35. See Amory Starr with Andrea Godschalk, *Underground Restaurant* (Pull Don't Press, 2013), for an excellent analysis of how the local food movement reflects efforts within the market economy that are radically progressive in their effects.

36. Bob Master, "The Zeitgeist Tracked Down Bill de Blasio: How the Rise of Occupy and Decline of the Neoliberal Narrative Helped Shape the 'de Blasio Moment,'" *The Nation*, December 26, 2013, http://www.thenation.com/article/177720/zeitgeist-tracked-down-bill-de-blasio#.

37. See J. David Goodman and Al Baker, "New York City Murders Fall, but the Police Aren't Celebrating," *New York Times*, December 31, 2014, http://www.nytimes.com/2015/01/01/nyregion/new-york-city-murders-fall-but-the-police-arent-celebrating.html?hp&action=click&pgtype=Homepage&module=second-column-region&region=top-news&WT.nav=top-news.

38. Schram, *Praxis for the Poor*, chapter 3. For the argument that Pierre Bourdieu articulated an understanding of how savvy participation in processes of social reproduction could lead to "the transformation of social fields, whether through incremental, but ultimately radical [change]," see Sherry Ortner, "Bourdieu and 'History,'" *Anthropology of This Century* 8 (October 2013), http://aotcpress.com/articles/bourdieu-history/.

39. Charles Lindblom, "The Science of 'Muddling Through,'" *Public Administration Review* 19 (1959): 79–88.

40. For a defense of incrementalism against the major critiques, see Michael T. Hayes, *The Limits of Policy Change: Incrementalism, Worldview, and the Rule of Law* (Washington, DC: Georgetown University Press, 1992).

41. Richard H. Thaler and Cass R. Sunstein, *Nudge: Improving Decisions about Health, Wealth, and Happiness*, expanded ed. (New York: Penguin Books, 2009).

42. The issue of whether to work toward more ambitious long-term change over pushing for immediate short-term gains is often falsely posed as a stark choice between social movement organizing and electioneering for mainstream candidates from the Democratic Party. See Reed, "Nothing Left." Yet these are not mutually exclusive. See Schram, *Praxis for the Poor*, pp. 49–108.

43. Schram, *Praxis for the Poor*, pp. 100–102.

44. For an argument supportive of an approach that approximates radical incrementalism, see Jeffrey Isaac, *The Poverty of Progressivism: The Future of American Democracy in a Time of Liberal Decline* (Lanham, MD: Rowman and Littlefield, 2003).

45. André Gorz, *A Strategy for Labor: A Radical Proposal* (Boston: Beacon Press, 1967).

46. David Harvey, "Neoliberalism" (paper presented to the Faculty Seminar on Neoliberalism, Hunter College, December 5, 2014).

47. Similar to the focus on challenging power relationships to get change is the emphasis on "tension points" in "phronetic" social science. For a definition of phronetic social science and its focus on tension points, see Bent Flyvbjerg, Todd Landman, and Sanford Schram, eds., *Real Social Science: Applied Phronesis* (New York: Cambridge University Press, 2012).

48. See James Ferguson, "Toward a Left Art of Government: From 'Foucauldian Critique' to Foucauldian Politics," *History of the Human Sciences* 24, 4 (2011): 61–68.

49. See Piven and Cloward, *Poor People's Movements*, pp. 23–39.

50. See Lisa Dodson, *The Moral Underground: How Ordinary Americans Subvert an Unfair Economy* (New York: New Press, 2011); and Carolyn Needleman and Martin Needleman, *Guerrillas in the Bureaucracy: Community Planning Experiment in the United States* (New York: John Wiley, 1974). For an insightful empirical investigation of legal-aid lawyering as a form of radical incrementalism, see Corey S. Shdaimah, *Negotiating Justice: Progressive Lawyering, Low-Income Clients, and the Quest for Social Change* (New York: New York University Press, 2011).

51. See Starr with Godschalk, *Underground Restaurant*, for how the local food movement is producing significant changes in the market economy that improve ordinary people's access to affordable and healthy foods.

52. Keith G. Benetele and Erin O'Brien, "Jim Crow 2.0? Why States Consider and Adopt Restrictive Voter Access Polices," *Perspectives on Politics* 11, 4 (2013): 1088–1116; and Lorraine C. Minnite, *The Myth of Voter Fraud* (Ithaca, NY: Cornell University Press, 2010).

53. Josh Boak, "Obama Takes GOP to Task for Diluting Voter Rights," *Fiscal Times*, August 29, 2013, http://www.thefiscaltimes.com/Articles/2013/08/29/Obama-Takes-GOP-to-Task-for-Diluting-Voter-Rights.

54. "The Worst Voter Turnout in 72 Years," *New York Times*, November 11, 2014, http://www.nytimes.com/2014/11/12/opinion/the-worst-voter-turnout-in-72-years.html?smid=nytcore-iphone-share&smprod=nytcore-iphone.

55. For an incisive analysis on the "disruptive" potential of Obamacare, see Lawrence R. Jacobs, "Health Care and the Future of American Politics," *Perspectives on Politics* 12, 3 (2014):631–42, doi: 10.1017/S1537592714001625.

56. Glenn Beck, "Cloward, Piven and the Fundamental Transformation of America," *Fox News*, January 10, 2009, http://www.foxnews.com/story/2010/01/05/cloward-piven-and-fundamental-transformation-america/.

57. Paul Howard, "Obamacare Is Killing Traditional Employer-Sponsored Health Insurance," *Forbes*, September 23, 2013, http://www.forbes.com/sites/theapothecary/2013/09/23/obamacare-killing-traditional-employer-insurance/.

58. Related to the issue of reinscribing the market logic of neoliberalism, a poignant criticism of President Obama's major misstep on promising people that they could keep their existing insurance under his health care reforms was that he fell into the trap of overemphasizing the individualistic perspective at the expense of pointing out that the changes he had signed into law should be evaluated in terms of how they improved our society as a collectivity. See Jonathan Chait, "Why Letting Everyone Keep Their Health-Care Plan Is a Terrible Idea," *New York*, November 1, 2013, http://nymag.com/daily/intelligencer/2013/10/letting-everyone-keep-their-plan-terrible-idea.html.

59. Michael Tanner, "Obamacare as Big Brother," *National Review Online*, August 14, 2013, http://www.nationalreview.com/article/355700/obamacare-big-brother-michael-tanner.

60. See Michael Lind, "Here's How GOP Obamacare Hypocrisy Backfires," *Salon*, October 28, 2013, http://www.salon.com/2013/10/28/what_the_tea_party_misses_if_you_hate_obamacare_youll_really_hate_what_the_right_wants_to_do_to_social_security/.

61. Thanks to Joan Schram for reminding me of the "camel's nose in the tent" metaphor that suggests how incrementalism can potentially proceed to the point where the whole camel is in the tent.

62. See Elisabeth Rosenthal, "Insured, but Not Covered," *New York Times*, February 8, 2015, http://www.nytimes.com/2015/02/08/sunday-review/insured-but-not-covered.html?smid=fb-share.

63. Steven Teles, "Kludgeocracy in America," *National Affairs* 17 (Fall 2013): 97–114, http://www.nationalaffairs.com/publications/detail/kludgeocracy-in-america.

64. Linda Greenhouse, "Law in the Raw," *New York Times*, November 12, 2014, http://www.nytimes.com/2014/11/13/opinion/law-in-the-raw.html?ref=opinion&_r=0.

65. Eric M. Patashnik and Julian E. Zelizer, "The Struggle to Remake Politics: Liberal Reform and the Limits of Policy Feedback in the Contemporary American State," *Perspectives on Politics* 11, 4 (2013): 1071–87.

66. Mike Konczal, "What Kind of Problem is the ACA Rollout for Liberalism?" *The Next New Deal: The Blog of the Roosevelt Institute*, October 23, 2014, http://www.nextnewdeal.net/rortybomb/what-kind-problem-aca-rollout-liberalism. Also see

Ross Douthat, "Could Obamacare Discredit Neoliberalism?" *New York Times*, October 23, 2013, http://douthat.blogs.nytimes.com/2013/10/23/could-obamacare-discredit-neoliberalism/?_r=0.

67. See Deborah Stone, *Policy Paradox: The Art of Political Decision Making* (New York: W. W. Norton, 2012).

68. Thaler and Sunstein, *Nudge*, pp. 17–21.

69. Anandi Mani, Sendhil Mullainathan, Eldar Shafir, and Jiaying Zhao, "Poverty Impedes Cognitive Function," Science, August 2013, 976–80, doi: 10.1126/science.1238041. Also see Sendhil Mullainathan and Eldar Shafir, *Why Having Too Little Means So Much* (New York: Times Books, 2013).

70. See Nicholas Kristof and Sheryl WuDunn, "The Way to Beat Poverty," *New York Times*, September 12, 2014.

71. Allison C. De Marco, Molly De Marco, and Alexandra Biggers, "Asset-Development among People Experiencing Homelessness: An Individual Development Account Model" (paper presented at the Annual Meeting of the Society for Social Work and Research, San Antonio, Texas, January 16, 2014), http://sswr.confex.com/sswr/2014/webprogram/Paper20657.html.

72. Matt Taibbi, "The Police in America are Becoming Illegitimate," *Rolling Stone*, December 5, 2014, http://www.rollingstone.com/politics/news/the-police-in-america-are-becoming-illegitimate-20141205.

73. Joe Soss, Richard C. Fording, and Sanford F. Schram, *Disciplining the Poor: Neoliberal Paternalism and the Persistent Power of Race* (Chicago: University of Chicago Press, 2001), chapter 2.

74. Jamie Peck, *Constructions of Neoliberal Reason* (New York: Oxford University Press, 2010).

75. See Soss, Fording, and Schram, *Disciplining the Poor*, pp. 297–98.

76. Lucy Heady, "Social Return on Investment Position Paper," *New Philanthropy Capital*, April 2010, p. 1, http://www.thinknpc.org/publications/social-return-on-investment-position-paper/.

77. Nancy Fraser, "Feminism, Capitalism and the Cunning of History," *New Left Review* 56 (March–April 2009): 97–117.

78. Thanks to Dianne Butera for underscoring the depoliticizing effects of neoliberal discourse as exemplified by "disruptive innovation." Clayton Christensen claims to have coined the term: http://www.christenseninstitute.org/key-concepts/disruptive-innovation-2/.

79. Wendy Brown, "Neo-Liberalism and the End of Liberal Democracy," *Theory and Event* 7 (2003), http://muse.jhu.edu/journals/theory_and_event/, and "American Nightmare: Neoliberalism, Neoconservatism, and De-Democratization," *Political Theory* 34, 6 (2006): 690–714.

80. On neoliberal paternalism, see Soss, Fording, and Schram, *Disciplining the Poor*, chapter 2.

81. See Nancy Fraser, "A Triple Movement? Parsing the Crisis after Polanyi," *New Left Review* 81 (May–June 2013): 119–32. Michel Foucault can be read as proposing a working through of neoliberalism to get to a more empowering individualism rather than nostalgically longing to return to the social protectionist state of Karl Polanyi's "double movement." See Peter Frase, "Beyond the Welfare State,"

Jacobin, December 11, 2104, https://www.jacobinmag.com/2014/12/beyond-the-welfare-state/. For the argument that Foucault ended up too complacent about neoliberalism as a way of practicing a new form of individualized freedom, see Dean, *The Signature of Power*, pp. 230–32.

82. Mitchell Dean sees Foucault as ending his life with the kind of thinking that almost, if not quite, amounts to an "apology" for neoliberalism. See Dean, *The Signature of Power*, p. 60. Yet Foucault can also be read less as apologizing for neoliberalism than as proposing working through it. He focused on not so much rejecting neoliberalism's individualism but on how we could get to a more empowering one, one that was not based on nostalgically longing to return to the social protectionist state intimated by Karl Polanyi's "double movement." See Peter Frase, "Beyond the Welfare State." In this way, Foucault shares with Piven and Cloward an interest in moving beyond the politics of resistance. Working on change, rather than only always resisting the status quo, could help accelerate the process to get to something better.

83. Piven and Cloward, *Poor People's Movements*, p. 37.

84. For Walter Benjamin, the "now time" for transformative change is when we find the strength to disrupt capitalism's persistent tendency to present the same old commodifying practices as new so as to redeem the past efforts to overcome oppression. See Walter Benjamin, "Theses on the Concept of History," *Illuminations: Essays and Reflections*, Hannah Arendt, ed. (New York: Schocken, 1969 [1955]), pp. 253–65.

85. Fraser, "A Triple Movement?"

86. See Thomas Nail, "Michel Foucault, Accelerationist," *Foucault and Neoliberalism AUFS Event*, January 5, 2015, https://itself.wordpress.com/2015/01/05/foucault-and-neoliberalism-aufs-event-thomas-nail-michel-foucault-accelerationist/.

87. See Ortner, "Bourdieu and 'History.'"

88. Walter Benjamin, *Selected Writings*, vol. 4, *1938–1940*, Howard Eiland and Michael W. Jennings, eds. (Cambridge, MA: Harvard University Press, 2003), p. 402.

89. Thanks to Eric Sidoti for reminding me of the importance of a long-range vision. See Shdaimah, *Negotiating Justice*, pp. 169–70, on the importance of a utopian vision for creating even incremental progressive change. Also see Erik Olin Wright, *Envisioning Real Utopias* (London: Verso, 2010); and Joel Rogers, "Productive Democracy" (paper presented at the American Sociological Association Annual Meeting. Denver, CO, August 2012) for an overview of his "high road capitalism" blueprint and the work of the Center on Wisconsin Strategy.

90. Dodson, *The Moral Underground*, pp. 189–200.

91. See Thomas Piketty, *Capital in the 21st Century*, Arthur Goldhammer, trans. (Cambridge, MA: Belknap Press, 2014), pp. 515–39.

92. See Dean Baker, "Economic Policy in a Post-Piketty World," *Truthout*, April 21, 2014, http://truth-out.org/opinion/item/23205-economic-policy-in-a-post-piketty-world.

INDEX

responsibility, personal
neoliberalism and, 4–5
Personal Responsibility and Work
Opportunity Reconciliation Act, 104
precarity and, 71
retirement, 206n102
retrograde incrementalism, 186–87
revolution, 47–48
rewards, 123–24
Riefenstahl, Leni, 217n35
rights
civil, 50–51, 218n58
social impact bonds and, 167–68
welfare rights movement, 95
Robbins, Bruce, 178–79
Robert Wood Johnson Foundation's
Advancing Recovery, 126
Robinson, Andrew, 72
Rogers-Dillon, Robin, 168
Rolling Jubilee, 56, 213n72, 213n74
Romney, Mitt, 64, 76, 214n78
Roosevelt, Franklin Delano, 94
Ross, Andrew, 54
Ryan, Paul, 46

Santelli, Rick, 39, 210n25
Schmitt, Carl, 68–69, 217n37
Schumpeter, Joseph, 10
Scott, Rick, 122
Second Chance Act (2008), 159–60
self-governance. *See also* melancholia,
middle-class
Mahmud and, 53
neoliberalism and, 25–26
semiotics, 82
cultural interpretive grid and, 88–89
culture and, 83
identity assumptions and, 89
semiotic structure of deservingness
binary codes and, 82–84
overview about, 81–84
persistence of, 106–8
social welfare policy and, 84–98, 90t
workings of, 84–98
Shapiro, Michael, 73, 218n52
Sidoti, Eric, 238n89

signals, 82
Silva, Jennifer, 65, 199n7, 216n28
Sklar, Martin, 203n48
Smith, Adam, 43, 147
Smith, Zadie, 209n19
social capital, 203n58
social change
politics of, 180, 181, 233n25
theory, 3–4
social impact bonds, 30–31
conclusions about, 171–72
coordination for, 158
CSRs and, 163
de Blasio and, 207n114
democracy trumped by capitalism
and, 169–71
excitement around, 161–62
explained, 153, 155–56
Finance for Good and, 162
global nature of, 153, 229n4
Great Britain and, 156
history surrounding, 155, 156
misdirection and, 166–67
model of, 158–59, 158f
origins of, 155
overview, 152–55
Pay for Success grants and, 157–58
performance measurement and,
153–54, 165–66
philanthrocapitalism and, 163–65
as PPPs, 162–65
reentry programs and, 161
rethinking, 162–65
rights and, 167–68
Second Chance Act and, 159–60
social policy bonds and, 155, 156,
229n7
social welfare funding and, 166–69
unknowns regarding, 161
"Social Impact Bonds: Investing for
Success" (Costa), 229n4
social movement theory, 3
social policy bonds, 155, 156, 229n7
Social Security, 83, 84, 168
Tea Party and, 40–41
Social Security Act, 94